HONEST OPPORTUNISM

HONEST OPPORTUNISM

THE RISE OF THE CAREER POLITICIAN

PETER RIDDELL

HAMISH HAMILTON · LONDON

HAMISH HAMILTON LTD
Published by the Penguin Group
Penguin Books Ltd, 27 Wrights Lane, London w8 5TZ, England
Penguin Books USA Inc., 375 Hudson Street, New York, New York 10014, USA
Penguin Books Australia Ltd, Ringwood, Victoria, Australia
Penguin Books Canada Ltd, 10 Alcorn Avenue, Toronto, Ontario, Canada M4V 3B2
Penguin Books (NZ) Ltd, 182–190 Wairau Road, Auckland 10, New Zealand

Penguin Books Ltd, Registered Offices: Harmondsworth, Middlesex, England

First published 1993
1 3 5 7 9 10 8 6 4 2

Typeset by Datix International Limited, Bungay, Suffolk
Filmset in Monophoto Sabon
Printed in England by Clays Ltd, St Ives plc

A CIP catalogue record for this book is available from the British Library
ISBN 0–241–12888–9

To all who have helped me understand politics, and to my godchildren and other young friends, for whom this book is, I hope, a warning as well as a guide.

CONTENTS

PREFACE

Why them? Why out of 57 million people have these 651 been selected by local political parties and elected by voters in their constituencies? Why out of 651 MPs have these eighty-five been chosen to sit on the Government front-benches as ministers and whips, faced by a similar number of shadow spokesmen a few feet away on the Opposition front-bench? And why, from these eighty-five ministers, have twenty odd been picked as members of the Cabinet, of whom one has become Prime Minister? What made them commit their lives to politics?

I have repeatedly wondered about these questions during my years of watching politicians at close quarters, first as a financial and economics correspondent of the *Financial Times* during the 1970s, then in the parliamentary press gallery as that paper's political editor from 1981 to 1988. It was then that the idea developed of a book about political careers, about why some succeed and others fail. Why did X remain on the back-benches for his whole career and why did the apparently similar Y reach the Cabinet? My final article as I left Westminster for Washington in October 1988 was on this theme and expressed my perennial sense of puzzlement about the nature of political careers. Politics is unlike other careers. While there is a hierarchy, there is no formal job structure, professional qualification, or objective yardstick of performance.

My thoughts developed during nearly three years in Washington while observing the US Congress and the very different career patterns in politics on the other side of the Atlantic. The book has taken its final shape since my return to London in the late summer of 1991 to become political columnist and commentator of *The Times*.

This book concentrates on the central role of Westminster in political careers. All leading British politicians spend most of their lives seeking election to the House of Commons, trying to stay there and to advance their careers there. This is unlike, for instance, America, where big city mayors and governors of states are nationally known and important political figures, or Germany, where leaders of provincial *Länder* have national influence. Of the five most recent American presidents, only George Bush and Gerald Ford spent any significant amount of time in Washington before entering the White House; the other three were all governors of states. In Britain, political life is centred on London and Westminster. The following chapters do not, therefore, consider the careers of local councillors or constituency activists, except incidentally where they are relevant in discussing preparation for careers in Parliament, and to wonder why some leading councillors wanted to become MPs while others were content to operate at a local level.

During its evolution, this book has changed from being primarily a description of how politicians succeed and fail; and has become instead a consideration of what motivates them, and the implications. Why do individuals become involved in the first place? What qualities and attitudes do successful politicians possess? As a result, the book is now about the nature of political life as practised in Britain.

As will become clear, one of my central conclusions is that British politics has become even more of a full-time career than is generally supposed. There has been a change this century, and particularly over the last generation, in the attitudes of the majority of politicians. Instead of life in the Commons being an offshoot of social and economic positions outside, it is now the centre of their lives and ambitions. Most MPs of even moderate success, let alone those who reach the Cabinet, have committed themselves to politics in their youth, frequently in their teens. There are late entrants, but these are increasingly the exceptions.

The idea of a career or professional politician (I prefer the former description) has been much discussed, notably in a stimulating paper by Anthony King (1981), to which I am much indebted, and in several studies of the life of an MP. But many of these works do not go far enough, either in establishing the very early age at which commitment to a political career is often made or in discussing the implications of this trend for public life in Britain. In particular, as in America, a whole series of ancillary occupations has grown up – special advisers to ministers and political consultants, as well as full-time local councillors – to act in part as stepping stones to careers in the Commons. Parliament has changed as a result.

This book follows a broadly chronological pattern, tracing the development of a politician's career from initial interest and then commitment, through early involvement at university or in a local constituency, to selection as a parliamentary candidate (often for a hopeless seat first), election to the Commons and then progress, or not, up the ministerial ladder. I concentrate more on the early stages, partly because they have been less discussed elsewhere but also because they highlight my views on the changing nature of political careers.

This approach offers the advantages of clarity, but it involves the risk of implying that all politicians are careerists in the pejorative sense. Of course, personal ambition plays a large part in the lives of most of us, whether journalists or MPs. But this type of analysis does not mean that politicians take all their decisions purely in relation to how they believe their careers will be affected. Ideology also plays a key part. There are many examples in this book of MPs who have chosen a path which appears to conflict with personal advance – for instance, the defection of thirty Labour MPs to the Social Democratic Party in 1981–2. Similarly, some Tory MPs, such as, for example, Nicholas Budgen, have resigned on an issue of principle at an early stage in their ministerial careers – in his case over Government policy towards Northern Ireland – at the cost of future preferment. Nor should it be assumed that, just because there are more career or full-time politicians, their advance is automatic or predetermined. Luck, chance and timing play key parts, as the generation of Labour MPs now in their forties and fifties can grimly testify.

The concluding chapter discusses the implications of the rise of the career politician for public life, for popular attitudes towards politicians. It looks at how a wider range of people might be attracted into national politics and how their talents and abilities might be better used when they arrive at Westminster. At present, too much effort and energy are wasted.

One of the curses, as well as the charms, of British politics is the frequency with which leading players change their names. Lord Home of the Hirsel and Lord Hailsham of St Marylebone have been the extreme recent examples, with several changes of name each during the course of their long careers as members of the Commons, Lords and the Commons again, and then finally as life peers. In other, less exotic, cases, MPs are knighted or become life peers. For the sake of simplicity I have used the name by which they were known at the peak of their careers: hence Margaret Thatcher or Mrs Thatcher, not Baroness Thatcher of Kesteven or the pedantic Lady Denis Thatcher. Similarly, I have referred to Sir Geoffrey Howe, since that is what he was known as by all when he was at the centre of politics.

Finally, a word on the title. There are several ways of describing a political career. The greasy pole, Disraeli's famous comment on becoming Prime Minister in 1868, gives the impression of ascent, setback, frustration and an elusive, and rarely attained, pinnacle. As such, it is a vivid description of a politician's life. But it has already been used as the title of the revealing memoirs of Reginald Bevins. Moreover, its very familiarity clouds the contrasts of political life, as splendidly suggested by Douglas Hurd's remark in the first chapter about 'the insidious pleasures of being elected to serve'. The ambiguous character of many political lives is most aptly and briefly conveyed by F. E. Smith's reference to 'honest opportunism'. That captures as well as anything the ambivalent attitudes and lives of career politicians.

Peter Riddell, June 1993

ACKNOWLEDGEMENTS

Much discussion of political careers draws heavily on the basic information in the regular Nuffield election studies produced by David Butler and various associates and in *The Times Guide to the House of Commons*, produced after each general election. These are invaluable and have been used here, but they tell only part of the story. They provide the basic framework for illustrating how political careers have changed since before the Second World War, but they do not explain what lies behind these changes. As will already be clear, I am interested in finding out why and when people first caught the political bug, how and when they decided they wanted to become MPs, and their attitudes to political life.

For this purpose I have looked in more detail at individual careers, based on biographies, interviews and profiles, as well as my own numerous conversations during the past decade. Whatever their other attitudes to the press, I have found few MPs reluctant to talk about their own lives, particularly what got them started. Of particular use throughout the book have been the profiles of MPs which appear in *House Magazine*, the invaluable weekly trade journal of Westminster, from which I have drawn. These have been written in recent years mainly by Julia Langdon and Fiona Millar. Their value is that they cover not just the great men and women of politics on the front-benches but also the rank-and-file back-benchers, those usually neither heard nor seen. I have also built up large boxes of newspaper cuttings and have used the many memoirs, biographies and autobiographies of politicians. While I have drawn examples from the past fifty years or so, the analysis concentrates on those serving in the Commons during the

1980s, though updated to take account of the very large intake of 140 new MPs after the April 1992 election.

The list of acknowledgements is potentially endless. This book is in one sense the result of conversations going back to the 1970s with politicians of all kinds, with political scientists and with fellow journalists who have watched all too many ascents up the greasy pole, as well as descents. More specifically, I am grateful for the thoughts of David Butler, Anthony King, Elinor Goodman and James Naughtie. Roger Liddle and Andrew Adonis were of enormous help in reading early drafts and offering invaluable comments. They prevented me from going down pointless culs-de-sac and pointed out new roads to explore. As with my previous books, Martin and Helene Hayman, and their sons, Ben, Joseph, Jacob and David, have provided distractions and encouragement in varying, welcome, proportions. While I was living in Washington the Pringles, Peter, Eleanor and their daughter Victoria, helped me understand both America and its politics. During the book's completion, Avril Walker offered both understanding and warm support.

I am grateful for the forbearance of Chris Holifield, my literary agent for this book, and to Andrew Franklin of Hamish Hamilton. They were patient even when it looked as if the book was disappearing into the endless future. The following, I hope, shows that a good idea eventually reaches fruition. While I owe many of the ideas to others, either directly or indirectly, the following interpretation, and any errors, are naturally my own.

INTRODUCTION

'What makes a British politician? First, a tradition of public service; then a dash of vanity and another of self-importance and, added to these, a streak of rebelliousness, a pleasure in good talk for its own sake, and in gregarious living. These, much more than the desire for personal power, are the qualities of the individual member. But the individual is shaped into his final form by the institution itself. It is Parliament which takes hold of the player.'

Richard Crossman, *The Charm of Politics*, 1958

'My belief is, when you get a chance, take it.'

Harold Macmillan, talking in 1979 to Alistair Horne, his biographer, about his succession to Anthony Eden

'I think what makes anybody become an MP is buried in the recesses of their psyche. I'd wanted to become an MP from the age of thirteen; it must just be that I'm insane. For me it was a combination of my psychological make-up, which means that I need the drug of politics, alongside an understanding that I had a facility for it, plus a framework of beliefs. These days what keeps me going is a mixture of anger and enjoyment.'

Jack Straw, interview in *House Magazine*, 4 July 1988

Around the Cabinet table on Thursday mornings sits a group of politicians who share a bond deeper and longer-lasting than their party allegiance and common membership of the Government. John Major and his fellow ministers have been committed, even addicted, to politics for at least twenty or thirty years. They are almost all career politicians, with little other experience except as a necessary preliminary to winning a seat in the Commons. Michael Howard, Kenneth Clarke and John

Gummer were – together with Sir Norman Fowler, the Conservative Party chairman – all active in politics together at
Cambridge thirty to thirty-five years ago, as was Norman
Lamont, a Cabinet member until his sacking in May 1993.
One senior supporter of Mr Major in the Tory leadership
battle of November 1990 said with a mixture of nostalgia and
glee that it was just like an election to the Cambridge University
Conservative Association (CUCA) or to the Union. Some ministers, such as Douglas Hurd, John MacGregor, William Waldegrave, Tony Newton and Michael Portillo, were advisers to
ministers, political secretaries or worked at Conservative Central Office before entering Parliament, while others, such as
David Hunt, were active in Tory politics while practising as
lawyers. No one can have been in any doubt about what most
of them have wanted to do with their lives since they were
aged twenty.

The weekly meetings of the Shadow Cabinet late each
Wednesday afternoon at Westminster are attended by MPs
with an equal devotion to politics. John Smith is surrounded
by colleagues who have spent most of their adult lives either in
the Commons or in jobs which have allowed them actively to
pursue a political career. Diverse though their routes have
been to the Shadow Cabinet, virtually all have lived and
breathed politics since their late teens and early twenties –
student politicians like Jack Straw and Gordon Brown, union
officials like John Prescott, workers at party headquarters like
Margaret Beckett and council leaders like Frank Dobson and
David Blunkett.

These are the new governing class, the successors to the
hereditary aristocrats who dominated Cabinets until early this
century. The current breed of politicians differs from them in
that their commitment to politics as a full-time occupation
does not derive from an outside social position, a title or
inherited wealth. Rather, politics is the sole focus and outside
standing is largely irrelevant. Consequently, British politics has

become a mainly closed world, confined to those who have made a youthful commitment to seeking a parliamentary career. It is like a religious order which requires an early vocation, or perhaps a post-entry closed shop. Douglas Hurd (1985) has remarked on the similarities with the priesthood:

An MP does what he does not for power, but for the more insidious pleasures of being elected to serve, which is like the dangerous pleasures of the priesthood in the way in which elected persons set themselves apart. By being elected they feel something has touched them and that is why I made this maybe rather far-fetched comparison with the priesthood.

Graham Greene would have relished the point. Elsewhere, Mr Hurd has drawn a parallel with a sort of trade union or masonry, since being elected is different from being appointed.

There is scope for late entrants to politics, like Paddy Ashdown, but they are, increasingly, the exceptions. Not everyone who starts early succeeds in politics – far from it; but virtually everyone who reaches the top has started early. All but four of the twenty members of the Commons in John Major's Cabinet formed after the April 1992 election became MPs before they were forty (ten before they were thirty-five) and eight first stood for Parliament in their twenties. Future Cabinet ministers who did not enter the Commons until their forties like Sir Patrick Mayhew or Michael Howard are the exceptions, and also in most cases their first serious involvement in politics, searching for a seat, began much earlier.

Almost all non-politicians or very late entrants who have later reached the Cabinet have, in effect, been brought in by the Prime Minister or party leader of the time, such as Frank Cousins and Lord Young of Graffham, who started off as a special adviser and was then chairman of the Manpower Services Commission before entering the Cabinet. One of few notable exceptions was Ernest Bevin, but he almost proves the point, since he would not have become an MP without the exceptional circumstances of 1940. He was elected an MP solely to become a minister, which he was for all but a few months of his time as an MP, and he was never at home in the Commons as such. Sir John Anderson, later Viscount Waverley, became an MP almost by accident in 1938, after a long career as a public servant, as discussed in Chapter 4. But within a few months he had become Lord Privy Seal with responsibility for civil defence. He wrote to his father, complaining:

There is, I fear, a definite prospect of my being invited to enter the Cabinet . . . It is rather a depressing prospect and knocks all my own plans for my future edgeways, but in these critical times I could not bring myself – with a long record of public service behind me – to refuse to answer a call from the head of the Government (Wheeler-Bennett, 1962).

Virtually no later politician would have even feigned such reluctance. Later, Sir John had the unusual satisfaction of becoming secretary of state at the Home Office, the department for which he had long been the permanent secretary.

Moreover, almost all the hereditary peers who have achieved real influence in post-war governments, rather than just grand-sounding titles, have been lifelong dedicated politicians, such as Lords Carrington, Home and Hailsham. The last two began their careers as members of the Commons and, having inherited in early middle age, renounced their peerages in 1963 in order to reach, or compete for, the top prize in politics. This is apart from former senior politicians in the Commons who become peers and remain in the Cabinet as Leaders of the House of Lords, like Lords Whitelaw and Wakeham. Lord Carrington is the sole holder of one of the top Cabinet posts not to have served in the Commons at all since an earlier Foreign Secretary, Lord Lansdowne, in the early 1900s. Lord Carrington's lack of Commons experience contributed to his difficulties, and resignation, over the Argentine invasion of the Falklands in 1982.

Lord Young's influence was dependent on having the ear of Margaret Thatcher, since he had no political base at Westminster and suffered as a result.

The vast majority of those reaching the highest level in politics have, therefore, started early in seeking, and obtaining, a seat in the Commons. Much can, of course, happen during the course of a political career to determine whether a promising new MP in his early thirties becomes a minister by forty, and is in the Cabinet by fifty. It is not just a matter of talent and ability. The safety or otherwise of an MP's seat is crucial, as Chris Patten, Francis Maude, John Maples and half a dozen other Tory ministers found when they lost their seats in April 1992 even though their party won the election. This is normally put down as luck, but then so is being selected in the first place.

In the past, most senior politicians moved fairly easily between seats. Until the 1919 and 1926 Re-election of Ministers Acts, MPs had to seek re-election on appointment to ministerial office. Most were successful but some, like Charles Masterman in 1914, were not and had to resign. There have also regularly been cases of ministers who have lost their seats while their parties have won nationally and remained in office. In some cases – for instance, Ramsay and Malcolm MacDonald in 1935 and Sir Frank Soskice in 1950 – they were successful in subsequent by-elections and continued in office. But others did not – most recently and notably Patrick Gordon Walker. Despite losing at Smethwick in the October 1964 general election, he was appointed Foreign Secretary in the first Wilson Government, but he lost a specially created by-election in January 1965 at Leyton and resigned. Gladstone, Disraeli and Macmillan all sat for more than one constituency, and Winston Churchill was the member for five different constituencies – Oldham, North West Manchester, Dundee, Epping and Wanstead – partly as a result of his various changes of party. In the past thirty years some politicians have survived defeat and returned to prosper in another constituency. Michael Foot, Bryan Gould, Tony Benn and Margaret Beckett are examples on the Labour benches, and Anthony Barber, John Gummer, Nicholas Scott and David Waddington on the Tory side. Other members shift to a different part of the country as a result of boundary changes, like Michael Heseltine did from Tavistock to Henley in February 1974. With typical adroitness Kenneth Baker managed to survive both defeat and the disappearance of his second seat in boundary changes by moving from Acton to St Marylebone and then to Mole Valley in Surrey.

But nowadays, boundary changes apart, it is much more difficult for a senior politician who is defeated at a general election easily to return at a subsequent by-election. The record of governing parties holding seats in by-elections is poor: the Tories, for example, only just retained Penrith and the Border after Willie Whitelaw became a life peer, and this contest was just a couple of months after the Tories' landslide victory in the 1983 general election. The Gordon Walker example has become a deterrent to the artificial creation of by-elections to bring defeated ministers back to the Commons. This was one of the main factors which persuaded Chris Patten to become Governor of Hong Kong after losing his seat in Bath in April 1992. The possibility of a by-election in a safe seat in central London was discussed, and urged on him by senior ministers and friends, but he rejected the option because of the risk of defeat.

A safe seat is therefore vital for an ambitious career politician. If you have a safe seat and your party is in power for a long time, like the Tories since 1979 or between 1951 and 1964, then you have a good chance of gaining preferment. By contrast, an MP, however talented, is likely to find life frustrating if his or her party is in opposition for long periods. Several times this century many politicians in one party or another have seen their careers in Parliament severely disrupted, and in some cases ended, by electoral convulsions when their party suffered large losses. This applied to many Tory MPs in 1906 (though it was easier then for prominent politicians, including party leader Arthur Balfour, to get back quickly because of the spreading out of polling days over three weeks until 1918); to many Liberal MPs in the elections of 1918 and 1922; to most Labour MPs in 1931; to many Tory MPs in 1945; and to many Labour MPs in the elections of 1979 and 1983. Some highly regarded current Labour MPs could go through their whole careers never enjoying office. The record of the past fifty years shows that some generations in one party or another are fortunate and prosper, while others do not. At present, of course, the generation of Tories at Cambridge in the late 1950s and 1960s is thriving at the top of John Major's Government, while few of their contemporaries on the Labour side are even in the Commons. Timing is critical. But the key characteristics of the career politician are commitment and energy, as well as good luck and timing.

Anthony King (1981) has offered a generally acceptable core definition of a career politician as someone who 'is committed to politics. He regards politics as his vocation, he seeks fulfilment in politics, he sees his future in politics, he would be deeply upset if circumstances forced him to retire from politics. In short, he is hooked.' That, as Professor King argues, does not mean that career politicians derive all, or even much, of their income from politics, or that they necessarily have to work at politics full-time, even though they would like to do so. Richard Rose (1987) has noted:

Politics is a calling very different from that of the business world, for many politicians forgo income in order to participate in Parliament. Advancement in politics requires the cultivation of political skills; and does not require many skills valued in other professions and occupations. Politics is a free-floating profession. MPs have no assurance of a regular and orderly promotion, as do bureaucratic employees. An MP's career is what he makes of it. What may be considered career planning in other occupations is usually described as the pursuit of ambition when practised by MPs.

Career politicians are obsessive; many MPs who have lost their seats are determined to return to the Commons. There is a high rate of recidivism. Nearly half of those who have lost their seats at general elections since 1970 have stood again (ignoring those who have unsuccessfully sought candidacies). And just under a third of defeated MPs have returned to the Commons at later by-elections or general elections. Francis Maude, the former Financial Secretary to the Treasury, would probably have entered the Cabinet in April 1992 if he had held his North Warwickshire seat. He has talked of a sense of personal loss and grief as in a bereavement. Nicholas Bennett, a junior minister at the Welsh Office who also lost in April 1992, said in a BBC interview, 'If you've got politics in the blood, it never goes away.' He was, at least initially, keeping up with *Hansard*. Both were keen to become MPs again.

Among earlier losers more fortunate in 1992, Mark Robinson, who was elected for Somerton and Frome after being defeated five years earlier, was quoted in the *Independent* in May 1991 as saying, 'Politics is like a bug. Once you get it, it is very difficult to shake off.' Similarly, Sir Derek Spencer, who lost Leicester South in June 1987 and was returned for Brighton Pavilion in April 1992, immediately becoming Solicitor-General, asked, 'Why throw up a six-figure income for the risks of politics? Basically, the excitement that comes from the uncertainty of it all. The feeling that you are at the centre of things. The opportunity to help individual constituents, which gives you a deep sense of personal satisfaction.' After his return to the Commons, he said (1992) it was like 'a dream going back into the chamber. I felt somebody was going to say, "OK. It's over – it's not real." Especially because, with all the new faces in the chamber, it's a bit like a film set to me anyway.'

We may or may not get the politicians we deserve, but we do get the politicians who believe we deserve them. British politics is largely self-selecting, involving a tiny political class. Only about 3 per cent of the electorate belong to a political party and probably less than 1 per cent are involved in the selection and reselection of parliamentary candidates – the crucial first stage of a political career. Most leading politicians succeed because of an act of will on their part. They are different from the rest of us because they make a specific choice at an early age which is then pursued with determination. In that sense, whatever their social background, they are abnormal.

Within the small political class, the successful are conformists. They do what is necessary to get selected as candidates and, when elected to Parliament, behave in line with existing norms of what is required to secure promotion. As the number of outsiders, the uncommitted, decreases, the pattern of preferment has become more institutionalized. Those aspiring to move up are expected to serve an apprenticeship, however short, at various junior levels – as a local councillor and/or officer in a constituency party, as a candidate in an unwinnable seat, then as victor in a marginal or safe seat, a spell as secretary to a back-bench committee, then time as a parliamentary private secretary to a minister, service in the Whips Office, promotion to under-secretary, minister of state, and then to the Cabinet. That, incidentally, is the career of John Major – 'the long road from Coldharbour Lane to Downing Street'. But it applies, with minor variations (for instance, not being a councillor or a whip), to half his Cabinet colleagues. The Labour ladder of promotion within the Commons is different. The Labour Whips Office has been much less of a training ground for its upwardly mobile MPs than has the Tory Whips Office. While two recent Tory leaders, Edward Heath and John Major, served in the Whips Office, no Labour leader has.

Roy Jenkins (1993) has complained about the formal hierarchy of political promotion 'under which everyone advances
through the whip's office to parliamentary secretary, to minister of state, to the Cabinet, and maybe to its head. This is an
innovation. Can one imagine Peel or Disraeli or Joseph Chamberlain or Lloyd George or Ernest Bevin as a junior whip? It
reduces, without obvious benefit to state or even party, the
business of government to the level of management promotion
in a bank or building society.' He is being rather grand.
Previous leaders may seldom have been ex-whips, but many,
including Gladstone, Churchill and Macmillan, did serve as
under-secretaries.

The ambitious adapt their lives accordingly. They take jobs
that will allow them to spend time as councillors, as local
party officers and to seek parliamentary candidacies. Self-
employed people with some control over their time, like
barristers or those running family businesses, have always been
well placed to pursue political interests. But there are few
other jobs permitting such flexibility. The ambitious have
increasingly chosen jobs related to politics. The list includes
trade union officials, full-time councillors, public affairs and
political consultants, members of policy think-tanks, special
advisers to ministers and shadow spokesmen and members of
the staffs of the parties.

Many of the ambitious have become more professional in
preparing for a full-time occupation. Only a minority, albeit a
growing minority, are professional politicians in the sense that
they have built up skills in these ancillary jobs. The term
professional has other connotations, associated with formal
qualifications and membership of an independent body super-
vising ethics and standards of conduct. So the designation of
full-time politician is preferable. He or she is a career politician
doing what he or she most wants to do.

This reflects the distinction which Max Weber drew between
those who live for and those who live off politics. The career

politician lives for politics in Weber's sense that, 'He who lives for politics makes politics his life, in an internal sense.' It is in many ways the ambition of the career politician to translate his or her commitment to politics as a life into an ability to live off politics. In Britain, it has been very difficult to live off politics unless you are an MP. The absence of state funding for parties and their own lack of resources have limited opportunities for full-time politicians who are not MPs. That may be changing to some extent in view of the growth during the 1970s and 1980s in the number of special and political advisers to ministers and front-bench spokesmen (in opposition financed by taxpayers thanks to what is known as Short money), of public affairs consultants and of full-time councillors. None the less, there is still a big contrast with the situation both in America, where there are many ancillary political jobs in Congress and the administration, and in Germany, where state funding, wealthy political parties and a diverse political structure (notably the strong regional *Länder*) support a large political class of advisers and officials.

But even MPs often find it difficult to live off, as well as for, politics. In the past, many Tory MPs had large private incomes, either inherited or from their own businesses. But that is true now of only a minority, which partly explains the desire of many back-benchers to supplement their incomes with consultancies and the like. Moreover, the growing number of women in work, and their increasing prominence in well-paid professional occupations, has benefited not only prospective female MPs but also, possibly as much, male politicians. A larger number of two-income households means that the relatively low salary of an MP is now, increasingly, supplemented by the sizeable income of the wife. The wife's earnings sustain the standard of living of the family and in effect support the husband's political career. Whereas a generation ago few wives of leading politicians would have had a full-time occupation – they would have been involved in part-time or voluntary work

– now most of the wives of politicians under fifty work full-time. There are plenty of Hillary Clintons among the wives of British politicians, including the spouses of several members of the Major Cabinet.

Parallel trends exist overseas. In his vivid account of the pursuit of office in America, Alan Ehrenhalt (1991) notes a similar rise in full-time politicians. In the more open candidate-based system of America, where parties matter much less in determining who stands, full-timers have driven out part-timers at all levels. Full-time campaigning for every post from the local school board upwards means that 'Politics in the 1990s is for people who are willing to give it vast amounts of time.' Lawyers involved in politics are not successful lawyers who have left thriving partnerships to run for public office, but are mainly political activists with law degrees. They are lawyers more by training than by profession. (Exactly the same applies in Britain. I once asked a distinguished lawyer/politician whom he would choose to defend himself on a murder charge; he produced a very short list – incidentally including John Smith – from the numerous barristers who are MPs. Similarly, many of the solicitors who are MPs come from small family practices rather than from large City or West End partnerships which demand a full-time commitment.)

Alan Ehrenhalt concludes that successful politicians 'got where they are through a combination of ambition, talent and the willingness to devote whatever time was necessary to seek and hold office'. His picture of the full-time politician is similar to the one emerging in Britain. In the past, politics, especially at local and state levels, was treated as a sideline to a main occupation, but no longer. Candidates now give politics their primary attention. There has also been a rapid growth in reasonably paid staff posts, both in Congress and in state legislatures, to provide the committed with the necessary training and experience to run for office. Bud Stewart, for twenty-six years city manager of Concord, a suburb of San

Francisco, says, 'The typical person who gets elected now is someone who grows up in the political process. Politics is a vocation for them.' Even though nearly everybody who holds office in Concord has another job somewhere else, since the official salaries are low, 'For most of them a job in private life is simply a way to make a political career possible. It is a means, not an end.'

A similar growth in the number of career politicians is noticeable even in the opposite type of political system, where parties are all-powerful in the selection of candidates, as in Germany. Under the variant of proportional representation in use there, members of the Bundestag elected in constituencies, as in Britain, are supplemented by those chosen from a list nominated by the parties in relation to voters' preferences between the parties. This naturally gives the party headquarters a key role and the ambitious ensure that they are in favour. As noted earlier, the sizeable, state-financed party headquarters and their associated research institutes replenish the pool of the talented and ambitious for recruitment to the Bundestag. In both Germany and France the dividing lines between party politicians and career civil servants are much more blurred than in Britain or America. Many ministers in Bonn and Paris have a long background of public service, rising up through the party machine and serving in local and regional government. A more detailed comparison in political careers between Britain and overseas is offered in later chapters.

In Britain as elsewhere, there has, of course, been a long tradition of full-time commitment by leading politicians. The citizen-legislator was always largely a myth. Indeed, as far back as Wolsey and Thomas Cromwell, many of the monarch's most prominent advisers were, in effect, career politicians. From the eighteenth century onwards, many leading politicians, and ministers, regarded their life at Westminster as a career. Being actively involved in the legislature and the executive was associated with the duties of a hereditary aristocracy. The

difference from now is that a political career was then open
only to the élite. Moreover, a political career was not a full-
time occupation. Until the Second World War, many MPs,
especially Tories, functioned independently of their existence in
the Commons. They were businessmen or landowners, not
dependent on the Commons for either their income or their
position in society. While many in the governing class have
always lived for politics, now most live off politics, in the
sense defined by Max Weber above. A related change is that a
greater number in the Commons now live for and off politics.

The myth of the grand career of politics has deep roots.
Since the late eighteenth century a parliamentary career has, in
the words of Edmund Burke, been regarded as an 'honourable
venture'. The lives of Pitt the Younger, Peel, Gladstone and
especially Disraeli became an inspiration for those attracted by
politics. This Romantic myth was encouraged by the flowering
of the political novel in the mid-nineteenth century – not just
Disraeli himself, writing the script for his own later triumphs,
but also Trollope and Eliot. Disraeli was candid in admitting
to his constituents in Shrewsbury in 1844:

There is no doubt, gentlemen, that all men who offer themselves as
candidates for public favour have motives of some sort. I candidly
acknowledge that I have and I will tell you what they are: I love
fame; I love public reputation; I love to live in the eye of the country;
and it is a glorious thing for a man who has had my difficulties to
contend against.

The classic expression of the 'glittering prizes' view of a
political career came in the words and deeds of F. E. Smith,
particularly in his Glasgow University Rectoral Address of
November 1923. He argued: 'Nothing is more apparent than
that politically, economically and philosophically the motive
of self-interest not only is, but must be, and ought to be, the
mainspring of human conduct.' He went on, memorably, to
state: 'The world continues to offer glittering prizes to those

who have stout hearts and sharp swords; it is therefore extremely improbable that the experience of future ages will differ in any material respect from that which has happened since the twilight of the human race.' In a later address to Aberdeen University, he praised 'honourable ambition' and 'honest opportunism'. As John Campbell (1983) argues in his biography of F. E. Smith, the 'glittering prize' remarks were taken out of context. His main aim was to express scepticism about the liberal internationalism of the post-war era, and he affronted enthusiasts for the League of Nations by maintaining that the only way to preserve peace was to be prepared for war. But, Campbell writes, 'Though in fact he was clearly referring to the rewards to powerful nations of military victory in war, he was widely taken to be urging on the students of Glasgow the personal rewards open to competitive ambition in the battle of life.' His own career was seen as exemplary in seeking glittering prizes, from cups to scholarships to office, wealth and fame. Campbell adds: 'So long as a man did not betray his friends or his principles, or breach the fundamental tenets of morality, he believed quite openly in ambition and despised the cant of those who pretended to be above it – particularly when by professing disinterested self-abnegation they somehow rose to be Prime Minister or Foreign Secretary.' He gloried in 'the endless adventure of governing men'.

Michael Heseltine has been the most striking contemporary example of this view, consciously building his life around the ascent of the greasy pole. I remember a conversation that took place at a critical point during the Westland saga, with apt irony at a party given by Jeffrey Archer just before Christmas 1985, when he asked, with evident irritation, 'Why shouldn't I be Prime Minister, then?' It was a question he kept asking, at least to himself, for nearly another five years until November 1990, and probably also after that.

Most political motives are complicated, as the quotations at the beginning of this chapter suggest. The comments by Richard

Crossman came from his review of Leo Amery's still stimulating *Thoughts on the Constitution* (1947). Amery wrote:

It is, indeed, as a never-ending adventure that political life most appears in retrospect, a great game with its 'Routs and discomfitures, rushes and rallies', its 'Fights for the fearless and goals for the eager'. A game in thinking back over which one may often be inclined to wonder 'had I done this, had I left that undone', sometimes tempted to feel that the struggle has been unavailing and to overlook the silent flooding in of unhoped-for results. On the whole one remains content to believe that the game itself was good, and that one played one's best for one's own chosen goals and by one's own rules.

The lure of glittering prizes and delight in the game should not be exaggerated. Most politicians become involved initially as a result of some ideological commitment, however vaguely defined, or a general concern about 'the condition of England'. This may be associated with family influences or with conversion and experience of life. The majority of MPs do believe in something beyond their own advancement, even if it is only their party right or wrong. This is reflected in their choice of parties. They may be influenced by the intellectual current of the day, but their decision is seldom made on a whim. Similarly, during their later careers, MPs frequently act against their own immediate career interests because of their views. A good example in the past generation has been attitudes to Europe. Roy Jenkins probably finished his chances of becoming Labour leader after he headed the group of sixty-nine MPs who defied the official party whip and voted for the principle of entry in October 1971, and then when he resigned from the deputy leadership a year later on the issue of a referendum on European entry. Many of the sixty-nine later became supporters of the SDP, though one who did not, John Smith, became Labour leader, backed by many previous critics of EC membership. Many of the younger non-MP supporters of the SDP would have advanced their careers, and prospects of becoming

MPs, more by remaining within the Labour Party instead of leaving.

When trying to unravel their own motives, politicians usually balance ambition and public service. As discussed in Chapter 5, many MPs find much of their satisfaction comes from their service to constituents. Many also become involved in response to some event: for instance, the Suez crisis in 1956 or the growing power of the trade unions. Sir Terence Higgins, a middle-ranking Treasury minister in the Heath years but ignored by Mrs Thatcher, said (1985) that the thought he could make a contribution 'about economics encouraged me into politics, plus the feeling about helping people in the constituency. My theme has always been economic, and attempts to escape from it have not been very easy – and indeed I don't really want to.'

While it is misleading to regard all career politicians as careerists in the narrow sense that they are just interested in advancing their careers, it is equally wrong to talk solely about policy and ignore personality. Few politicians become involved without an inner core of ambition. In his classic study of political life, Henry Fairlie (1968) concludes that, while ambition is the quality in a politician which many people seem to find most objectionable, it is, in fact, one of the most necessary virtues: 'It is humbug in a politician not to recognize that he is moved by it, and to pretend that he is driven solely by a concern for the people's good or even by a divine call.'

That is also the view of William Waldegrave, who has tended to be discounted as an aristocratic intellectual. He echoes (1985) Enoch Powell's line on ambition:

Any politician who tells you he isn't [ambitious] is only telling you he isn't for some tactical reason; or, more bluntly, telling you a lie. There are people in public life and in the House of Commons who are not ambitious other than to get into the House of Commons and represent their locality. There are other people, the hired charges as it were, who get in because the party needs people to be ministers.

I certainly wouldn't deny that I wanted ministerial office; yes, I'm ambitious.

The motives of politicians are examined in more detail in later chapters. But the key point is that the nineteenth-century Romantic tradition saw politics as an adventure as much as a cause, and one which applied only to the few. The assumption in both nineteenth-century political novels and the careers of those who sought the 'glittering prizes' was that only a few would compete. Most in the political class were content to observe the rise and fall of the stars. Pitt the younger, Chancellor of the Exchequer at twenty-three and Prime Minister at twenty-four, was a committed politician by any definition, as were Disraeli and Gladstone, for all their varied intellectual and personal interests. But they were exceptions. Most MPs did not aspire to be like them. Until well into the twentieth century, there was a clear division between men of office and perpetual back-benchers who retained a wide range of outside interests.

For a considerable time after the 1868 Reform Act, MPs were regarded as representatives of interests and locations. Writing in *The English Constitution* in 1867, Bagehot described the House of Commons as composed of 658 persons 'collected from all parts of England, different in nature, different in interests, different in looks, different in language'. This was replaced by a class view of representation following the extension of the franchise in 1884 and the split in the Liberal Party over Irish Home Rule in 1886. The Tories, or rather the Unionists, under Lord Salisbury and Balfour presented themselves as the defenders of property against the radical threat of the Liberals and then, gradually from 1906 onwards, of Labour. David Cannadine (1990) has described the dramatic change from 1880 onwards in the social composition of the House of Commons. In 1880, of 652 MPs, as many as 394 were nobles, baronets, landed gentry or their near relations, and 325 had an interest in land. Youngest sons of peers followed their fathers into the Commons. Even as early as 1883, *The Times* was reporting, 'Members have been heard during the last few weeks asking whether it was any longer an assembly of gentlemen.' That was premature. But by the 1930s less than a tenth of MPs had a close landed connection and on the Tory side they were overshadowed by those from the professions and business. The plutocracy had taken over from the hereditary landed aristocracy. Many more millionaires served in the inter-war Parliaments than in the nineteenth century. Landowners and gentry were more concerned with survival.

Most MPs on both sides continued to regard themselves as foot soldiers, or at least as solid regimental officers, rather than as members of the general staff, whether they were knights of the shire or long-serving trade union officials. Service in Parliament was not a full-time occupation and there was usually plenty of time for all but a handful of the most committed to follow outside interests and country pursuits. Even if there were fewer ministerial aspirants or 'serious' politicians in the Commons before the 1900s than there are now, this does not mean that the competition for office was any less intense then. The demand for posts may have increased, but so has the supply. In pre-1906 administrations half the posts in the Cabinet were taken by peers and only just over two dozen MPs were members of the Government at all, including whips. Three times as many MPs are now in the Government, even excluding parliamentary private secretaries. So, as discussed in Chapter 6, many of the ambitions of the career politicians have been satisfied by an expansion in opportunities. The Empire has disappeared as a source of employment for former ministers or those in mid-career, as in the cases of Lords Curzon and Halifax – with the notable recent exception of Chris Patten. But there are now politically and socially acceptable alternatives in running quangos and in directorships in the private sector.

Attitudes to political careers among MPs began to change with the further widening of the franchise in 1918 and the replacement of the Liberals by Labour. After the Second World War Leo Amery noted in 1947

a great change in the composition of the House of Commons itself. The House of fifty years ago consisted almost entirely of frock-coated top-hatted men of substance, younger sons, landlords, big business men, leaders in the professions, none of them dependent on politics for a living, few of them able or willing to give their whole time to public work. It was, in fact, composed of the men who in the literal sense of the word owned and directed the country. Since then the House has been changed out of all recognition. In 1895 the House was nearly equally divided between the landowning class, big business, and the professions, the last mainly lawyers. In the present [post-1945] House, professional men in the widest sense of the word form the main body of some 250, with 170 manual workers or ex-manual workers as the second largest group, and with the balance, most in the opposition ranks, divided between business and the old landowning and services class ... What is more, membership has become a very different occupation. Members today are expected to be at the House not only all the afternoon and evening, but in ever increasing proportions for committee work in the morning. The 'best club in London' has become an overworked legislation factory ... Politics are thus becoming more and more, for those who take them at all seriously, an all-time or most-of-the-time profession.

It is one of those delightful ironies of politics that, at about the time these views were being put forward, the underrated and astute Leo Amery was giving advice on a political career to a precocious fourteen-year-old wearing a school blazer whom he had heard address a Conservative conference in Central Hall, Westminster. Over tea in Eaton Square, one of the great figures of the Imperial Tradition offered some precepts for life to someone who was to become one of the exemplars of post-war meritocratic Conservatism: he should be widely read and become financially independent. The young prodigy was Peter Walker. According to his autobiography, appropriately entitled *Staying Power* (1991), he built his subsequent career around those two sensible pieces of advice. Mr Walker proved to be one of the most successful, and at any rate durable, career politicians of his time, serving as a member of the Cabinets of both Edward Heath and Margaret Thatcher (before leaving voluntarily earlier in the year of her downfall, 1990).

Leo Amery's warnings may seem either prescient or premature, but the trends he identified have gathered pace over the years. Anthony King (1981) has suggested a number of indicators to mark the rise of the career politician: for example, the increasing number of MPs being first elected in their forties (and increasingly in their thirties) as opposed to both older and younger; the increasing number of seats a prospective member fights before being elected; and the increasing number of members staying in the Commons until retiring in their sixties. He has also suggested a series of categories moving from less to greater commitment among Cabinet ministers since the Second World War. These range from those who have come into politics out of a sense of duty and were or are never really at home, such as Frank Cousins; via those who have entered politics more or less by accident and might be equally content elsewhere, such as Oliver Lyttelton, and those who, while committed to politics, are partly detached and have other interests, such as Roy Jenkins; to, finally, the totally committed, such as Harold Wilson and Margaret Thatcher. He reports a steady reduction in the number of the less committed and a corresponding increase in the proportion of the totally committed between the Attlee and Churchill administrations in the decade after 1945 and the final Wilson, Callaghan and Thatcher administrations.

Another way of looking at the growth in the number and character of career politicians is to examine what MPs were doing before they were elected. Did they pursue an independent career and then decide in their thirties and forties that they would like to become MPs, as was the frequent pattern before 1945? Or did they take on jobs from their early twenties onwards which were entirely secondary to their main goal of winning a seat in the Commons? Did they, in the language of Westminster, ever have 'proper' jobs? MPs can be divided into three groups: first, full-time politicians who earned their living working as a special adviser, on the staff of a political party or in the various ancillary jobs discussed above, like full-time union officials or consultants; second, those in an intermediate position in jobs which are not long-term careers but are intended to facilitate political activity; and third, those in so-called 'proper' jobs, wholly independent of politics. These distinctions are inevitably subjective, but at least they should be consistent across time.

The main conclusion is that there has been a steady increase in the number of those who are already full-time politicians when they are elected to the Commons, as well as of those in the intermediate category. The total of full-time politicians (for both the Tories and Labour) rose from 11 per cent of new MPs in 1951 to nearly 31 per cent in 1992. By contrast, the proportion of new MPs in 'proper' jobs fell from 80 per cent to 41 per cent between 1951 and 1992. These figures point to a dramatic change, but it is still true that nearly half of new MPs, and more than half of existing ones, held 'proper' jobs before being elected. The relative change has considerable implications, which are discussed in later chapters, but it would be wrong to ignore the continuing large number of MPs for whom arrival in the Commons is the pinnacle of their career and who are content to play, or resigned to playing, a supporting role.

A large part of the explanation for the rise of the career politician lies in the increasing specialization of all jobs over the past fifty years. Virtually every trade or occupation now demands a full-time commitment. The days of the gentleman amateur have gone, except in some of the more exotic byways of journalism and in the running of professional sport. Very few MPs can afford to treat politics as an amusing diversion. No MP can now have both a seat in the Commons and a career at the top of business, the law or even the trade unions (none of whose leaders is now an MP). This is unlike even the pre-1939 era when, as Michael Moran (1989) has written, the Tory ranks contained a sprinkling of senior industrialists such as Sir Alfred Mond, a founder of ICI. 'Before the First World War, for instance, it was perfectly possible to combine a successful career at the top of business and at the top of politics. Neither sphere demanded the exclusive commitment of time and ambition now required.' Philip Stanworth and Anthony Giddens (1974) looked at 460 leading companies and showed that in the last quarter of the nineteenth century some 36 per cent of chairmen had been MPs at some stage of their career. The total was still 19 per cent in the inter-war era, when the influx of businessmen after the 1918 election prompted Keynes's jibe about 'hard-faced men who had done well out of the war'. But by the late 1960s and 1970s only 4 per cent of chairmen of sizeable companies had ever served as MPs. By the 1980s the only prominent company chairmen in the Commons were Sir Edward du Cann of Lonrho and James Prior of GEC (after he left the Cabinet in 1984); otherwise, one of the few more traditional business figures was Sir Peter Tapsell, a successful stockbroker and investment adviser, who has never been a minister.

In general, those wanting to reach the top in any large organization have had to give up the idea of running for the Commons. Political ambitions are frowned upon as a sign of not being seriously committed to the company. Only the self-employed, such as lawyers, small businessmen and farmers, or those in public sector jobs allowing time off, such as teachers and lecturers, are able to pursue political ambitions, whether on their local council or in the Commons.

The growth of government has also imposed greater

demands, not only on ministers themselves but also on MPs aspiring to be ministers and those seeking to scrutinize the activities of government. MPs now also devote much more attention to their constituents, answering letters and holding local surgeries (a trend much deplored by both Churchill and Attlee). The expanding role of the MP as welfare officer shows how members now see their job as a full-time occupation. Approaching the job in this way, MPs now seek fulfilment by being active both in monitoring government and in looking after their constituents. This is not inconsistent with the continued involvement of many, especially Conservative, MPs with out-side interests, whether in business, in the law or as consultants to companies. That primarily reflects their desire to supplement their incomes and to keep in touch with outside bodies, while in no way detracting from their ambitions as career politicians. Few MPs ever turn down the offer of a government job, even though it means they may have to give up substantial outside incomes. Their political careers almost always come first.

Moreover, it is increasingly difficult to transfer into politics in your late forties or fifties. The competition for candidacies in winnable seats, and the time required, mean that someone with a demanding post in a big organization finds it very hard to stroll into a constituency, as occurred until the 1950s. A lengthy apprenticeship has, in almost all cases, to be served by anyone wanting to enter the Commons and to be considered as a potential minister. The specialization and compartmentaliza-tion of careers noted above mean that leaders in other occupa-tions neither want nor are able to become full-time politicians in their forties or fifties. Of the 140 new MPs elected in April 1992, only twenty were aged over fifty.

These trends have changed the character of Parliament and of British politics. Whatever their differences of ideology, local origin, previous employment and even accent, new MPs are much more alike – entering the Commons in their thirties or early forties, ending their previous employment (which they may have already done to prepare for a campaign if selected for a safe or winnable seat) and eager, on the whole, to work full-time as MPs for many years.

To Denis Healey, who retired from the Commons in 1992 after forty years' service (1992):

The big difference between my early years in the House [and now] is the change in the class structure of the two parties. That was largely the result of the welfare state reforms introduced by the Attlee Government. When I first came in, I should think that at least half the Labour MPs were clearly manual workers – miners, engineers or factory workers. The bulk of Tory MPs were clearly gentry and that has changed enormously. Now the majority of Labour MPs come from the professions, particularly the public services. Meanwhile Mrs Thatcher took her party away from the landowners and gave it to the estate agents, so the average Tory MP is indistinguishable from the Labour one. The physical difference has gone.

Denis Healey exaggerates; while there may have been a narrowing, though not an elimination, of publicly noticeable physical and social contrasts between MPs, there are still important differences of origin and occupation.

The changes have disturbed some of the old-stagers. Sir David Price, a stalwart Tory back-bencher and former junior minister who left the Commons in 1992 after thirty-seven years, noted in a pre-retirement reflection (1991):

We certainly have more career politicians amongst us who have little else in life but politics than in 1955. We have far less of the other type of member who came into the House in middle life with no ambition to be other than a decent local MP – the country squire, the successful local businessman, the old type of trade union leader, the redoubtable northern alderman. The new type of member is more knowledgeable about the details of modern government – possibly took a degree in politics or sociology. He or she is more professional in their approach, having worked in the media, academia, public relations or advertising.

Looking around the Commons at the new members elected in April 1992, there were admittedly a handful who had achieved some fame and distinction beforehand. The most prominent were Glenda Jackson with her Oscars for acting and Sebastian Coe with his Olympic gold medals for running – and for those with more oleaginous tastes, Lady Olga Maitland, the gossip columnist, and Gyles Brandreth, the television personality. Most of the other new MPs may have done reasonably well in their chosen jobs – failures and bankrupts are seldom selected by constituency parties. But few were previously at the top of their profession or occupation. In the past not only were leading industrialists often members of the Commons but so were prominent literary figures. In the late eighteenth century, Sheridan, Burke and Gibbon were all members (though the latter was silent throughout his service), while in the nineteenth century Macaulay was prominent. In this century, Hilaire Belloc, John Buchan and A. P. Herbert were members; Julian Critchley has amused in his wry way over the years, but he is not in the same league.

The absence of members of such outside distinction has resulted in a narrowing of focus within Parliament. A House where Geoffrey Dickens and Andrew Faulds are regarded as characters has obvious deficiencies. A loss of originality, individuality, even of eccentricity, was one of the complaints of many of the retiring MPs in 1992. This is not to say that all MPs are alike – Identikit meritocrats; Glasgow machine politicians still face public-school barristers, bankers and stockbrokers. But these much debated social differences are not only fewer, or rather more subtle, than they were; they are also much less important than the desire of the vast majority of MPs to treat politics as a career, and preferably a full-time occupation.

The argument should not, however, be overstated. New MPs may start out ambitious and single-minded, but a taste of failure and disappointment can lead to greater detachment.

Alastair Goodlad, who was unexpectedly dropped from the Government in 1987, when only forty-three, reflected (1988):

People who think of a political career are probably unwise; it's more helpful to think in terms of a political life. The vagaries of politics are such that it is not possible to plot a career in the same way that you would in other fields. It is much better to seek to forward things you believe in, in all the ways available to you, rather than to fine-tune a ministerial career.

But such reflections do not extinguish the flame of ambition. Alastair Goodlad returned to the Government in 1989 and resumed his rise up the ladder of preferment.

The changes in the nature of the Commons have not been costless, as Lisanne Radice and her fellow authors (1990) have written in their study of MPs. Increased experience and knowledge of politics have to be balanced against corresponding lack of experience and knowledge of the world outside politics. Greater ambition may be linked to greater partisanship and greater dogmatism. 'The public may believe it gets a better deal from such tireless and committed individuals, training themselves all their lives for their political goals; they might also remember Shaw's sardonic suggestion that those who single-mindedly pursue public office should be considered to have disqualified themselves from holding it.' Sir David Price, whose regrets at the changes were noted above, acknowledges that the new style of member might possibly be a better social worker than the old style – 'But are they wiser? Have they as much experience of life?'

Career politicians can be inward-looking. MPs prefer the company of those in the political world, whether fellow members or even political journalists, to those outside, including sometimes their own constituents. Those within the political world talk the same language, and understand the same nuances – almost a code of their own, which often sounds alien and incomprehensible to outsiders. Politicians inhabit a private intellectual and social world, largely separate from those running large companies or the professions. Their priorities are differ-ent – notably trying to stay in office and retain their seats, which can produce a short– rather than a long-term perspective. Their role as full-time politicians also produces an innate preference for activity, whether as a minister or a back-bencher. Thatcher-ite maxims about government being best when it governs least have been contradicted by the volumes of legislation since 1979. Reining back the public sector suits the activist/career politician just as much as expanding public spending. Tory sceptics about the role of government, like, for instance, John Biffen became and Nicholas Budgen, are out of fashion in the modern Com-mons. The expansion of the select committee system since 1979 has, in part, been a safety valve to permit the energies of full-time back-benchers to find an outlet in a way which is either useful or harmless, depending on your viewpoint.

The rise of the career politician raises the question of whether the public is being well served by such a closed world of rulers. Do the processes by which the ambitious advance their careers and get selected work against the choice of those who might make good ministers and even back-benchers? Are the attributes needed for selection – single-minded commit-ment, focus and energy – contrary to those needed by a successful legislator or minister? Are we, in short, choosing people by criteria which are irrelevant or harmful to their later roles in Parliament? Are many people of talent and proven ability in other occupations being excluded by the need to become involved so young? Are the new breed more partisan and out of touch than their predecessors? Has the rise of the career/full-time politician contributed to a broader public disil-lusionment with Parliament and the political process? The following chapters explore the motives and the route to the top of our leaders, before considering whether the process of selection should be broadened.

2

FIRST STIRRINGS

'In 1923, at the age of seven, I had an operation for appendicitis ... It took place on the day of the general election, called by Stanley Baldwin, who was seeking a mandate to introduce tariff reform protection for Britain's industries. That evening my parents came to see me in hospital as I came round from the anaesthetic. As they lingered, I kept urging them to leave so that they would be in time to vote for Philip – my hero Philip Snowden.'

Harold Wilson, *Memoirs, 1916–64*, 1986

'Mainly by intuition I came to believe in what we would now call capitalist non-interventionist economic theories and to discard completely the fashionable paternalistic and Socialist doctrines of the mid-1940s. So even at fourteen years of age I had conceived a distrust of Socialism and a sympathy with the liberal free-market views which, unknown to me, Professor Hayek was expressing in *The Road to Serfdom* – a book I was not to read for almost forty years.'

Norman Tebbit, *Upwardly Mobile*, 1988

'John [Major] sat in the Strangers' Gallery and watched a debate. The whole experience hit him with the force of a cannon ball. "I was pretty clear I wanted to go back to the House of Commons. Indeed, so clear was I that I wouldn't actually go back very often and listen to the debates because it was frustrating to go there and not be a part of it. I feared I might never get there."'

John Major, looking back on his first visit to the Commons aged thirteen, in Nesta Wyn Ellis, in *John Major: A Personal Biography*, 1991

Most career politicians become hooked when they are in their teens. A familiar pattern appears in the vast majority of

profiles, published interviews, biographies and personal conversations with MPs. They start being interested in politics when
they are very young and many become determined to follow a
political career by the time they are twenty. It does not matter
which party the MP is from, or what his or her social background is, the same phrases recur: 'At the latest when I entered
the sixth form I decided I wanted to be an MP' (Barry Jones,
Labour); 'I think I probably wanted to be an MP ever since I
was about twelve' (Tony Newton, Conservative); 'I joined the
Labour Party at sixteen in Shropshire' (David Blunkett,
Labour); 'I was interested in politics as a child' (Peter Bottomley, Conservative); 'I started taking leaflets around with my
mother when I was about two and remember going to a trade
union meeting with my father when I was about five' (Ian
McCartney, Labour); 'I don't know why but I had this desire
to be an MP at a very early age – like other kids want to be
ballet dancers or engine drivers' (Janet Fookes, Conservative);
'At the age of eleven I decided that I wanted to be an MP'
(David Amess, Conservative).

But why did these youngsters from such a wide variety of
backgrounds become interested in politics, and which qualities
turned that interest into what for many of them became a
vocation, or even an obsession? This is the most fascinating,
and elusive, question in all political biographies and autobiographies – and often the most inadequately answered. Take a
teenager, born in 1943 and growing up in Brixton in the 1950s,
who experienced a marked change for the worse in his standard
of living and circumstances in his formative years. Why should
he become a Tory at a time when the fashion among his
contemporaries was to move to the left?

No one has yet satisfactorily explained why John Major
became such an active Tory so young. His biographers write
as if it was inevitable, even though Bruce Anderson (1991) and
Edward Pearce (1991) agree that there was no politics or
political discussion at home. None the less, his parents appear

to have been instinctive, patriotic Tories. There is no dispute that he became interested in politics early, like most politicians, and that he formed his ambition to become an MP after visiting the Commons to listen to a debate when he was thirteen. His biographers differ over whether he began to be active politically 'not much later', when he ran into some Young Conservatives canvassing in Brixton market and began to help them (according to Anderson), or two to three years later, when he was canvassed by the Conservative Party and joined on the spot (according to Wyn Ellis). Either way, he was involved by his mid-teens and soon began his career as a soap-box speaker. He had also formed his strong, and long-standing, dislike of racial discrimination by this stage.

Bruce Anderson argues that John Major had little doubt about his choice of party:

At no stage, however briefly, did he have a left-wing phase. It might have seemed more natural for a poor boy from a poor part of London to resent the *status quo* and identify with the Labour Party, which claimed to represent the poor – but John Major rejected these claims. Like most teenagers, he did have radical enthusiasms, and was instinctively anti-establishment, but in his south London, the establishment was a Labour one; in his eyes, Labour was the party of the *status quo* ... John Major could not see what benefit the poor derived from Labour rule.

That is not entirely convincing, since the ruling Labour group in those days was moderate and mainstream by any standards, even if somewhat paternalist.

These theories, though, are still mainly only descriptions, rather than explanations, of what he did. They leave a puzzle, or rather two puzzles: why did John Major decide to pursue a political career with a determination which struck friends and acquaintances by his late teens and early twenties, and why did he become a Tory? The sincerity of John Major's account of the development of his views is not in doubt. His decision to seek a political career reflects his reaction, as a teenager, to the change for the worse in his family circumstances after the move to Brixton. This linked with the business difficulties and illness of his aged father, and, for a time, his mother. He left school uncertain and confused. Political activity provided, not for the first time, an answer to feelings of personal insecurity and inadequacy. It gave him an opportunity to prove himself.

Half a century earlier a youngster from a similar social background who lived just a few streets away from where John Major grew up in Brixton also became committed to politics. He was Herbert Morrison, later Deputy Leader of the Labour Party and a leading figure in government from 1940 to 1951. In his case he opted for Labour, not the Conservatives. Morrison's biographers, Bernard Donoughue and George Jones (1973), write, 'He was not born into it [Socialism], nor bred in it, nor was there any sudden revelation. It was a gradual intellectual conversion.' While he was working in a Brixton shop, Morrison first became interested in politics at around the age of sixteen. Politics were rarely discussed at home, since the family followed the unquestioning Conservatism of his father, a policeman. His political consciousness was first awakened by street orators – a forerunner of John Major's liking for soap-box speaking both as a young man and as Prime Minister. Morrison had initially been attracted by the great preachers whose thunderings crammed the churches. He was also told by a phrenologist who read his head that he might one day be Prime Minister, which stirred his existing ambitions.

The related questions of why politics and which party can still be answered in many cases by family background and views. This is no longer primarily a matter of heredity, though some of the traditional political families are still represented in the Commons. The names Churchill, Soames, Hurd, Hogg, Brooke, Channon and Aitken have been heard in the Commons for much of this century, and earlier in some cases. (David Faber, a grandson of Harold Macmillan, also won a seat in 1992). In recent Parliaments only about twenty to thirty MPs (just twenty-four after the 1992 general election) have been either the sons or the daughters of former members – fewer than earlier in the century.

Virtually all of these MPs are in the same party as their parents, though there have been a few exceptions. One of Baldwin's sons became a Labour MP, and the son of Jimmy Thomas, one of Labour's founding generation, became a Tory. Sir Nigel Fisher was the long-serving Tory MP for Surbiton until 1983, when his son, Mark, entered the House as the Labour MP for Stoke-on-Trent Central. In the opposite direction, Michael Irvine, the son of Sir Arthur Irvine, a Labour Solicitor-General, was the Tory MP for Ipswich for five years from 1987. The fathers of both Tony Benn and Greville Janner were Liberal MPs before they switched over to become Labour members. A similar move was made by Michael Foot's brother Dingle; their father had been a prominent Liberal MP.

For these hereditary political families, continued involvement is not surprising. Douglas Hurd is the third generation of Tory MPs from his family. His first political memory was his grandfather's election campaign at Devizes in 1935, when, aged five, he and two brothers were dressed in blue and were placed as a demonstration of Tory solidarity in the front row of a Liberal meeting. At about the same time he was also introduced to Lloyd George, 'shorter than I thought and with dramatically white hair'. In his unexpectedly self-revelatory autobiography, Roy Jenkins (1991) almost takes it for granted that he would become interested in politics in view of his father's activities as a leading official of the Miners' Federation, as a district and county councillor, as a member of the National Executive of the Labour Party, and, from 1935, as an MP. Politics were part of the daily background to his life, including visits to his home by many of the great Labour figures of the era. He also accompanied his father to party conferences and meetings. When he was fifteen, he started visiting the House of Commons regularly after his father became an MP: 'I was an indefatigable listener to debates (a habit I fear I did not subsequently keep up).'

Daughters as well as sons are affected. Llin Golding, whose father, Ness Edwards was Labour member for Caerphilly for twenty-nine years, remembers (1990) delivering leaflets when she was six years old: 'I became used to the MP's lifestyle as a child.' Emma Nicholson (1990) was similarly imbued with politics very young, since her father, three uncles, ten cousins and numerous relatives from earlier generations had served in the House: 'I was born into a very political family and my own political leanings started when I was about four or five. I had my sights set on a political career throughout my schooldays.'

While there are now few Cecils or Churchills in the House of Commons, there are a surprising number of MPs who grew up in a politically interested family. Their parents may not have been national leaders but they were often important local figures, active on the town council, in a constituency party or in their union branch. Just as many sports stars – Sebastian Coe and Steffi Graf are merely two obvious recent examples – had almost fanatically dedicated fathers to push their careers, so too did many MPs grow up in homes already steeped in politics. Looking at the personal histories of 200 recent and current MPs, family influence appears to have been crucial for a remarkably high number, particularly those living in communities with a firmly established class identity.

Margaret Thatcher was born into politics as much as any of her Tory predecessors. Hugo Young (1989) vividly describes how politics infused the atmosphere in which she was reared. Her father, Alderman Alfred Roberts – without question one of the biggest influences on British politics this century –

handed on to his daughter not only his values but also the
example of the attractions of the political life. As important as
his precepts was his practice, as a prominent local figure on
the board of everything that mattered in Grantham as she
grew up. At the age of ten, in the 1935 general election, she
was running canvass lists and messages between polling stations and party headquarters. She was already attracted by
politics, and was a vigorous and single-minded participant in
debates at her local girls' grammar school. But it was not until
much later that she thought about pursuing a parliamentary
career. As an adolescent she did not believe such a full-time
political career was possible, because of a shortage of money.
While Alderman Roberts was officially an Independent all his
time on the council, as well as a believer in municipal activism,
he signed the nomination papers of the Conservative candidate
and MP in 1935. His values were those of the thrifty and
successful shopkeeper he was. As argued in my own study of
the first Thatcher term (1983), Thatcherism, as it became
known, was

essentially an instinct, a series of moral values and an approach to
leadership rather than an ideology ... an expression of Mrs
Thatcher's upbringing in Grantham, her background of hard work
and family responsibility, ambition and postponed satisfaction, duty
and patriotism. Her views were 'born of the conviction which I
learned in a small town from a father who had a conviction approach', as she put it in an interview in January 1983 on London
Weekend Television's *Weekend World* programme.

Mrs Thatcher inherited a paternal commitment to politics
which sustained her throughout her career.

Many Labour MPs were similarly born into politics, even if,
like Mrs Thatcher, not to an automatic assumption that they
would enter the Commons. That is the key difference with the
older generation of hereditary MPs, although both groups

have politics in their blood. Several middle-aged Labour MPs from Wales talk of the influence of family, both on their party preference and on their desire to go into politics. Robert Harris notes (1984), for example, in his biography of the former Labour leader:

What is clear is that Neil Kinnock did not, like most of his colleagues, acquire his Socialism. He was born into it. Politics is discussed in south Wales with the enthusiasm and spontaneity which in England is devoted to sport or the weather. This was especially true in Tredegar in the 1950s, when the MP since 1929 was Aneurin Bevan. All the Kinnocks supported the Labour Party.

Barry Jones recalls (1985) that his grandfather sold the *Daily Herald* when it was regarded as a radical newspaper and his father was a union activist: 'My father subsequently became constituency chairman to my predecessor, Baroness White, and later was a full-time employee of the party as an agent; that makes four generations of us, because my son stood for Parliament too.' Similarly, Denzil Davies talks (1985) of being brought up in a small village in west Wales, where his father was a strong unionist who lost his eyesight in an industrial accident. Davies remembers going with his father to a local solicitor appointed by the union to try and get some compensation from his father's employer, without much success. That was his first experience of politics in the broadest sense.

Likewise, in south London between the wars, George Brown, Deputy Leader of the Labour Party from 1963 until 1970, quickly assimilated the prevailing values of the trade union and labour movement. According to his autobiography (1971), he found his way to the Labour committee rooms in Southwark when he was seven or eight and persuaded the then leader of Labour politics in Southwark to allow him to run errands and to deliver leaflets. He was also involved in vigorous debates at school and by seventeen was vice-president of the Streatham constituency Labour Party and a member of the National

Advisory Committee of the Labour League of Youth. Even if he may have allowed some exaggeration to creep into his memory, George Brown was committed to politics by his teens. Growing up in Birmingham in the 1930s, Dennis Howell (1989) recalls that all his father's family were Labour supporters, as was his mother; being taken to a local by-election meeting when he was thirteen really started his lifelong interest in politics.

A strongly Labour family background is related not just to class origins but also to geography, and is most striking among MPs from party strongholds in Scotland, Wales and the northern industrial cities. For instance, while John Smith's father was a primary school headmaster in Ardrishaig, a small village in Argyllshire, he was part of the distinctively Scottish, rural radical tradition. His father was a Christian Socialist, rooted in the Presbyterian legacy, as well as a subscriber to the *New Statesman* in its most high-minded days under Kingsley Martin. These down-to-earth values of right and wrong, fairness and practicality, are clearly visible in John Smith today. There is no trace of metropolitan trendiness. For all his image as the responsible mainstream leader, he is even less part of the English establishment than was Neil Kinnock. The former Labour leader did, after all, live in Ealing in west London, while John Smith has always retained his home base in Scotland. Not surprisingly, the son joined the Labour Party while at school. After leaving his father's primary school, he went to Dunoon Grammar School, which produced fellow Labour MPs George Robertson and Brian Wilson. This family influence is true not only of an older generation of Labour MPs but also of some still in their thirties and early forties, especially outside the south-east. Henry McLeish (1991) says his political roots go back to his grandmother, who had been a member of the Labour Party for seventy years when she died aged ninety-one. The traditional side of the Labour Party was, he says, a considerable influence: 'It is very common in Scotland.' But social changes mean that family influences are not as strong for some younger MPs, as discussed below. Although more have had middle-class jobs, until recently about half were the children of manual workers.

On the Conservative side, strong political commitment among parents is less often mentioned. This may partly be because support for the Conservatives was, and is, assumed in many middle-class households, and does not have to be asserted publicly. Tony Newton (1988) says his parents were not interested in politics: 'They both ran a mile when anybody suggested they should stand for the local council.' His mother was one of the many millions who voted Labour in 1945 and then said they would never do it again. He believes that his father, who was a small shopkeeper in Harwich on the Essex coast, would never have wavered from voting Tory. Mr Newton says he formed an interest in politics at a very early stage, even before he was in his teens.

I don't know what generated my interest. It may have had a little to do with the fact that the MP for Saffron Walden was one of the great figures of that period of British politics, namely Rab Butler. I have always been a Conservative, but again I don't actually know why, except you might attribute it to the natural forces of a middle-class Tory background.

Alistair Burt, a junior minister, says (1989) that neither of his parents was really political, 'although I was well aware that I was growing up in a Conservative household'. He became hooked on the fun of politics after someone from the local Conservative Association came round and put a board up on a tree in his parents' front garden during the 1964 election: 'I thought this was amazingly exciting.'

Family influences seem to have been crucial in the decision to become involved in politics for roughly 40 per cent of the more than 220 MPs whose family histories I have examined in detail in preparing this book. By contrast, the remaining 60 per cent decided to become politically active for broadly ideological reasons – that is, in reaction to external events or as a result of being converted. In most cases they chose the party of their parents or what might be expected from their social background, but family ties were not the immediate cause of their involvement. The significance of family influence seems to be declining among younger MPs. This is hardly surprising in view of the general loosening of class ties and the greater social and geographic mobility of the past twenty to thirty years. But there is a distinction between the parties: family influences are proportionately more significant among younger Labour than younger Tory MPs. Many Labour members, even the younger ones, have grown up in strongly working-class communities, especially in Scotland, Wales and northern England, whatever their current social standing and occupation. This is less true of those Labour MPs who have grown up in southern England.

However, more of the young, university-educated and professionally qualified MPs say their desire to become politically involved was the result of a conscious decision, rather than something predetermined by their family backgrounds. They have either been converted ideologically or reacted to some major political event, or, more likely, responded to a mixture of the two over time. Of course, one would expect such articulate people to claim that they had reached their own decisions and not merely followed a family tradition. In practice, the line is often blurred between family influence and a decision based on some external event.

Timing matters a lot. Different generations react in different ways. This affects decisions about whether to become politically involved and which party to support. For a generation of MPs of both main parties now aged over seventy and largely retired from the Commons, the inter-war Depression and the rise of Fascism were the key events; Churchill's ascendancy and the austerity and controls of the Attlee Government helped bring a younger group of Tories into politics; Suez and the materialism of the Macmillan era pushed many young graduates towards both Labour and the Liberals; and the failures of the Wilson era and worries over British decline produced a reaction which inspired many of the Tory MPs who entered the Commons after 1979. Individual politicians have also often had a key influence on the decisions of aspiring politicians: in some cases prominent local figures or family friends, but also national leaders. Several MPs mention the impact of Winston Churchill, Aneurin Bevan, Hugh Gaitskell, Harold Wilson, Iain Macleod, Jo Grimond and Margaret Thatcher.

For the older generation, the approach of the Second World War was crucial. Denis Healey (1989) says the arts so dominated his life at school that he had little interest in politics then, though he made a speech against Nazism in the debating society at Bradford Grammar School. He did, however, resign from the Officer Training Corps, because the poets of the Great War had converted him to pacifism and because he found it senseless to train on a wooden Lewis gun. It was not until 1936, when he was nineteen, just before going up to Oxford, that 'politics first presented me with the challenge which has shaped my life'. He went on a five-week cycling trip through Europe to the Salzburg Festival, talking to a lot of young Germans, including members of the Hitler Youth. 'The freemasonry of the young gave me an invaluable insight into European society on the eve of war.' As a result of that holiday, 'for the first time I began to take a continuing personal interest in politics'.

Edward Heath, one of Denis Healey's contemporaries at Balliol, also visited Germany at about the same time, and that experience influenced his post-war view of European development. By contrast, Margaret Thatcher, eight years younger than Healey, did not travel to the Continent for the first time until well after the Second World War, when she was an adult and much of the rest of Europe was in ruins. Her main foreign influence at that stage was America, Britain's great ally in the war, especially as thousands of young airmen from across the Atlantic were stationed around her home town of Grantham. While Margaret Thatcher had no direct experience of fighting, Edward Heath (and Denis Healey) did. This contrast influenced her subsequent view of Europe in relation to America, while the Europeanism of Edward Heath and his generation was a reaction to the horrors of war.

Several Tory MPs were affected by Churchill's leadership during the Second World War and, in particular, by his defeat in 1945, followed by experience of life under the Attlee Government. Mrs Thatcher often referred to 'Winston'. As the extract at the beginning of this chapter shows, Norman Tebbit's interest in politics started early, before he was fifteen: 'As I saw the programmes of the Labour Government unfold I became more fiercely convinced that Socialism was bound to fail and that in its failure it might well turn towards the authoritarianism which was spreading over East Europe.' Kenneth Baker has also said that the first political voice he remembers hearing was Winston Churchill's, speaking on the nine o'clock news, while he was an evacuee in Merseyside.

A younger generation of Tories reacted against Harold Wilson's period in office and the sense of national decline which developed during the 1960s and 1970s. Chris Patten has said that he had been impressed in his teens by the writings of Anthony Crosland, so that if he had been old enough to vote in the 1964 general election he would have supported Labour. But it did not take much of Harold Wilson's regime to see that idea off and he was soon a committed Tory. Peter Lilley, who is roughly the same age, became convinced he was a Conservative while he was at Dulwich College – partly, he says (1991), 'in reaction to my left-wing friends, who seemed to be very negative and authoritarian in their attitudes'. Michael Fallon (1991), a junior education minister until he lost his Darlington seat in 1992, says he started to be politically aware at school in the late 1960s, when he read the Black Papers on education, which warned about the dangers of a fully comprehensive, egalitarian type of education. He says these struck an immediate chord: 'I understood for the first time what the Wilson Government was up to with its social and educational engineering.' David Heathcoat-Amory, a senior whip before becoming a Foreign Office minister in May 1993, said (1990) that even though his uncle was Chancellor of the Exchequer under Harold Macmillan, he was not drawn into politics by him. 'It was the failure of the post-war consensus politics which made me realize the game was up and that more radical reforms were necessary. It was as though the country was slipping into shoddy retirement. I spent a year abroad after Oxford and I could see how little respect we received overseas.'

Even where the interest of future MPs in politics was first sparked by an outside event, rather than by previous family preferences, most young men and women chose the party which might have been expected from their home background. There is the important caveat, though, that in Scotland support for Labour, or the Liberal Democrats, is much more normal for children of the professional middle classes. But what of the rebels against their class background – the public school Labour MPs and the working-class Tories? Here, external events and experiences were crucial. Tam Dalyell, an Old Etonian, had been chairman of the Cambridge University Conservative Association; he was nominated for that post by John Biffen, a future leader of the Commons. Mr Dalyell changed his party allegiance after two years of national service as a trooper. He joined the Labour Party at the time of Suez and was also heavily influenced by the late John Mackintosh, a leading political scientist and Labour MP. In an earlier generation, Tony Crosland reacted against the strict religious background of his parents, who were Plymouth Brethren, and the 'clearly formed political views' of his father, a senior civil servant, who was a Liberal. Susan Crosland, his widow, has recorded (1982) how at Highgate he 'joined the Left Book Club. As he grew more and more politically minded, he felt the sheer illogicality of his family's position.'

Tony Blair is one of the few people educated at public school (Fettes) and Oxford still at the top of the Labour Party. His father was brought up in a shipbuilding family in Govan in Glasgow, but in the 1950s moved to Durham, where he was a lecturer in law at the university, as well as a Tory. Tony Blair (1990) says, 'I have never found my background a problem with working-class voters – only with middle-class journalists. I am certainly not a Socialist through guilt, which is an unhealthy political motivation. I like to think I am a Socialist by instinct and reason.'

Ray Mawby, a former shop steward who left school at fourteen, became a Tory and an MP for a rural part of south Devon for twenty-eight years. His mother deplored her son's Toryism. He admitted, 'It would take a psychiatrist to discover why I went Conservative in the first place.' His obituary noted that it may just have been cussedness, since he enjoyed argument and was used to opposing his surroundings, including, unfortunately, the Commons, where he was rather a sad figure by the end. Of a later generation, Patrick McLoughlin was the son of a mineworker. He decided quite early on that he wanted to be part of the decision-making process. He admits (1991): 'My school life was not successful – I wasn't particularly good academically – but there was always that determination that I would like to become an MP. The trouble was that, coming from my background, I didn't really know how to become involved in politics.' He joined the Young Conservatives aged sixteen and in time became a district councillor, all the while still working underground and being challenged on his views by fellow mineworkers. Terry Dicks is another working-class Tory. He grew up in a tough area of Bristol, with a lavatory at the bottom of the garden. He was an eleven-plus failure. His interest in politics began when, after leaving school at fifteen with no qualifications, he was working as a clerk at the Imperial Tobacco Company, and he then went on to the London School of Economics aged twenty-nine. He felt some things needed to be said and that politics, and Parliament, offered a platform from which to say them.

The one group where few MPs picked their party from their family backgrounds has been the Liberals. Many have come from left-leaning, radical or Nonconformist homes, but few from families with a tradition of specific commitment to the Liberal Party. For David Steel (1989), spending his early teens in Kenya was crucial: 'The formative years between the ages of eleven and fifteen were to provide me with the beginnings of political awareness and a deep-seated opposition to racism in all its manifestations.' His father was a leading Church of Scotland minister who was prepared to challenge the authorities in Kenya, and that probably pushed the young Steel in the direction of politics. By contrast, Menzies Campbell, Steel's contemporary, came from a Labour family. This is rather surprising since both by appearance and by background – a former Olympic athlete and successful advocate – he looks like a typical Scottish Tory. But his father was a member of the Independent Labour Party and there was a lot of political discussion at home. He believes (1989) that his first political stirrings began over Suez: 'I had this gut feeling that it was wrong. I was drawn to Liberalism rather than the Liberal Party because, like a lot of people, I was captivated by Jo Grimond. He seemed to me to represent something quite innovative and exciting in politics.' David Steel, who helped secure Grimond's election as Rector of Edinburgh University, shared this view. Grimond, an inspiring orator at his best, had a particular influence on Scottish Liberals.

Even David Alton, a much younger Liberal who grew up in London in a working-class Labour family which admired Harold Wilson, remembers (1987) that in the 1964 and 1966 elections he was very impressed by Jo Grimond. He seemed to be saying the kind of things I believed. He spoke up for the underdog and seemed to be talking a lot of common sense. Then in 1967 I started to look at the political parties seriously and I didn't like the corporate state approach of Labour and I thought the Conservative Party stood for the maintenance of privilege. In comparison, Jo Grimond seemed like a breath of fresh air.

Alan Beith, who grew up in a Conservative working-class family, also reacted against the Tories as the ruling class, while, to him, Labour tried to tell ordinary people what they ought to want: 'So the attraction of Liberalism – which had no tradition at all in our family – was considerable, because of its general emphasis on the individual.'

These descriptions do not, of course, explain why one teenager rather than another became politically interested and, more importantly, involved. After all, not every child from a highly political family becomes active; only a minority do. While many of the children of the first generation of Labour leaders themselves became politically involved – the names Henderson, MacDonald, Greenwood, Benn, Marquand and Summerskill echo down the decades – few of the children of members of the Wilson Cabinet did so. Indeed, many reacted negatively to the political careers which had so obsessed their fathers and became rather anti-politics. This, in turn, suggests that family influence may be declining. But even where there is not a strongly political family background, many people are unmoved by even the most dramatic public events.

Do politicians, whether successful or aspiring, have some personality trait which predisposes them towards a political career? This is dangerous territory, where almost everything is speculation and little is provable. There is, no reader will be surprised to learn, a vast American literature on this theme which is inconclusive, apart from suggesting that politicians are unbalanced to varying degrees. Anthony King (1981) has summarized this work:

Politicians are said to displace private emotions on to public objects, to suffer from lack of self-esteem, to experience difficulty in making meaningful relationships, to be hungry for power, to be hungry for acclaim, to be hungry for personal recognition, to be hungry for all sorts of things. But in fact no one has the faintest idea of whether or not any of this is true.

This diverting literature suggests that psychological theories may have something to say about the more extraordinary political leaders – not just Hitler or Stalin but also Lyndon Johnson and Richard Nixon. But they do not really help very much with explaining about why the average back-bencher or junior minister became interested in politics. Even so, this work throws an interesting sidelight on to the political stage, if not exactly a spotlight.

Harold Lasswell was the pioneer of the American approach of applying Freudian theory to political lives. In his *Psychopathology and Politics*, first published in 1930, he described the 'political man' as one who turns to public life to realize his private motives. However, Lasswell offers few useful explanations of what such a displacement means: 'No doubt the general answer is that the selection of certain public objects depends upon the "historical" accident of the patterns offered by the personal environment of the individual at critical phases of growth. It is safe to predict that more politicians rise from families with political traditions than without them.' But he acknowledges that this tells us little. So, he writes:

If the psychopathological approach to the individual is worth the trouble, it must disclose a variety of relatively novel circumstances which dispose individuals to adopt, reject, or modify the patterns of act and phrase which are offered in the environment. Provisionally, we may assume that the puberty phase of biological growth, which coincides with increasing social demands, may be the period in which the attitudes toward the invisible environment most rapidly crystallize.

Or to put it more bluntly, as the more empirical investigation in this book of individual careers suggests, future politicians become interested and committed in their teens.

British writers have been wary of such speculations, apart from some work by Leo Abse and, most revealingly, an unusual book by Lucille Iremonger, herself the wife of a former MP. Her book *The Fiery Chariot* (1970) was subtitled 'A Study of British Prime Ministers and the Search for Love'. She looked at the lives of British Prime Ministers from Spencer Perceval to Neville Chamberlain and noticed how many had lost a parent in childhood or in early adolescence – some twenty-four out of forty. This is an extraordinarily high figure and compares with a loss of just 1 per cent of either parent for children aged up to fourteen, in 1921. However, none of the Prime Ministers after Chamberlain suffered such bereavement until James Callaghan, though John Major's father was sixty-four when his son was born and was ill for much of his son's teenage years. In America, President Bill Clinton is a classic example of this pattern. His father was killed in a car crash three months before he was even born. For more than two years he was brought up by his grandparents while his mother went away to pursue her training as a nurse. However, even when a parent did not die, some of the earlier Prime Ministers suffered loss of the love of one or other parent. The mothers of both Wellington and Rosebery also detested their sons.

Mrs Iremonger concentrated on the two-dozen Prime Ministers between Spencer Perceval and Chamberlain and detected a pattern: 'Not only had many of these men suffered the traumatic and unusual experience of lack of love in their early years. So many were abnormally sensitive, reserved and isolated. So many demonstrated the most powerful drives for attention and affection.' She went on to look at various developments of Freudian theory, notably the Phaeton complex, which fatherless or abandoned children might have – that is, the desire to possess everything in order to convince oneself that one has nothing. For her the key was the deprivation of love rather than just the absence of a parent from any particular cause. So she broadened her list from just those who had lost a parent in their youth to those who had suffered parental rejection. This contributed to later characteristics observed in many of these Prime Ministers, such as insatiable need for total love, drive for attention, recklessness, isolation, abnormal sensitivity, depression, austerity, aggressiveness, extreme reaction to bereavement and a belief in magic.

Her conclusion is that the nation has been led by men with exactly the opposite type of personalities from the ones that the public would ideally have sought. She suggests, not unreasonably, that the country wanted as leaders men

who above all mixed happily with their fellows, who were essentially gregarious rather than reserved and isolated, who shared a taste for common pursuits and relaxations, from team games to agreeable social occasions, who were the reverse of the thin-skinned and ultra-sensitive, who responded to the blows of fate, whether of death or of disappointment in love, with more rather than less stoicism and philosophy than the ordinary man.

But it got the reverse. She suggested that the stereotype of the actual leader would have a 'hypersensitive nature, and suffer from incapacitating psychosomatic illnesses, often at times of greatest stress. He will remain throughout his life isolated from his fellow men, nauseated by his junketings, and exhausted by their relaxations.' There are many examples to back up this analysis, from Aberdeen's extreme reaction to bereavement to Rosebery and MacDonald's sensitivity about depressions.

Mrs Iremonger's path is intriguing rather than conclusive. Are the majority, who grow up with contented and happy family backgrounds, to be governed not by people like them but instead by a minority of sad, singular and lonely men, the loveless products of their loveless childhoods? Is that reflected in the chasm between the people and Parliament? While most are happy to be perennial spectators, 'the miserable, energetic Phaetons have driven themselves inexorably on to stand among the few at the mountain peak, perhaps rivals only with each other for supreme power and the frightening tasks which deter all others'.

There is insufficient evidence from personal histories of MPs' lives to say whether these theories can be applied to the politically active as a whole, as opposed just to a handful of political leaders. Many politicians appear to have been loners when young, and often also during their parliamentary careers. Herbert Morrison recalled (in Donoughue and Jones, 1973) that in his youth, 'I was moody, lacked self-confidence. I was unhappy and I kept apart from other youngsters. I became introspective. You know what that means – it may crack you up, or it may make you determined to stand on your own. You've got to stand on your own feet.' Cases certainly exist of orphans or those who have lost a parent before their mid-teens; David Blunkett, for example, not only went blind because of a rare defect when very young but also lost his father in a works accident when he was twelve. Patrick McLoughlin, from a mining family and himself a miner, struggled against many disadvantages to become an MP. He never really knew his father, who died of lung cancer the day after his son's seventh birthday. He admits his father's death had an effect on him; his mother had to go out to work at 6.30 a.m. and the children had to look after themselves. Terry Dicks was born a spastic with cerebral palsy and at one stage it was suggested that he should go into a home, but he overcame all these difficulties. John Major had an unusual upbringing by elderly parents, but there is no doubt of their affection for him. And there are plenty of other examples of leading politicians who have grown up in happy and contented families. Perhaps, like on an interview panel for aspiring army officers and civil servants, a pyschiatrist ought to be included on every selection committee for a parliamentary candidate – though whether to weed out the unbalanced or to pick future leaders is an open question.

Another way of looking at the issue is provided by survey evidence of political involvement. Politics in Britain is, after all, a minority activity, in which most people are content for a small number to reach decisions on their behalf. An extensive survey of 1,600 adults carried out in the study on political participation by Geraint Parry and others (1992) confirms that voting is the only political act undertaken by most people, rivalled only by signing a petition. But a small number of people do get involved in a surprising number of ways: more than 20 per cent have contacted a local councillor, nearly 15 per cent have attended a protest meeting, and between 11 and 14 per cent have got together in informal or formal groups of various kinds. But very few become involved in party campaigning in any way: less than 9 per cent have attended a rally, only about 5 per cent have been involved in fund-raising and a mere 3.5 per cent have canvassed. According to the survey, some 7.4 per cent of the sample described themselves as party members, more than double the figure suggested by other evidence. People's definition of party membership may be looser than paying an annual subscription. But there is a big difference between being a member of a political party and being active. More than half never attend any party meetings at all each year and a quarter attend only one to five meetings a year, with the balance claiming to be more active.

The Parry study argues that just 2.2 per cent of the adult population can be described as party campaign activists. The authors suggest as a 'guesstimate' that the size of the national and local elected and administrative political élite in Britain might be around 50,000. The party campaign activists are not a representative sample of the whole population. They are well-off (some 58 per cent come from the top quarter of the population by income), they are well educated (over 40 per cent have either a degree or a further-education qualification) and well over half are from the salariat (57 per cent). Moreover, two-thirds of them are women, especially noticeable in the Conservative Party.

However, political activism appears to have declined over the past two decades, at least as measured by membership of a political party. Patrick Seyd and Paul Whiteley (1992) argue that 'as British society was becoming more affluent, citizens' interests were becoming more diverse and pressure groups were better able to represent these diverse demands than parties. In addition, people's greater concern with individual lifestyle was reducing the numbers willing to become involved in such time-consuming public activities as party membership.' Many natural activists have opted out of party involvement altogether and now identify more with specific single issue groups, in the environmental or conservation field, or organizations which began to expand in the late 1960s and early 1970s like Shelter and the Child Poverty Action Group.

Why, then, do people become involved in party politics? Many economists argue that it is not rational for any individual to participate in politics. This is because the political process produces collective goods, such as defence and law and order, which all share whether or not they have contributed to their provision. An individual's efforts on behalf of a political party or candidate have no relationship to the benefits of any policies enacted afterwards, which everyone will enjoy. That ignores the fact that the political process produces much more than collective goods. Politicians can change the tax system or award contracts to favour one specific group, while patronage is often dispensed to those backing a successful candidate. Political scientists argue that there is a bigger flaw since they maintain that individuals are motivated to join a party and become active because of a variety of personal incentives. Seyd and Whiteley have developed this theory on the basis of a survey of more than 5,000 Labour Party members which was

carried out at the end of 1989 and at the start of 1990. This
confirms the conclusions of the more general study of political
participation carried out by Geraint Parry and others, and
discussed above. Political activists are not typical socially of
the electorate as a whole, and even less typical of Labour
voters. They are middle-aged, better educated, better paid and
much more likely to be owner-occupiers than the average
person. In the case of Labour Party members, they are also
much likely to work in the public sector, as 63 per cent of
the Seyd and Whiteley sample do. This partly reflects the high
proportion of teachers and lecturers among Labour members.

The survey also provides insights into why some become
active and others do not – the central puzzle of most political
careers. Labour members and activists are revealed as altruistic
in the sense that many are motivated by a desire for a more
equal society and by general goals such as reducing unemployment – accounting for roughly half the reasons for joining the
party. Some of these attitudes are handed down from generation to generation. These figures are a reminder of how
ideological influences are often the initial incentive for many
people to become involved in politics. This is in contrast to a
narrowly defined careerism, a desire primarily to advance
oneself personally. The survey found that just under a quarter
of Labour members wanted to work with like-minded people
and be politically active. The authors conclude that 'ambition
plays a very important role in explaining why some are activists
while others are not. One of the strongest motives for activism
is political ambition, or a desire to build a career in politics at
the local or national level.' This reflects not just a desire to
invest in a career in politics as such but also sheer enjoyment
of the political process for its own sake. Labour activists have
clear incentives to be involved as a result of their day-to-day
political work. In all parties there are plenty of political
junkies who relish ward meetings, election campaigns and the
like, as others would enjoy bird-watching or stamp-collecting.

It is their hobby and the height of their ambition is to hold office in a local constituency party or to be a local councillor.

If we are only a little nearer explaining why some rather than others become politically involved, it may be simpler just to list some of the early indications of a political calling or temperament – a version of 'Don't put your daughter on the stage, Mrs Worthington.' Among the signs to watch out for are an unusual interest at a young age (at the latest in the early teens) in politics and current affairs, a liking for reading a lot (especially biographies and history), an argumentative disposition, active involvement in a school debating society and strong opinions. A contemporary of Sir Geoffrey Howe at Winchester remembers (in Hillman and Clarke, 1988) how he was a frequent speaker at the school's debating society: 'There was no doubt he was determined to get on in the political world from a very early time.' From an earlier generation Herbert Morrison was noted as a boy for reading a lot. The first stirrings are evident even in the most unlikely cases. The last school report on Clement Attlee as he left Haileybury for Oxford noted (in Kenneth Harris, 1982) that the future Prime Minister 'thinks about things and forms opinions – a very good thing ... I believe him a sound character and think he will do well in life. His chief fault is that he is very self-opinionated, so much so that he gives very scant consideration to the views of other people.' As a child he liked to argue about politics and personalities in Parliament. In this light it is curious that Attlee was later, misleadingly, regarded as meek, self-effacing and modest.

The danger is that such young men and women can become obsessive and narrow. The very enthusiasm that fires their early interest in politics can also lead them to exclude much else. Politics can become all-consuming in their lives, even when, as aspiring politicians, they first become actively involved at university and in a local party.

3
BECOMING ACTIVE

'I have often been shocked, looking back, to think that in June 1940 I was almost as cast down by defeat for the presidency of the Oxford Union as by the fall of France.'

Roy Jenkins, *A Life at the Centre*, 1991

'By any standards, the Cambridge of the late 1950s and early 1960s produced an exceptional number of politicians, including no fewer than eight Cabinet ministers for different Thatcher administrations: Leon Brittan, Ken Clarke, John Gummer, Michael Howard, David Howell, John Nott, Norman Lamont and myself. In addition, there have been two European Commissioners – Christopher Tugendhat and Leon Brittan – and a whole raft of ministers and MPs like Peter Lloyd, Peter Viggers, Peter Temple-Morris, Hugh Dykes, Nicholas Budgen and Michael Latham.'

Norman Fowler, *Ministers Decide*, 1991

'I joined thinking that there would be a really good chance in about ten years of getting on the local council if I worked really hard ... By the time I went to my second branch meeting I was chairman and secretary of the Young Socialists and on the local government committee. By the time I went to the third, I was membership secretary of the party and on the executive committee.'

Ken Livingstone on joining the Labour Party in 1968 (by 1971 he was on Lambeth Borough Council), in John Carvel, *Citizen Ken*, 1984

Photographs of the famous when they are young are always revealing. Subsequently familiar faces are still partly unformed as they look out awkwardly and a trifle smugly. The undergraduate politicians already seem to be thinking of later days, whether it is the youthful Harold Macmillan in 1914 or an earnest Michael Foot in 1933. Norman Fowler's memoirs (1991), quoted above, contain a photograph of a stately Macmillan at the height of his powers in 1960, accompanied by an already middle-aged-looking Fowler, while both are watched eagerly by a boyish John Selwyn Gummer and by Peter Viggers, future ministerial colleagues. For some all this is rather embarrassing – the young behaving in a prematurely old way, self-importantly mimicking the attitudes and style of members of the Commons at their most pompous. It is honest opportunism at its most enigmatic, when dedicated careerists start ascending the greasy pole; when the establishment starts replenishing itself. Political scientists describe such student activity as part of the socialization of future leaders.

Whatever the description, many future MPs translate their adolescent political interest and aspirations into a firm commitment when at university. Three or four years as a student often provides the first test of whether these noviciates have the talent, energy and personality to pursue a lifetime career. Not all who succeed prosper later, and many who reach the top were not active then, but politicial activity at university and college remains the first sighting of many future stars. The bonding, still primarily male rather than female, and the networks formed there are often what carries the ambitious politician forward. The friendships and rivalries formed between the ages of eighteen and twenty-one carry on through the twenties and thirties into the House of Commons.

Later achievement can, of course, make the earlier activities look more glittering in retrospect. Every half-remembered remark is treated as a pointer to future brilliance. But it is misleading to see in the deeds of the twenty-year-old undergraduate politician predictors of the success of the fifty-year-old Cabinet minister. Apart, perhaps, from William Pitt the younger and Gladstone, few future high-flying careers have looked predetermined. Many influences intervene: health, family ties, changes of interest and view, timing, an adverse political climate – all of which is commonly called luck. But the early clues can be illuminating.

Political ambition operates like a magnet, attracting those already with an interest. Over the years clusters of future MPs have appeared from time to time at Oxford and Cambridge, and, more recently, at Glasgow and St Andrews. The National Union of Students has also proved to be a nursery, particularly for future Labour politicians. The tradition of early political involvement at university goes back at least to the formation of the Cambridge Union Society in 1815 and the Oxford Union Society in 1823. Among the early stars at Cambridge were Macaulay. Percy Cradock notes (1953) how already at the Union Macaulay's approach to speaking had displayed 'a mature style, and the effects could be overpowering'. Typically of the period, Macaulay's political opinions underwent changes while at Cambridge. He came up as a Clapham Tory and for a while was Tory spokesman in the Union, then had an intervening stage when he came very near to being a Radical, before going down as the Whig he remained, both in Parliament and as a historian. Among his contemporaries were Alexander Cockburn, later Lord Chief Justice; Bulwer Lytton, who, at the time, was also one of the lovers of Lady Caroline Lamb; and Benjamin Hall Kennedy, better known to generations of schoolchildren as author of *A Latin Primer* and later in fictional form as Dr Skinner in Butler's *The Way of All Flesh*.

A few years later at Oxford the first star of the Union was Gladstone, who made his mark by taking a strong line on an issue – in opposition to the extension of the parliamentary franchise – which he would later champion. He spoke for three-quarters of an hour against reform in 1831, warning that the inevitable result would be revolution. Even so upright a figure as Gladstone got carried away in his undergraduate exuberance. As secretary of the Union he recorded how there was 'tremendous cheering from the majority of one', and he once spoke at great length against a motion, before voting for it. In his engrossing book, *The Oxford Union* (1984), revealingly subtitled 'Playground of Power', David Walter describes how

Gladstone and the Oxford Union did one another a great deal of good. The future Prime Minister learned his speaking technique there. Indeed, the union probably persuaded Gladstone against a career in the Church and swayed him in favour of politics instead. The society even, indirectly, provided him with his first seat in Parliament. Lord Lincoln, a friend from his days at Eton, was so impressed with his anti-reform speech that he persuaded his father, the Duke of Newcastle, to offer him one of the seats in Parliament which he controlled. As a result, Gladstone was able to enter Parliament before his twenty-third birthday. More than anyone else, Gladstone put the Union on the map. His career kindled the idea of the Union as a nursery of statesmen.

The myth of the 'nursery of statesmen' became entrenched during the course of the nineteenth century. Among political leaders involved in the Oxford Union in later years were Lord Robert Cecil, later Lord Salisbury and Prime Minister; Asquith, who was (according to his biographer Roy Jenkins, 1964), 'mostly' putting forward the orthodox advanced Liberal point of view with his own peculiar combination of lucidity, force and precision'; and Curzon, who was president of the Union during what one contemporary described as 'the brief interval which must intervene between Eton and the Cabinet'. In the 1890s, presidents of the Oxford Union included two future Lord Chancellors, F. E. Smith and John Simon, as well as the writer-politicians Hilaire Belloc and John Buchan. F. E. Smith epitomized the 'glittering prizes' approach, combining flowery oratory and a determination to impress, and at times shock, the great and the established to advance his career at all times. David Dutton (1992) notes how Simon and Smith developed a close relationship which lasted thirty-five years, until Smith's death:

Though there seems to be no truth in the legend that the two men decided by the toss of a coin which of them would join the Conservative Party and which the Liberals – their political affiliations were fixed before they even met – Simon and Smith did agree that neither in his future legal career should take silk before the other. It was a pact which was maintained. The two men took silk on the same day in February 1908, though Simon upset his rival by making his application without consulting Smith in advance.

The ever present danger, clear then as in all subsequent generations, was of young men taking themselves too seriously. The tone of self-congratulation was summed up by F. E. Smith's tribute to Gladstone on his death: 'In one sense we should not even yield up our claim to the House of Commons. We cannot forget that, if the splendid maturity of his life was theirs, ours, and ours only, was its brilliant dawn, and our claim to mourn over its pathetic end is not less.' Former presidents who became great men like Cardinal Manning encouraged such inflated expectations as when, at an anniversary dinner, he talked about the young men before him who were

to form the material of future legislators, not prompted by the low ambition of calculating minds, but by the high aspirations of men who desire to do good service to the Commonwealth, and who are now training themselves in all the fire of youth, the vigour of their fresh intellect, and the energy of their will, set upon our great public service, in the Oxford Union.

It may all have been harmless bombast, but I would guess that there were a few 'calculating minds' in the audience working out how their careers might flourish.

A revealing sidelight on some of the interpretations of the political personality discussed in the previous chapter is provided by a comment in David Walter's book about John Buchan's ability to overcome his shyness. He says: 'It is a curious pyschological phenomenon that many of the Union's greatest successes have been men who are shy in private, people who find it easier to communicate with an audience of a thousand than with an audience of one.' Similarly, John Simon overcame much of his youthful shyness and became an effective speaker.

These clusters of the like-minded ambitious who later made a mark in public life recur over the years. In Oxford, the pre-1914 generation included Harold Macmillan, Walter Monckton, A. P. Herbert and Harold Laski. In the 1920s Oxford boasted future ministers such as Leslie Hore-Belisha, Michael Stewart, Dingle Foot, John Boyd-Carpenter, Quintin Hogg, Derek Walker-Smith, Gerald Gardiner and Alan Lennox-Boyd. In Cambridge at the same time, the Union stars included R. A. Butler, Selwyn Lloyd, Geoffrey Lloyd, Patrick Devlin (the barrister, and later judge, described as the F. E. Smith of his generation), Hugh Foot (the later Lord Caradon) and the future Archbishop of Canterbury Michael Ramsey. So during the course of a decade the two Unions produced two future Lord Chancellors as well as two future Foreign Secretaries.

The point about such lists of rising stars is not just who shows the first signs of early promise while active in university politics, but also how groups of the politically interested cluster together. Quintin Hogg, Michael Stewart and John Boyd-Carpenter were presidents of the Union within a year of each other. Most of the key figures of the Labour right and centre up to the mid-1980s were at Oxford either just before 1939 or in the decade after the war. Denis Healey (1989) notes how a dozen of his Balliol contemporaries in the late 1930s met again as MPs after the war:

including Ted Heath, Julian Amery, Hugh Fraser, Maurice Macmillan and Tony Kershaw, who became ministers in Conservative governments, and Roy Jenkins and Niall MacDermot, who, like me, became Labour ministers. All of us had been active in student politics. Despite wide differences on other issues, all of us had fought against Chamberlain's policy of appeasing Hitler. All of us fought Hitler directly when appeasement failed.

Roy Jenkins notes: 'What an extraordinarily concentrated political society Balliol, with its entry of no more than eighty a year, then was.' Politics, he acknowledges, consumed a vast amount of his time, but, given the dramatic events in Europe and in contrast with later Oxford generations, 'It is to the credit of the tone of Oxford politics that, while there was inevitably plenty of the manoeuvring for personal position and petty gossip which goes with it in any closed circle, there was also serious interest in the content of politics, both national and international.'

There was an intensity of political debate in that period, notably in the Munich crisis of autumn 1938 and the Oxford by-election of that year when rebel Tories like Edward Heath joined with Labour supporters to back A. D. Lindsay, the Master of Balliol, as Popular Front candidate in opposition to the official, and pro-Munich, Tory, Quintin Hogg. Denis Healey argues: 'We were perhaps the most political generation in Oxford's history.' But bitter arguments developed in 1939–40 after the Hitler–Stalin pact and the Soviet attack on Finland about attitudes to the war. Most on the left, including Denis Healey and Iris Murdoch, both then Communists, stayed with the non-interventionist, fellow-travelling majority in the Labour Club, while Tony Crosland and Roy Jenkins broke away to form a new Democratic Socialist Club, which was loyal to the Labour Party nationally and supported the war. Denis Healey writes in his memoirs that he 'was sorry to say I opposed them, more from inertia and indifference than from conviction'.

Lifelong friendships started then. Roy Jenkins records (1991), in a passage reminiscent of the style of Anthony Powell, how in the autumn of 1939 Tony Crosland came

to my rooms, probably on some minor point of Labour Club business, and having settled it, remained uncertainly on the threshold, talking, but neither sitting down nor departing, for nearly two hours . . . Thereafter, I saw him nearly every day until he left Oxford in the

summer of 1940 ... Our friendship persisted on an intense but
fluctuating basis for nearly four decades. Not only was his character
engaging, his personality was dazzling and his intellect was of very
high quality. He had maddening streaks of perversity, was in my
view not at his best as a minister, but was the most exciting friend of
my life.

Susan Crosland (1982) describes how her late husband and
Jenkins became good friends: 'Tony found it pleasant to have
Roy around, treating him rather as a senior partner treats the
junior ones.' Denis Healey (1989) recalls that: 'Tony Crosland
then considered himself a Marxist, but could not nerve himself
to join the Communist Party outright. I knew him less well
than I knew Roy, because he was at Trinity, though I found
his offhand brilliance most engaging.'

Tony Crosland (completing his degree in 1946 after war
service) and Tony Benn were presidents of the Oxford Union
in 1946–7. It was in that period that Crosland made what
became a famous joke at Benn's expense, as recorded by the
latter's biographer, Jad Adams (1992):

Benn made an intervention in one of Crosland's speeches to the
effect that it was important for Labour undergraduates to discard the
taint of intellectualism. Crosland replied that in order for the honourable gentleman to discard the taint of intellectualism it was first
necessary for him to acquire it. This has frequently been repeated as
if it were a mature judgement by one middle-aged politician on
another, rather than an aside in an undergraduate debate. It later
became a standing joke between Benn and Crosland.

Adams, a generally sympathetic biographer, records a
number of characteristics of the youthful Benn which would
later become familiar – notably his enthusiasm, his eccentricity,
his outspokenness, his support for democracy and his tendency
to stand for elections. Because of his father, then a prominent
Labour minister, he already had extensive connections in the
party, but these developed during his Oxford period. For

instance, he met the ubiquitous Hugh Dalton, the sponsor of a generation of bright young Labour men, in Crosland's rooms.

The records of the Oxford University Conservative Association show a stellar burst in the late 1930s, with a succession of presidents starting with Edward Heath. He narrowly defeated the pro-Franco John Stokes, later a Tory back-bencher with John Bullish/Colonel Blimp views, much to the delight of parliamentary sketch writers. Heath was followed by Hugh Fraser and Julian Amery. In 1946–7 the then Margaret Roberts was succeeded as president of OUCA by Edward Boyle, while in 1957–8 six successive presidents of OUCA went on to become MPs, including three future Cabinet ministers: Kenneth Baker, Tony Newton and Paul Channon. It was the same in the 1967–70 period, when seven presidents of OUCA later became MPs, including William Waldegrave.

The most widely discussed recent undergraduate generation is the Cambridge one of the late 1950s and early 1960s. The group was certainly not unique; as seen above, plenty of former presidents of OUCA become MPs. The Cambridge 'mafia', as it has popularly become known, is striking instead because of its degree of success, since so many have reached the Cabinet. At the time, and in the eyes of many subsequently, they did not seem to be outstandingly talented compared, say, with the late 1930s Balliol group of Edward Heath, Denis Healey and Roy Jenkins. They obviously were not, and are not, as clever as these three. In an entertaining profile of the group in the *Guardian* of 10 October 1988, Andrew Rawnsley wrote that as a group they appeared to have struck most of their university contemporaries as a curiosity – the fag-ends of the conservative 1950s, when the rest of student Britain was about to make a sharp left turn into the 1960s. To themselves they were the vanguard of a new, self-consciously liberal, meritocratic Tory Party. Indeed, while they prospered and advanced politically during the 1970s and 1980s, few of their contemporaries on the left have made any mark at Westminster.

The *Guardian* article quotes John Dunn, a Socialist contemporary in the Cambridge Union and now a leading political theorist at the university:

It didn't strike me that I was in the presence of people that would run the country. They were all tremendously unformidable. The most impressive, in an out-of-date sort of way, was Leon Brittan, who was clearly very bright and a fluent orator. But most of them seemed to be in a stage of prolonged adolescence. It was inconceivable that they would be running the country, even scary.

He remembers John Gummer as 'in many ways a ludicrous figure' in a duffle coat; Kenneth Clarke as 'actually quite nice', with his jazz-playing and snooker; and Norman Lamont as something of a smoothie, with corduroy jackets.

The picture that emerges is of rather self-satisfied young men interested in their careers to the exclusion of much else, though they should not always be presented as serious. They all had fun. But they regarded the union as a mini-parliament where they were able to develop skills for their later careers. They could also mix with the leading politicians of the day, who might advance their careers. Norman Fowler unconsciously caught the self-important tone in his memoirs (1991) when he reports on the aftermath of a disastrous Cambridge Union debate for the Tories on the traditional 'no confidence' motion in October 1960:

A day or two after the debate I was working in my rooms at Trinity Hall – which I shared with another future Tory MP and minister, Peter Viggers. There was a knock at the door. Two younger undergraduates a year behind me entered and explained the purpose of their visit. They were worried at the damage the Union debate had done to the Conservative cause and they wanted urgent action to correct the position. The first of the undergraduates was a law student from Caius College called Kenneth Clarke and the second another law student from Peterhouse named Michael Howard. Twenty years later I recruited Ken Clarke as my parliamentary secretary at the Department of Transport. Thirty years later when I left the Government I handed over the Department of Employment to Michael Howard.

It is all a bit twee, like those Hollywood films of the 1940s which featured lines like, 'Mozart, I would like you to meet a young composer from Bonn, Beethoven.' But the group did exist, and it did prosper.

Unlike earlier generations, Norman Fowler and his contemporaries were not members of the ruling class enjoying themselves. Rather they were the sons of professional men and small businessmen, often first-generation university students who had emerged from some of the best of the old grammar schools (Clarke from Nottingham High School, Howard from Llanelli Grammar, and Fowler from King Edward VI Grammar in Chelmsford). Like many of the future MPs and ministers of the Thatcher era, they were the successful products of the Butler Act of 1944 and the opening up of educational and social opportunities during the 1950s. But that resulted in a commitment to success. Ambition was worn on their sleeves. Norman Fowler records how 'undergraduate careers were taken seriously. Having reached university, we were anxious to make the most of it and were ambitious about what we wanted.' A critical profile of Norman Lamont in the *Sunday Telegraph* in March 1991 noted that to understand him 'one must remember he was chairman of CUCA – and has that in common with many present and former members of the Government. Being chairman of CUCA often brings an instinctive understanding of the concept of the career plan – for without one in embryo it is unlikely that most chairmen would have reached that office in the first place.' Much the same has been said of an earlier generation of Tory undergraduates like Michael Heseltine. In at least two books (1985 and 1987) Julian Critchley has described how, over dinner at an Oxford restaurant called Long John's, Michael Heseltine would take 'from his pocket an envelope and draw upon it a chart of his progress within and beyond Oxford. Downing Street was the goal towards which he strove; the date, the 1990s.'

The Cambridge group were in part lucky in their timing. They entered Parliament during the 1970s and reached the age when they might become ministers – their late thirties or early forties – just when the Tories started a long period in office. People with their astuteness, speaking abilities and, above all, ambition are always likely to thrive in such conditions. While the group has maintained close contact, not least because so many sit round the Cabinet table, they have advanced their careers separately. Michael Howard defeated Kenneth Clarke for the presidency of the Union, which Clarke later won. They each sought candidacies; four of them stood for hopeless seats in their twenties. Norman Fowler warns, however, that the group was not a 'mafia' in the sense that its members spent all their time together. 'Nor, when we left, did we act as an entirely self-supporting group. Given that we spent a good deal of the time competing with one another for the same constituencies, that was impossible. Yet we have remained friends in spite of the inevitable vicissitudes of politics.' When they arrived in the Cabinet in the 1980s, they were often on opposite sides – Gummer and Clarke were counted as Euro-enthusiasts, while Howard and Lamont were more sceptical. In May 1993, Kenneth Clarke replaced Norman Lamont as Chancellor. This was primarily at the urging of Norman Fowler, who later sharply rebuked Lamont for his resignation statement. So there has not been a cohesive Cambridge 'mafia' acting to further each others' later careers.

Oxford and Cambridge do not have a monopoly of such early political networks. The Oxbridge influence at the top of the Labour Party has declined over the last decade, partly as a result of the creation of the Social Democratic Party in 1981. Twelve of the thirty-one former Labour MPs who either left to join the SDP or were elected in by-elections in the 1981–3 period were graduates of Oxford or Cambridge, including all the original leaders – Roy Jenkins, Shirley Williams, Bill Rodgers and David Owen. So also were many of their leading supporters and aides, who might otherwise have become Labour MPs. John Smith's twenty-strong Shadow Cabinet team elected in July 1992 included only four members – Tony Blair, Michael Meacher, Chris Smith and Bryan Gould – educated at Oxbridge, and only three after Gould's resignation two months later. By contrast, Harold Wilson's Cabinet in 1974 included eleven graduates of Oxford and Cambridge. This matches a more general decline in the number of Labour MPs educated at Oxbridge, only partly reversed after the 1992 general election. Many local Labour parties are less willing to adopt London-based, Oxbridge-educated professionals.

Many of the new Labour leaders have emerged from student politics at the Scottish or English provincial universities. Some were involved in national debating competitions or became prominent via the National Union of Students, like Jack Straw. Neil Kinnock, for example, was president of the union at University College, Cardiff. Several of the new Labour MPs who entered the Commons at the 1992 election had been presidents or vice-presidents of the students' unions at their universities – Richard Burden (York), John Denham (Southampton), David Hanson (Hull) and Alan Simpson (Nottingham). John Denham had also been active in the British Youth Council, like Peter Mandelson, another new entrant in 1992. The atmosphere in these students' unions may have been less rarefied – some would say less precocious – than at Oxford or Cambridge, and there was less of a sense of a future élite forming. But skills of political organization and public speaking of a more direct – and for the Labour Party of a more practical – nature were often acquired.

Joan Ruddock has recalled (1989) how she went to Imperial College, London, where she joined 'the Labour Club and became very active in the international students' body; my influences come very much from the world of international relations rather than domestic politics'. Similarly for Joan Walley (1990), her interest in politics became 'more formed' after she left her home town of Stoke and went to Hull University. 'It was 1967 and a time of great student unrest. I wasn't in a political party but I was involved in campaigns for greater student democracy.'

There are examples of groups of future political leaders congregating together at some universities. John Smith was part of an intensely political generation at Glasgow University in the late 1950s which also included Donald Dewar; Alexander Irvine, the successful barrister who has become Lord Irvine of Lairg; Menzies Campbell, the Liberal MP; John MacKay, then a Liberal but later a Tory MP, minister and life peer; and Donald MacCormick, the television journalist. They have stayed friends in spite of political differences. Another contemporary was Teddy Taylor, the last successful standard-bearer of working-class Conservatism in Glasgow. These students were involved in undergraduate debating, which in Scotland is rather more vigorous and less genteel than at Oxford and Cambridge. A contemporary at Edinburgh University at the time was David Steel, who has also maintained close links with his Glasgow opposite numbers. In 1960 Steel, Dewar, MacCormick and George Reid, a future Scottish Nationalist MP, were on the first post-war delegation of Scottish students to go on an exchange tour of the Soviet Union.

Donald Dewar recalls (1985), 'Glasgow University in those days was a most unusual political establishment. The Labour Club had 600 members and the Labour Party itself was very wise and encouraged students to get involved. There was a real effort to draw people in, and that, combined with the Glasgow debating tradition, started me on the road.' Dewar helped his close friend John Smith, when still a student, to fight the East Fife by-election in 1961. He organized a group of about fifty people to cross from Glasgow to St Andrews to help in the campaign. John Smith was chairman of the Glasgow University Labour Club in 1960 and he helped Glasgow win the *Observer* Mace debating trophy. Then, as later, his speeches were not noted for great oratory but for their wit and careful marshalling of facts.

If the Cambridge 'mafia' adapted to, and thrived under, Thatcherism, many of Mrs Thatcher's most zealous and enthusiastic supporters were graduates of St Andrews University in the first half of the 1970s, notably Michael Forsyth, Michael Fallon, Robert Jones and, slightly earlier, Christopher Chope. An *Observer* profile of Michael Forsyth in September 1990 at the climax of his battles as chairman of the Scottish Conservative Party, as the voice of Thatcherism north of the border, noted:

During the mid-1970s St Andrews seems like the last redoubt of the kind of hard-faced Toryism which has never much impressed Scottish voters. The radical young things who huddled together there reading Hayek and despising even their own party seemed eccentrics at best. Most people did not know that tomorrow, or at least a large chunk of it, belonged to them.

Michael Forsyth flourished there, becoming president of the university's Conservative Association and chairman of the Federation of Conservative Students. Michael Fallon (1991) joined the Conservatives at St Andrews and remembers: 'The Tories there were very liberal, market-minded and merito-cratic: not at all wedded to paternalism.' They were 'very quick in spotting the U-turn of the Heath Government and inveighing loudly against this'. At about the same time, Edward Leigh, a future close ally of the St Andrews graduates in the No Turning Back group of Tory MPs, arrived at Durham University. He recalls (1991):

It was when I walked into the Durham Union Society that I acquired this political bug which became all-pervasive. I have always tended to rebel against the generally prevailing ethos. So, partly because everything was so left-wing in the 1960s, I moved to the right. I decided that I really wanted to go into politics rather than the navy.

All this student political activity does not just create networks of friends and rivals which persist later on in people's lives. It mainly exposes the young to political life – its setbacks as well as its pleasures in the competition to get elected to office in student political and debating societies. Young boys, and a few girls, who were interested in current affairs at school can see if they have a talent for politics, whether they enjoy speaking in public and all the manoeuvring of elections and campaigning. Many do not and opt for other careers, but many do and decide to pursue a career in Parliament. But skills can be learned which are valuable whatever occupation is later taken up. William Rees-Mogg, who stood for election in the Oxford Union many times, had, after being defeated for the presidency by Jeremy Thorpe, to decide whether to try again and go all out for a first-class degree. He had been advised by his tutor that the presidency would not make a great deal of difference to his academic chances. He stood, won – and ended up with a second. In retrospect, Lord Rees-Mogg believes he made the right choice, since the presidency is rarer than a first and shows evidence of public attributes, indicating what people can achieve in the rough and tumble of ordinary life. The powers of persuasion which he eventually learned at Oxford subsequently proved to be invaluable, he told David Walter (1984). Fifty per cent of modern administrative life consists of persuading people in committees, making a case competently and amusingly in a short space of time.

The most obvious result of undergraduate political activity is greater fluency. Shy boys become self-confident. Julian Critchley notes, in his aptly subtitled 'Unauthorized' biography of Michael Heseltine (1987), how young Oxford Tories were,

over several generations, given speakers' classes by Mrs Stella
Gatehouse,

a chain-smoking parson's wife of indeterminate age and cheerful
disposition . . . On Wednesday afternoons ambitious young Conservatives would assemble in a dingy upstairs room above a milk bar to be
taught how to take the pebble out of their mouths . . . We were told
to stand erect, synchronize our few gestures and project our voices to
the back of the hall. Those in whom she had some confidence were
sent out to address afternoon meetings of the local Tory ladies.

Learning how to speak fluently has obvious advantages, but
it can easily turn into glibness. It can make it easier for the
new MP to adapt to the conversational style of the House of
Commons with its give-and-take in face of interruptions and
need to think on your feet – in contrast, say, to the more
formal style of the US Congress. David Walter (1984) writes of
the Oxford Union, 'The qualities which it admires in its
leading performers are powers of persuasion, panache and wit.
Knowledge is of much less consequence.' An Oxford Union
style has become almost a pejorative term for the slick show-
manship of a Jeremy Thorpe or a Gyles Brandreth, the last
faint echoes of the F. E. Smith tradition. Walter acknowledges
that the Oxford Union style is sometimes meant disparagingly
to suggest that a speaker is 'good at playing with words but
short on ideas and substance. What the society's products do
have in common is an interest in public speaking as an art.' Jo
Grimond has argued that the Union approach has encouraged
'the view of politics which expresses itself in clichés suitable
for speeches and articles'. Harold Macmillan in old age took a
sympathetic view of the advantages, while deploring the tendency for young people to take up fixed party views rather than
listening, hearing and talking. As he said:

The Union was fun because it was an opportunity to learn something
of the parliamentary system, to which I always had ambitions. It was

organized like the House of Commons. The president, like the Speaker, was in the chair. You addressed the chair. There were front-benches and back-benches and so forth, and it was the drill of the House of Commons as it had been since it was founded by Mr Gladstone and his friends.

Similarly, Edward Heath remembers when he 'first went into the House of Commons in 1950, I felt I was coming home. It was perfectly natural . . . I think we avoided all the strange feelings which many new members have – How do I settle down here? How do I handle that?'

Mixing with the great figures of the day is obviously a spur. As earlier generations of undergraduates were dazzled by F. E. Smith, Lloyd George or Winston Churchill, so the young men and women of the 1960s were often inspired by Iain Macleod, Dick Crossman or Enoch Powell. Most of the great, and rising, figures of British politics are only too eager to address student audiences. Edward Heath remembers Winston Churchill coming down in 1936 to speak to Conservative undergraduates. After he had made a 'tremendous' speech, some of the undergraduates went back to the rooms of Churchill's great friend Lindemann, 'the Prof', at Christ Church. 'Churchill came there and talked until very late into the night, far past the time when we ought to have been back in college. He went finally at about 2 a.m., to stay at Blenheim.' David Hunt recalls (1988) how, when he was chairman of Bristol University Conservative Association in 1964–5, he invited all of the then Shadow Cabinet and ten came. David Hunt is an example of someone who made his mark in this way, as well as by winning debating championships and establishing a reputation for organization (increasing the membership of the association fourfold). These attributes in time took him to the top of the Young Conservatives nationally and to the chairmanship of the British Youth Council.

The impact of visits by leading politicians can vary. I

remember how, after a Cambridge Union debate in the early summer of 1968, one of us impressionable undergraduates asked Tony Crosland if he had read Paul Foot's recently published, and highly critical, political biography of Harold Wilson. Politicians read few books, but Crosland, always the exception, had, and replied, 'I hadn't realized what a shit Harold was until I read the book.' A typical piece of Crosland exaggeration to impress the young perhaps, but it was startling to hear a leading Cabinet minister talk about his Prime Minister in that way. After many years of contact with leading politicians, it is easy to forget the impact which an indiscretion or a candid comment can have on someone new to that world. Contact with leading politicians can also bring students down to earth when they are not so impressive. Norman Fowler records how, after having listened to a rather tedious speech from Selwyn Lloyd, the then Chancellor of the Exchequer, one of his friends remarked, 'I could do as well as that.' Fowler added, 'Doubtless there are undergraduates at Cambridge today thinking precisely the same thoughts as they listen to us. There is nothing like getting close to politicians to make politics appear more accessible.'

But undergraduate activity can also give a distorted view of politics, suggesting that the game is the only thing that matters and the ends are somehow secondary. David Walter (1984) reports that, even in the Oxford Union of the 1920s,

speeches of the time give the impression that most members took themselves much more seriously than the political issues which they were debating. Not for the first time, the acquisition of office in the Union became a burning ambition for its most active members. Elections, though always interesting, became an obsession which has often since distorted the Union's proper function and make it an object of ridicule and derision for non-members. Endless intriguing and gossiping about personalities and their position on the slippery pole is endemic to politics. When, however, it becomes an exclusive concern and all-consuming object of interest, it betrays a depressing narrowness of mind and lack of imagination which can only stunt the development of the budding politicians at the Union.

The Oxford University Conservative Association in 1991 produced a brief pamphlet on its history since its foundation in 1924. The early battles over Fascism and appeasement involving Edward Heath and his contemporaries gave way during the 1950s to an inward-looking preoccupation with elections and personal careers. There is a recurring theme of electoral corruption, factionalism and college tickets. The history notes, somewhat piously, that, 'a vital association attracts able and ambitious members who will cheat the system to win the prestigious key positions if it proves necessary'. In the mid-1950s there was a system of postal voting, much approved later by some of the Oxford Tories of the time when they became ministers under Mrs Thatcher. 'When George Gardiner came up in 1955 it was rumoured that a senior OUCA figure (since a Cabinet minister) had obtained his committee post by removing ballot papers from the pigeon holes and filling them in himself.' Gardiner was too poor to compete in the common malpractice of signing up people from secretarial colleges and paying their membership fees of half a crown to ensure their support, so he decided to print his own ballot papers instead, with friends faking different signatures. He was duly elected president of OUCA.

Although an investigation was launched when the duplicated papers were found, there was no firm evidence against him. However, the Master of Balliol read about the investigation in *The Times* and, when he saw Gardiner's name, decided to look into the matter. If caught, Gardiner would have been sent down, so he decided to confess to OUCA's senior member, Lord Blake. His resignation was accepted without question so as to avoid a scandal and Tony Newton took his place as president.

George, later Sir George, Gardiner became a political

journalist, then a Tory MP, when he was a strong right-wing supporter of Mrs Thatcher. He became the highly successful, and respected, organizer of the right-wing 92 Group slate for the annual elections to Tory back-bench committees, though in this case each MP has to turn up and postal voting is not allowed.

Undergraduate political activity therefore offers a mixture of contact with leading politicians, an opportunity to learn some of the skills of politics and, above all, in many cases, a test of the ability to survive in debates and to win elections. But is it all just an apprenticeship in careerism, or does the experience influence people's later views? The intense debates of the late 1930s certainly shaped the Denis Healey–Roy Jenkins–Edward Heath generation. The highly political atmosphere at Glasgow in the late 1950s and early 1960s affected not only the debating style of John Smith, Donald Dewar and their group but also shaped their right-wing Labour views. They all wore suits and were too early for the flower-power generation. The Cambridge set of the same years has been seen as flexible in their later political careers, at first embracing Edward Heath's approach and then endorsing Thatcherism in response to the change in intellectual fashion. In answer to the question, 'What kind of Conservatives were we?', Norman Fowler (1991) writes:

In those days the terms wet and dry had not been invented. Had they been, most of us would surely have been categorized as wets. In the main we were in favour of joining Europe and supported the wind of change in Africa. We took a determinedly liberal view on most social questions, and although unemployment was not an issue we assumed it was unthinkable for it ever to return to pre-war levels. If we were to rebel against the official line, it was much more likely to be to the left than the right.

Fowler notes that he moved a motion that 'Public schools do more harm than good', though he warns that in Union debates you were not necessarily expected to agree with the motion you were proposing since the skill was to take up any brief. 'We were not automatically Conservative and thirty years earlier you would have found some of us in other parties.' But he cautions against generalizing about the views and motivations of nearly two-dozen undergraduates who happened to be at one university at the same time. 'Most belonged to the liberal wing of the Conservative Party – but that does not accurately position Nick Budgen. Most were not devoutly religious – but that does not remotely include John Gummer.'

Norman Lamont has said of his Cambridge days, 'I suppose we were all Butskellites then, I'm not sure what you'd say now.' Edward Heath, then a rising star of the party and an economic liberal, was their hero during the 1960s. The election of Heath, somebody from a grammar school like them, was seen as a great revolution, a move by the Tories into a more meritocratic era, when people like them might advance. Opposition to a stuffy aristocratic Tory establishment had also been expressed by many of the Oxford generation of the 1950s like Michael Heseltine. Criticism of a Tory establishment of a different kind also bound together the St Andrews set of the late 1970s and early 1980s.

Many later MPs held views at university very different from the ones they later espoused. Indeed, many belonged to a different party. John Biggs-Davison, later a right-wing Tory and strong supporter of the Ulster Unionists, was a Communist at Oxford in the late 1930s. Among future Labour MPs, Tam Dalyell was prominent in the Conservative Association at Cambridge in the 1950s, as Phillip Whitehead was at Oxford at the start of the 1960s. Future Tory MPs Sir Peter Tapsell and Sir Geoffrey Johnson Smith were both Labour supporters at Oxford in the 1950s.

Many future politicians saw little point in student politics. In the pre-war generation, Iain Macleod preferred bridge and racing, while Willie Whitelaw was busy on the golf course.

Harold Wilson was active in the Liberal Club at Oxford but was never involved in the Union. Of a later generation neither Chris Patten nor Michael Portillo was active in politics at university. Some were too shy. Peter Lilley, who had become convinced he was a Conservative while at school, says (1991) that when he went up to Cambridge, 'I was certainly determined to get into politics, but I was a very shy and diffident youth. I didn't get involved in the Union except as an avid listener to the likes of Norman Lamont, Michael Howard and John Gummer, who were slightly older than me. I never had the courage to speak.'

Others disliked the approach to politics of their fellow undergraduates. David Owen was up at Cambridge in the second half of the 1950s. He notes (1991):

Surprisingly, despite these highly political events in 1956 [the Suez crisis and the Soviet invasion of Hungary] and the response they evoked in me, I did not become involved in party politics at Cambridge. I never joined any political party. I went along to the Cambridge Union and took out a life membership for ten pounds but the one debate I attended put me off. I disliked, and still do, the mannered style of both the Oxford and Cambridge Union debates and have only rarely accepted invitations to debate, preferring to speak and answer questions.

Some of Dr Owen's critics might say this attitude to debating and the style of politics of the Oxford and Cambridge Unions was reflected in the way he distanced himself from his fellow members at Westminster. He was never a clubbable man. From a later generation, Tony Blair, who was at Oxford in the early 1970s, says (1990), 'I became interested in left-wing politics there through my friends, but I was never much involved in student politics. I couldn't be bothered with that. I have always had a fairly practical turn of mind and student politics at Oxford, at any rate, never seemed very practical.'

Political involvement at university is a mixed predictor of

what people do in their later careers. Many former presidents or chairmen of university political societies, and presidents of the Oxford or Cambridge Unions, have had a distinguished later political career, but many have not. Of 218 presidents of the Oxford Union between 1900 and 1975, a total of fifty went on to become MPs (twenty-nine Conservative and thirteen Labour, with seven Liberals and one independent). This compares with thirty-five who went into journalism and broadcasting, twenty-five barristers and judges, and thirteen academics. It is, however, notable that of the fifty MPs, thirty-two became ministers. This is a remarkably high proportion and suggests that the qualities of ambition and determination needed to become a minister were present in embryo form in undergraduate days. Similarly, of 117 presidents of the Oxford University Conservative Association between 1924 and 1975, thirty-five later became MPs, including twenty-four future ministers. This is again a high striking rate and suggests that university politics is serving its self-assumed purpose as a nursery for success in the House of Commons.

An alternative view is that this is a self-fulfilling prophecy in view of the shared values and styles between Oxbridge undergraduate politics and the House of Commons. The late Michael Stewart argued that people who are successful at the Oxford Union do not necessarily go on to success in politics because of their Union triumphs. It may simply be that people who have above average gifts and a keen interest in politics are likely to do well both in the Union and afterwards. But, as noted above, future political leaders often appear in clusters and many twenty- and twenty-one-year-old stars either fade or distinguish themselves in careers other than politics. These are matters of chance, timing, changes of view and changes of interest. People also develop in different ways. It is not just athletes who often peak around the age of twenty; so too do some debaters and politicians. Others develop later. A sizeable proportion of former presidents of the Oxford and Cambridge

Unions and the political societies never make much of a mark in politics, or in some cases in other careers either.

John Dunn remembers that potentially the brightest star of the Cambridge Tory generation of the late 1950s and early 1960s was a president of the Union and chairman of CUCA called Colin Renfrew. He substantially reduced the Labour majority at a by-election in Sheffield Brightside. But he gave up politics and became a leading archaeologist and Master of Jesus College. Some active undergraduate politicians become judges or civil servants, like Leo Pliatzky and Nicholas Henderson of the pre-war Labour group at Oxford.

More recently, the Tories' record of success in elections and repeated Labour failures have affected careers. Norman Fowler argues that, in contrast to the success of his contemporaries in the Conservative Party, Labour did virtually nothing to recruit undergraduate talent. The evidence from Cambridge in the late 1960s illustrates the dangers of making premature predictions of political success. On the Tory side, two Cambridge graduates of that time, David Mellor and Richard Ryder, reached Cabinet rank and another five have also become MPs. However, while all but one were very active in politics at Cambridge, they were not regarded as future stars at the time. They were not as prominent as Edward Heath or Michael Heseltine had been as undergraduates. Several of the leading Tories of the time have instead followed careers as barristers. On the Labour side, only four of the late 1960s generation became MPs, with only two in the Commons after the April 1992 election. This is partly because of Labour's lack of success nationally, as hopeful candidates have been defeated and others discouraged from standing. It is also partly because of the general shift in Labour selection away from Oxbridge-educated candidates. Some possible future Labour MPs left to join the SDP. The stars of the left at Cambridge in the late 1960s have been involved in the voluntary sector, the health service and the Civil Service.

The unpredictability of what happens in future careers is highlighted by a story which Nigel Fisher (1973) tells in his biography of Iain Macleod about Macleod's time at Cambridge before the Second World War:

A friend of those days remembers meeting him one morning in the courtyard of Caius. Iain had just paid a visit to his tutor, who had advised him that the best university degrees were not obtained at the bridge table or on Newmarket Heath. His tutor had quoted the name of another Caius undergraduate as a model of the hard work and academic prowess which would take him to the top of any profession. Twenty years later, Macleod, newly appointed as Minister of Health, was being conducted round the department by the permanent secretary and introduced to the staff. In one office he recognized a middle-grade official whose face he could not immediately place but whom he soon remembered as the young man who had been held up to him at Caius as an example of certain success in later life. The recollection appealed to his dry sense of humour and he told me the story with pleasure some years afterwards.

This chapter has concentrated on political activities at university because that is where so many future MPs first become actively involved and form political links which last through most of their careers. Some 245 Tory MPs – or 73 per cent of the total – elected in April 1992 went to university, including 151 to Oxford or Cambridge. On the Labour side, some 166, or 61 per cent, were university graduates, including forty-four from Oxford and Cambridge (figures from Byron Criddle's chapter in Butler and Kavanagh, 1992). But many MPs did not go to university or college and first became politically involved through local constituency parties or via trade unions. Take two south London boys who grew up in the 1950s and 1960s. John Major's early interest in politics was noted in the last chapter. At the minimum age of sixteen he joined the Young Conservatives. According to Bruce Anderson (1991):

[he] displayed a taste for the slog-work of constituency politics. In

particular, he showed a tireless enthusiasm for canvassing, and was happy to knock on doors in the roughest bits of Brixton on the filthiest winter evenings. In the small world of Brixton Young Conservatives, he began to develop the reputation that has stayed with him throughout his political career, at each successive level: of a man who could be relied on to get things done.

He was active in election campaigning, so by the time he was twenty-one he was already 'one of the most prominent figures in the Brixton Conservative Association'. In 1964 he fought his first election, unsuccessfully, for Lambeth Borough Council, only just being old enough to stand.

Two years younger than John Major, Ken Livingstone became active slightly older, at the age of twenty-three, about a mile away from Brixton in Norwood. Characteristically, he went against the grain, joining the Labour Party in 1968, just a couple of months before the spring riots in Paris. John Carvel (1984) notes that this was 'a time when almost every socialist of his age was deserting Labour for the headier comradeship of Trotskyism and other brands of insurrectionist policy'. Livingstone says that he did not realize when he joined the Labour Party just how totally debilitated it had become. While many activists had gone off to join other left-wing groups, Livingstone believed that social change could only be achieved through the Labour Party. But in the absence of the left-wingers, his interest and commitment meant that he soon occupied several posts in the local Young Socialists and was a member of the local party's key committees. He was ensconced in Norwood Labour politics before the left-wingers returned from their various sects. Like John Major, Ken Livingstone discovered that youthful energy soon brought influence and position.

Similarly, Robert Atkins, later a close friend of John Major, recalls (1991) his rapid early advance in politics:

My politics were entirely self-generated. I joined the Young Conservatives in 1963; within months I was chairman of the branch in

Hornsey and so it went on. I was chairman of the Greater London Young Conservatives at a time when it was a very radical organization and by 1968 I was a Haringey councillor. I lost my council seat in 1971 and had lost my vice-chairmanship of Greater London Young Conservatives. It was excellent for me. It brought me down to earth and made me realize I wasn't anything like as good as I had thought.

For a whole generation of younger Tories, like John Major and Robert Atkins, the route into politics from the 1940s until the 1960s was provided by the Young Conservatives. Norman Tebbit (1988) remembers:

As I reached my fifteenth birthday I joined the newly formed Young Conservatives . . . I was not only from a different social background but I was much younger than most of the other members. The secretary of the branch, Colin Turner, was some ten years older than me and from a very different family background, and further distanced by his RAF war service as a navigator during which he had reached the rank of Squadron Leader and won his DFC. Yet it was he who made the effort to bridge the gap and bring the still shy and awkward schoolboy that I was into the mainstream of the activities of the branch. I was soon elected to the committee and sent as a representative to area and national YC meetings and political school weekends.

Several other politicians report having a mentor like Colin Turner was for Norman Tebbit. When still an active Young Conservative in his teens, John Major was much helped by Ken Payne, whose election campaigns he assisted.

On the Labour side, trade unions have traditionally provided a route into active politics, and still do for the minority of Labour MPs that start out as manual workers. Kevin Barron worked in the mining industry in south Yorkshire and was sent on a National Union of Mineworkers' scholarship to Ruskin College, Oxford. He says (1990) he became very political in the late 1960s, influenced by issues like miners' wages.

So in the early 1970s he went to Ruskin; even though he did not pursue any more qualifications than his diploma in Labour studies, the experience 'opened up my horizons. It took me out of the community in which I had always lived and exposed me to different classes, nationalities and cultures.' This led on to further involvement in the NUM, at local and area level, and eventually a parliamentary candidacy for a safe seat. There are only six other current Labour MPs who went to Ruskin, including Alan Meale, John Prescott and Dennis Skinner. The latter's debating style may seem far removed from the traditional Oxford Union approach, but in its very different way Oxford marked him like it has so many other MPs. John Prescott has recalled (1992) how, when he went to Ruskin aged twenty-five, 'All of a sudden my mind was opened up to the pleasure of learning, of shaping the bullets with which to fight. Ruskin gave me self-confidence in mobilizing my arguments. It taught me that I had no need to feel inferior to anybody.'

Future MPs become involved in politics in numerous different ways. But the early stages generally always involve the translation of an early, adolescent interest in current affairs and debating into active participation in some collective activity, whether a local branch or a university debating society. John Major found a role, an identity, in his campaigning and work for the Young Conservatives in Brixton in the late 1950s and early 1960s, at the same time as John Smith was developing his self-confidence and learning how to capture the attention of an often irreverent audience in Glasgow University debates.

Robin Cook captures (1982) the often haphazard path into politics of many:

I'm always distrustful of those people who produce one great symbolic event to explain their politics. I didn't consciously set out to become an MP or to have a full-time life in politics. I became active in the Labour Party when I was still young, in my teens, and I was chairman of the Students Labour Association in Scotland. As always when you become active in the party, if you are willing to take it on, there are plenty of people willing to propose you for something. My most powerful political post was secretary of Edinburgh City Labour Party – that was real power – everything since then has been a declension in power.

4

SELECTION AS A CANDIDATE

'Powerful filters ensure that only certain types of individuals arrive at Westminster. These filters are political, social and legal.'

Peter Richards, *The Backbenchers*, 1972

'My attraction to some of the local members in what was a safe Labour seat [Greenwich] with a large middle-class vote was that I was a member of the executive of the Fabian Society, connected with the Co-operative movement, and a full-time trade union official. In the Labour Party these credentials are the equivalent of Eton, Sandhurst and the Guards in the Conservative Party.'

Richard Marsh, *Off the Rails*, 1978

'To my astonishment, a little after the general election of that year [1955], I was driving a tractor along the road when someone stopped me and said they were looking for a new candidate at Lowestoft. "You're a young man; you're just the type of person we want. Why don't you let your name go forward?" I didn't even know they needed a candidate ... Almost immediately I found myself the prospective candidate for the Lowestoft constituency. Everything had happened so quickly that I was selected as their candidate without having been approved by Conservative Central Office.'

James Prior, *A Balance of Power*, 1986

In 1971 two aspiring Conservative politicians returned to London in low spirits having lost out, not for the first time, at a selection conference to pick a parliamentary candidate. The two were aged either side of forty, a time when contemporaries were well established in their careers. They wondered when, and even whether, they would find a seat. But fortune was kind. Before long both gained selection for safe Tory seats.

One was Nigel Lawson and the other was Douglas Hurd. Both were ministers within eight years and in the Cabinet within twelve to thirteen years. The successful candidate in the selection for the Tory nomination for Macclesfield, and in the subsequent by-election, was Nicholas Winterton. Throughout a Commons career of more than two decades he has remained on the back-benches, never even close to office. He has been increasingly maverick, or independent-minded (according to taste), in his opinions and behaviour, often clashing with the Tory whips.

This story highlights the arbitrary and apparently haphazard way in which parliamentary candidates are selected. The only unusual part is that Mr Lawson and Mr Hurd were older than most future Cabinet ministers when they were eventually picked for safe seats. As Austin Mitchell argues in his entertaining and informative *Westminster Man* (1982):

Top jobs become more challenging with every step up the ladder but Parliament is front-end loaded: getting the job is more difficult than doing it . . . Getting into Parliament is a lottery rather than a career choice, and not for the scrupulous or squeamish; a question of survival, a reward for sheer brass nerve, thick-skinned perseverance, or simply good luck.

Getting selected is the key obstacle in most political careers. The later electoral contest is a formality in the vast majority of cases. Most candidates face either virtually certain victory or equally certain defeat – even though most do not feel so secure. Even those defending impregnable party bastions are often nervous until they see the bundles of votes mounting up at the count. It is perhaps fortunate for the democratic process that most candidates, and sitting MPs, believe they cannot ignore their constituents. They fear that otherwise calamity will strike, normally in the form of a Liberal Democrat community politician. But the odds are mostly clear. In the last seven general elections, starting with 1970, at most 12 per cent of

MPs defending their seats were defeated. The average was just 8 per cent. At each election more MPs have retired than have been defeated – a total of 468 at the seven elections, compared with 389 who have been defeated. This comparison overstates the risk since over the seven elections some seats changed hands three or, in a few cases, four times, even after adjusting for two boundary changes. Most MPs were much safer. Admittedly, a handful on each occasion (six in 1992) have stood down in seats which the Opposition later captured. These figures exclude MPs who leave the Commons between general elections, either through departure for another job or because of death. There were 135 by-elections between 1970 and 1992. When added to the number retiring from Parliament at each general election, these figures further underline how most new MPs are starting a job where the risk of defeat is relatively low. The careers of a clear majority of MPs will end through voluntary retirement or death, rather than through defeat.

In view of the key importance of the first stage of selection, there is a large literature on the subject (Ranney, 1965; Paterson, 1967; Rush, 1969; Alison Young, 1983; as well as parts of Mitchell, 1982; and Radice *et al.*, 1990). Before looking at the central issues for this book of how people are selected and what motivates them, it is worth examining some of the filters mentioned by Peter Richards in the quotation at the beginning of this chapter. Legally, only British subjects aged over twenty-one can stand for Parliament. This is now broadly defined to include not just those formally counted as British citizens but also citizens of the Commonwealth and of the Irish Republic. Among those disqualified from standing are the certified insane; English and Scottish peers (subject to limited rights of renunciation thanks to Tony Benn and the 1963 Peerage Act); priests of the Churches of England, Scotland and Ireland and the Roman Catholic Church (though not Welsh clergy and Nonconformist ministers); permanent civil servants, members of the police and armed forces, and judges (defined as those holding 'offices of profit under the Crown'); bankrupts for five years; and anyone convicted under the Corrupt and Illegal Practices Prevention Act. Otherwise, anyone over twenty-one can stand where they want without any residential requirement and only having to deposit a minimum sum of money, raised from £150 to £500 after the 1987 general election.

The main political parties themselves act as the primary filter for prospective candidates. A basic requirement is that someone seeking selection has to be a member of the party. This limits the choice to less than 3 per cent of the electorate. Unlike, say, America, where candidates often change their party affiliations, and survive, in Britain evidence of a longer-term involvement is necessary. Moreover, outsiders very rarely succeed. It is a long time since a genuine independent won a mainland British constituency at a general election. The rare exceptions have been sitting MPs who have renounced the whip of their former parties and have sought re-election under their own colours. In almost all cases they have at best succeeded for perhaps one or two general elections. Even though most MPs come from the main parties, there is no shortage of candidates. The main parties believe they should have standard-bearers in all constituencies and others stand to attract publicity and to make a point. In spite of the increase in the size of the deposit, the number of candidates at the 1992 general election was a record 2,948, or an average of 4.5 per constituency.

To gain selection by one of the main parties it is not enough just to be a member of a party; certain other criteria have to be fulfilled. Potential candidates have to demonstrate a commitment to politics, both by displaying a degree of interest and knowledge and by becoming active, in a local constituency party and/or as a local councillor. The first hurdle to be overcome is getting on the approved list of candidates of the parties. For the Tories, this involves writing to the party vice-chairman responsible for the candidates' department, always a back-bench MP. An aspiring candidate has to have three sponsors, preferably including one MP and a party constituency chairman. Initial interviews are conducted by an area agent, then by the vice-chairman himself in London, and, finally, there is a twenty-four hour selection board spread over two days. Only about half succeed in getting on the approved list of candidates. What this process mainly ensures is that someone is on a list at Conservative Central Office, which is then sent to constituencies looking for a candidate, while the potential candidates are notified of vacancies. Tom Arnold, the party vice-chairman responsible for candidate selection in the 1987–92 Parliament, has explained the qualities sought in a Tory candidate (as quoted in Adonis, 1990):

Are they leaders? Could they weld a Conservative Association together, lead it into an election campaign, and, if successful, represent the constituency in the House of Commons? Are they well-rounded individuals who can cope with the stresses and strains of public life, domestic pressures and constant travelling? The Conservative Party is not looking for experts, but it is looking for men and women who have a good working knowledge of contemporary politics and a proven track record of experience in the party, and who above all know their own minds.

The Labour Party's approach is similar in many respects to the Tory one. There are two lists of approved candidates – an A list consisting of trade-union-sponsored candidates and a B list of non-sponsored candidates. For the A list a nominee has to be sponsored by a union affiliated to the Labour Party, and the unions carry out their own vetting and interviews. For the B list, and some separate regional lists are kept, nomination has to be by a local constituency party. An applicant then has to submit a resumé of his or her career, plus a statement of intentions. These applications are considered at party headquarters. Such procedures are mainly intended to weed out the obviously unsuitable, whether extremists of various kinds or people with criminal records or other personal blemishes. In Labour's case, getting on the list is a minor hurdle and for potential candidates is mainly a means of finding out about vacancies. It is peripheral to the manoeuvring involved in actually getting selected.

The real choice is made by local parties. National headquarters may have a preference, but in general any overt intervention by head office in London can be counter-productive. The exception is that the Labour Party's National Executive Committee has the power to impose candidates on local parties during by-elections, and did so a number of times in the 1987–92 Parliament. This was to exclude unsuitable left-wing candidates, such as sympathizers with Militant, the Trotskyite entryist group which had a sizeable presence on Merseyside. The Labour Party nationally also has the power in certain circumstances to reject a candidate selected by a local party and has done so, in effect imposing its own nominee at a general election.

Precise procedures vary between the parties and from constituency to constituency, but in general there are several stages, especially in safe seats. A large number of applications is reduced to, say, ten to fifteen who are interviewed before a smaller short list of at least three and up to five or six is drawn up. The final choice is by a larger selection conference – in effect, the main activists in the local party. In the Tory case, the whole Association then ratifies, and only rarely rejects, the choice. In the Labour Party, initial nominations come from ward parties and affiliated organizations such as union branches, though the number of nominations is not decisive in the final choice. Labour has also changed its procedures for selecting candidates after prolonged and, at the time of writing, continuing debate. Neil Kinnock had sought from 1984 onwards to secure selection by all local party members rather than just by activists on the General Management Committee. This proposal was blocked by the trade unions. The 1987 conference considered three options: the existing system, one member one vote, and an electoral college consisting of a mix of one member one vote and union involvement. The union block vote ensured that the electoral college was adopted, under which at least 60 per cent of the votes were given to local party members and a maximum of 40 per cent to affiliated organizations, mainly unions. This system, however, left open the issue of how union branches should consult their members, in particular whether a ballot should be held. All short lists also had to include at least one woman candidate. This hybrid system of selection was widely regarded as unsatisfactory and after the 1992 general election the leadership pressed for a full system of one member one vote.

Looking round the benches in the House of Commons – Labour as well as Tory – the selection procedures cannot be said to have a 100 per cent success rate. Some pretty odd people get elected who could not be described as 'well-rounded individuals' even by close friends, let alone their long-suffering whips. Selection is seldom a mark of excellence or future potential, but rather a reflection of the particular skills of presentation involved in being picked. A sharp local populist reaffirming the eternal verities of crown, country and hanging may have an advantage in Tory selections over a more reflective metropolitan figure. What is needed is a certain cunning, persistence, self-confidence and, above all, a determination to be selected. In short, successful candidates have to be committed to pursuing a full-time life in politics.

A wide variety of routes exist for aspiring MPs to gain selection. There are now few cases of the almost casual nomination and selection described in the quotation from James Prior at the beginning of this chapter. Sir John Wheeler-Bennett's account (1962) of how Sir John Anderson, later Viscount Waverley, became an MP in 1938 has a nostalgic ring. Ramsay MacDonald's death had left a vacancy among the representatives for the Scottish universities. One of its other MPs was talking to one of the members for Cambridge University who noted that Sir John was shortly going to receive an honorary degree on returning from his term as Governor of Bengal (he had earlier been permanent secretary at the Home Office) and suggested his name. A telegram was sent to Sir John on his ship travelling home:

Though he found the offer of a seat in Parliament attractive, it was a new idea to him and he required time to consider whether he really wished to enter upon a political career. Certainly he would never have sought election in an ordinary constituency, for he would not have lent himself to the rough and tumble of an election campaign. But the university seats were contested by a postal vote, so that this particular objection did not arise. On the other hand, however, though he had imbibed much of his father's Gladstonian Liberalism, John had never been a party man and had no desire now to adopt a party label.

In the end, he agreed to stand as a National Government candidate, without any party label, because of his conviction that a former member of the Civil Service should not become an adherent of any political party. His address to the graduates of the Scottish universities adopted a tone of Olympian detachment:

I am not a party man. Having for more than thirty years, as a matter of duty, studiously avoided any party affiliation, I could not now, without a tinge of hypocrisy, assume any party label even if I did not feel that by doing so I should be, to a considerable extent, undermining the basis of the only claim I can legitimately make to the confidence of any electorate – that of a public servant.

Other easy paths to the Commons have also disappeared. Paul Channon may have inherited his father's old constituency in Southend when still only twenty-three, but that is now highly unusual. On the Labour benches, however, Greville Janner succeeded his father in Leicester and Hilary Armstrong took over her father's old seat in Durham. Two women Labour MPs, Llin Golding and Irene Adams, also inherited constituencies from their husbands, in both cases via by-elections in the middle of Parliaments. But in most cases the sons and daughters of MPs have to look to different constituencies from their fathers.

In even the most hopeless seat there is some competition for the Tory or Labour nomination. None the less, at almost every election there are examples of last-minute selections – for instance, Tony Blair at Sedgefield and Charles Kennedy in Ross, Cromarty and Skye in 1983. Charles Kennedy recalls (1988) that he was a graduate student aged twenty-three in America, – thinking there would not be much prospect of being in Parliament until his early thirties – when he received a phone call to be told that a new constituency had been formed in the Highlands. They asked

Why didn't I throw my hat in the ring. So, I did. They shortlisted me, so I then had to decide what to do. I blew the $500 I had in the bank on a weekend return ticket from Indianapolis to Fort William, spoke at the hustings, and then went back to the States. A couple of weeks later they told me I'd won the postal ballot.

He went on to spring one of the surprises, and rare victories for the then SDP, of the 1983 election by defeating Hamish Gray, a minister of state in the Thatcher Government.

Nowadays, however, most parliamentary candidates go through a long process of travelling round seats, while the majority of MPs have previously fought another constituency before being selected for the one they now hold. This is in sharp contrast to the position before 1939, when the vast majority of Tory MPs in particular entered the Commons at their first attempt. Even in the early 1970s between two-thirds and three-quarters of MPs were successful at their first contest. But now most aspiring MPs are expected to try a hopeless or marginal seat first. All but five of the twenty-strong Major

Cabinet formed after the April 1992 election had previously fought another seat. Seven, including the Prime Minister himself, had fought two earlier contests before winning their current seat. The exceptions were three who had worked for Edward Heath (Douglas Hurd, John MacGregor and William Waldegrave) and two of the newcomers to the Cabinet in April 1992 (John Patten and Gillian Shephard). Similarly, on the Labour side, all but five of John Smith's twenty-strong shadow team (including himself and his deputy) had previously fought seats before entering the Commons. The exceptions were Jack Cunningham, Tom Clarke, Frank Dobson, Harriet Harman and Marjorie Mowlam. Four members of his original Shadow Cabinet – Margaret Beckett, David Clark, Donald Dewar and Bryan Gould (before his resignation in late September 1992) – had experienced defeat. They had been in the Commons, usually for one Parliament, before losing and then coming back for another constituency. Of the 140 new MPs elected in April 1992, a total of eighty-eight in all parties had previously fought another constituency; in four cases four or more times, including contests for the European Parliament. Among new Labour MPs, the proportion is less than might have been expected – thirty-seven out of sixty-nine – but that is partly because of a search for new candidates after the defeats of the 1980s and a preference for local nominees, as discussed later in the chapter. Finding a winnable seat is often a 3,000-metre steeplechase rather than a 100-metre sprint.

On the Tory side, there are several well-trodden paths to Westminster, too well trodden for some tastes. A classic route has been via service in the Conservative Research Department, or, particularly over the past twenty years, as a special or political adviser in 10 Downing Street or in a minister's private office in Whitehall. Six members of the Major Cabinet entered politics after this apprenticeship, as did nine of the newly elected Tory MPs in 1992. The Conservative Research Department has been a nursery of mainly Oxbridge-educated talent since the 1930s. John Ramsden (1980) points out in his comprehensive study of its history up to the late 1970s: 'The department has been a valuable training ground for future politicians; the old boys of Old Queen Street [its then headquarters] have included Henry Brooke, Lord Longford [a Tory in the early 1930s when still Frank Pakenham], Iain Macleod, Enoch Powell and Reginald Maudling.' He might also have included Gordon Campbell, a future Scottish Secretary. Since Ramsden wrote, the list of future Cabinet ministers can be extended to include Douglas Hurd, Norman Lamont, Chris Patten (one of its directors), Tony Newton (a deputy director) and Michael Portillo, while Nigel Lawson was nominally attached to the department when acting as a speech writer for the Tory leader in 1963–4.

The myth of the importance of the department as a formative influence in the careers of future political stars was established by the post-war trio of Macleod, Maudling and Powell, working under the leadership of R. A. Butler. Maudling wrote of the excitement for a young would-be politician of working in close proximity to such historic figures as Eden and Churchill, providing the background material for speeches. These three, all with war service, saw their time in the department as a prelude to political careers of their own. According to Ramsden, Enoch Powell had 'the reputation of being humourless and difficult to work with; he drove himself extremely hard, but he expected the same commitment from everyone else and he made no concessions to the more junior employees who had a less single-minded approach'. Macleod and Maudling, he reports, often had convivial lunches together at Crockford's, where the former was still playing bridge in his spare time. 'There were long hours of argument between Powell and Macleod, sometimes long into the night at Powell's bachelor flat in Earls Court Square, arguments in which Powell would usually take a rather doctrinaire right-wing position, while Macleod jumped about in the centre of Tory politics.'

Among the alumni of the department in the 1950s were Lord Balniel, John Biggs-Davison, Peter Tapsell, Richard Sharples, Anthony Berry, Paul Dean and Gordon Campbell. In the 1960s the list included Michael Alison, Eldon Griffiths, Keith Speed, Barney Hayhoe, Michael Spicer, Carol Mather, John Wilkinson and Tony Newton. In the 1970s, apart from Chris Patten and Michael Portillo, the list included Nigel Forman, David Nicholson and Alan Howarth. After the general election of May 1979 twenty-five former officers of the Conservative Research Department were Tory MPs. During the 1980s, an overlapping route developed through the expansion in the number of special or political advisers to ministers – a more interesting job than working in Conservative Central Office when the Tories are in government. These advisers have often started in the department, but they have to resign as advisers when they are selected as parliamentary candidates. Among the former advisers elected to Parliament from 1979 onwards were Michael Portillo, Douglas French, Christopher Butler, David Lidington, Rod Richards, Charles Hendry and Peter Luff (who managed to work successively for Edward Heath and Lord Young, before taking over Peter Walker's seat at Worcester), as well as former members of the Downing Street Policy Unit such as John Redwood and David Willetts. Several others stood as candidates or sought candidacies. Serving as political secretary to the Tory leader, whether in opposition or in Downing Street, has also been a regular path to the Commons. The list includes Douglas Hurd, William Waldegrave, John MacGregor, Richard Ryder, John Whittingdale and Judith Chaplin (who died less than a year after entering the Commons on the brink of a ministerial career).

Although less well known, many Labour MPs have also emerged from party headquarters and from working as special advisers. The roll call is as distinguished as on the Tory side. Denis Healey was secretary of the international department from 1945 to 1952, during which time he played a key role in

nurturing continental Democratic Socialist parties in the difficult post-war period when they faced a strong Communist
challenge. He recalls (1989) how six years at Transport House
had given him a unique insight into the problems of the post-
war world, but 'on the other hand I had been neither excited
nor impressed by what I had seen of party politics'. But the
alternatives came to nothing, so after the 1951 election he
decided 'after all to try for Parliament'. Among his successors
were David Ennals, later a fellow Cabinet minister, and Tom
McNally, who held the post from 1969 to 1974 and was later
political adviser to James Callaghan as Foreign Secretary and
Prime Minister. He then became a Labour MP and moved
over to the SDP. Mike Gapes, a later head of the party's
international side, entered the Commons in 1992, gaining an
early opportunity to use his experience by joining the Foreign
Affairs Select Committee. Two heads of the research department became MPs – David Ginsburg, its head from 1952 to
1959, who never made much impact in the Commons, and
Peter Shore, head from 1959 to 1964, who became a long-
serving Cabinet minister. Margaret Beckett, Labour's Deputy
Leader from July 1992, served as a research officer, as did
Geoffrey Robinson and Joyce Quin. Gerald Kaufman was
parliamentary press liaison officer for Labour, working in
Downing Street in the late 1960s, while Peter Mandelson was
the party director of campaigns and communictions in the late
1980s. He was one of five new Labour MPs elected in April
1992 who had worked for the party nationally.

Outside party headquarters, many aspirant Tories have been
active in the Bow Group, which was founded in the early
1950s as an association of graduate Tories to discuss new
policies. The most prominent early luminary was Sir Geoffrey
Howe, who, while developing his legal career, was busy writing
pamphlets. Before his marriage, he shared a flat with Patrick
Jenkin, a Cambridge friend and later a fellow minister, who
was also involved in the group. Sir Geoffrey provided the

organization and research backbone. Hillman and Clarke (1988) quote his old friend Ron Needs about the 1950s:

Geoffrey was quite clear in his mind, I am sure, at that stage that that [politics] was what he was going to do and the whole of what he was doing was geared to making an impact in political circles, even though he was at the same time aiming to develop his career in the law. That was why, even though he was not yet in Parliament, one could speculate that he could be Prime Minister.

Among other Tory MPs involved in the late 1950s were Tim Raison, Tom Hooson, David Howell, Peter Lloyd and a precocious Leon Brittan. 'Leon Brittan first made his mark in London politics at the Bow Group, travelling as a student from Cambridge to meetings at the Constitutional Club and amazing graduate members with his self-confidence from the floor as he held forth, thumbs tucked under his jacket lapels.'

Many of the Cambridge generation discussed in the previous chapter became involved in the Bow Group during the 1960s. Peter Lilley, who was too shy to do more than watch the stars of the day when he was at Cambridge, found that later, after he got involved in the Bow Group, he 'eventually realized that if you put yourself into it, you can overcome diffidence'. He wrote pamphlets, including an alternative, pre-Thatcherite manifesto in 1973 which warned that the Heath Government was heading for a crash (1991).

Copies of *Crossbow*, the group's quarterly magazine, read during the late 1960s like a manual on how to become a parliamentary candidate. The issue for January–March 1968 – prepared by an editorial board including Leon Brittan, Jonathan Aitken, Julian Critchley, Norman Fowler, Norman Lamont and Christopher Tugendhat – included an article by the suitably anonymous Psephologue entitled 'What Vacancies at Westminster?' This listed Tory MPs aged sixty or over and speculated about which might announce their retirement before the next general election: 'A few are already known and rumours abound about many others, though it is impossible to distinguish between those who it is thought "will" and desirable "shoulds", a rough guide can be given by listing Tory MPs in descending age order.' The author drops a few not very subtle hints that they might hurry their decision, no doubt to make way for thrusting young Bow Groupers: 'There are those whom even a careful student of *Hansard* could be excused for not recognizing – perhaps these are more than usually active in their constituencies, perhaps not.' The article concludes:

Sadly, illness and death will claim their victims. But to those who must make a personal choice, either to retire if they are already MPs, or to seek election if they are not, the first Marquis of Halifax proferred sound advice when he said: 'It would be well for the business of the political world if young men would study longer before they went into it and old men were not so long before they went out of it.'

Surprisingly, that issue of *Crossbow* did not include any recipes for hemlock.

The close interest, bordering on obsession, with parliamentary candidacies was reflected in other issues about the same time. In the July–September 1968 edition, Christopher Brocklebank-Fowler, the chairman of the Bow Group, later a Tory MP and the only Conservative to cross the floor to join the SDP in 1981, questioned the way people got on the candidates' list at Central Office: 'I am sure that the quality of candidates would be considerly improved if candidate selection and training were approached in a more positive way.' He went on to complain that:

The majority of people on the list as it stands, either have independent means, or are self-employed in their own small businesses, or are dedicated career politicians for whom employment in early life is only a means of earning sufficient money to take part in politics.

There are too few successful middle managers from large companies on the list. This lack is partly due to the disinterest at this level in industry in becoming MPs. It is also true that those who work for big corporations receive little or no encouragement to take part in politics in parallel with their business career. The majority of large employers discourage it, and in some cases even forbid it. These attitudes may well have contributed to the ever widening gap in understanding between industry and government. The Conservatives have not done sufficient to attract candidate material from industry and commerce, nor have they done much to convince the large corporations that there would be a positive advantage to them in supporting young politicians ... An injection of experienced executives and managers into Parliament would go a long way towards improving the relationship between government and industry, and at the same time improve the quality of Parliament itself.

Exactly the same complaints are heard a quarter of a century later; indeed, big companies have become even more like enclosed bureaucracies discouraging rising executives from becoming politically involved. *Crossbow*'s diary also returned to this problem of industry's hostility to the involvement of its employees in politics, noting that a Greater London councillor had lost his job and a parliamentary candidate complained of difficulties in finding one because of their involvement in politics. The anonymous author asked what career the political aspirant could safely choose.

The Bar's demands make the combination with politics less easy than it once was. In other professions partners are likely to be troublesome. Teaching doesn't pay well enough, although it gives one the time. Not everyone can go into public relations. The City's all right, although the image is just a shade unfashionable. Running one's own business is fine, but likely to be too time-consuming in the early stages. Journalism or television – very popular this line, but it can be a bit precarious, unless you're with a very sound outfit. The best solution of all is undoubtedly to be born rich. Failing which? The alternative tradition is to marry an heiress.

As the election approached, *Crossbow* maintained its concentration on candidacies with articles on Tory primaries, an account by Elspeth Howe on the televised Reigate primary (at which she spoke and which her husband won against Christopher Chataway), a semi-parody of a candidate's speech to secure certain adoption for a safe seat, and a list of likely Bow Groupers in the next Parliament. After the Tory victory in June 1970, the issue of October–December 1970 contained a celebration of the Bow Group in power and statements of view from four new MPs. The issue also included a tribute by Nicholas Scott to Iain Macleod, who had died suddenly that summer, as well as a ticking-off for the new Education Secretary, a certain Margaret Thatcher. In the item 'Black Mark', the author, Mentor, criticizes Mrs Thatcher for her circular on comprehensive education – then very much in vogue in fashionable Tory circles like the Bow Group.

This is a classic case of an unnecessary decision being badly taken for reasons of political dogmatism, the educational consequences of which could not only be a step back in some areas but a wrong step forward in others. Mrs Thatcher was perhaps the victim of her own catch phrases. But as a result she has done nothing to help progressive education authorities and much to bolster reactionary ones.

Little did these Bow Groupers know how much most of them would be seeking her favour and praising her only a few years later.

These excerpts give some of the flavour of the frantic search by that generation for the first step on the parliamentary ladder. Several succeeded in 1970 itself – Norman Fowler, Kenneth Clarke and John Gummer (though he lost his seat in 1974). Some had to wait until slightly later – Norman Lamont at a by-election in 1972 and Leon Brittan in February 1974. Michael Howard, after a couple of unsuccessful attempts, concentrated on the Bar and did not enter the Commons until 1983. But he quickly caught up some of his old friends, entering the Cabinet only a few months after Norman Lamont.

In the Labour Party, the routes to candidacies are more diffuse, generally because there are fewer London-based professionals seeking and obtaining seats in the provinces. More Labour candidates, and MPs, have been local men and women, and this trend has increased since the political upheavals of the early 1980s. A classic route for a Labour MP is through involvement in a trade union. The unions did after all create the party at the beginning of this century and still sponsor a sizeable number of Labour MPs. Sponsorship often follows, rather than precedes, election to the Commons and generally is not of direct financial benefit to a candidate or MP personally but involves payment of a proportion of election expenses, and other costs of a constituency party. This can create a relationship of dependency in which the local party looks to a trade union as a financial prop, and therefore the dominant local union can determine who the Labour candidate is. While there are still a large number of union-sponsored MPs, half or more in recent Parliaments, the relationship has changed. That is partly because of the decline in employment and of union membership in some traditional industrial sectors. So fewer industries dominate a particular constituency or area. The NUM still seeks to promote miners and its own officials in mining-dominated constituencies but there are many fewer of these, even in South Yorkshire, let alone central Scotland or south Wales, than there were even in the 1970s. Some unions have looked more to university lecturers, lawyers and middle-class professionals to sponsor, in the hope that if they succeed politically they will remember the interests of the union. The TGWU, for instance, has sponsored both Neil Kinnock and Peter Shore, while the GMB has sponsored those well-known boilermakers John Smith and Gerald Kaufman. The old NUR (now RMT) used to sponsor mainly railwaymen but increasingly opened up to backing middle-class professionals. This was because they could not find working railwaymen of the calibre to win selection conferences. The union's recent sponsored members have included Robin Cook, Tam Dalyell, Frank Dobson (whose constituency of Holborn and St Pancras at least includes several mainline railway stations) and Keith Hill.

Involvement in union branches has traditionally provided a training ground comparable to university political societies and unions where people can develop self-confidence in speaking and discussion with others. The number of former manual workers becoming MPs has fallen sharply (down to 22 per cent of Labour MPs after the 1992 election, according to Byron Criddle in Butler and Kavanagh, 1992). They are increasingly overshadowed by former full-time union officers with further education, but there are still some. Peter Snape is a good example. He became a railwayman at fifteen, spent six years in the army before rejoining the railways, then became very active in his local Labour Party and was elected to the council. As he has said (1988):

I discovered I quite liked local politics and became chairman of the finance committee and leader of the Labour group. Then the NUR asked me if I was interested in going on the union's parliamentary panel. I agreed, but not with any great hope, or ambition, to get to Parliament. I always regarded that as somebody else's role and responsibility. It's the old business, you need a lot of luck in politics, and I happened to be in the right place at the right time – when they were selecting in West Bromwich. I'd only been to West Brom once before the selection conference – to watch a football match – but I was selected.

Ron Leighton was a printer in Fleet Street, in the era when the unions were still a dominant influence. He recalls (1987) meetings of his union chapel:

I think it was a great training for my entry into politics, because all of those members were able to get up on their hind legs and put their case and speak. It was a part of the nature of their lives, in the same way, I suppose, as some people who go to public school are taught to get up and speak without inhibition.

At that stage, he says, the thought of becoming an MP had never crossed his mind. It happened as a result of the collection of a petition calling for the abolition of nuclear weapons tests. He came up to Westminster to present the list to an MP. 'He said he'd noticed me before at a union meeting, and would I be interested in standing as a candidate in the constituency next to his? I really was flabbergasted because I thought all MPs wore black jackets, striped trousers and carnations and spoke nicely.' He had a go, was selected for the seat (Middleton and Prestwich in the Manchester area) and he knocked about 10,000 off the Conservative majority.

Then the MP who'd invited me there in the first place advised me to disengage. Within fourteen months we had another election and that seat was won, so if I'd stayed there I would have come into the House in 1966. I do sometimes wonder what would have happened if I had come in then, rather than in 1979 [after being rejected as a candidate at Stoke in 1966 and fighting and losing Horsham and Crawley in February 1974].

He finally entered the Commons for the Newham seat which Reg Prentice had previously held, before his move to Daventry after switching to the Tories.

Adam Ingram became a full-time union official in Nalgo and this led to involvement in the East Kilbride Labour Party and a place on the local council. He claims (1990) that during this period, in the early 1980s, he never even thought of himself as a parliamentary candidate. But in 1983 he fought the Tory-held seat of Strathkelvin and Bearsden. 'I came third and it whetted my appetite for doing it again – suddenly the adrenalin was flowing very fast.' Then in 1985 he was selected for his home seat of East Kilbride, following the decision of Maurice Miller to step down. 'Even though I had been very involved in local politics and felt sure I would win the seat, I still had to organize very hard.'

A large number of future Labour MPs started as local councillors. Robert Hughes, the veteran anti-apartheid campaigner and MP for Aberdeen North, recalls (1988) that he became a councillor in 1962.

Then it's the old story. There was a rural seat which we'd no hope of winning and they couldn't find a candidate. They asked a number of people to consider it and I was the only one to turn up. Politics is like a drug and, having once fought a seat, it got into my system and I couldn't get rid of it.

Sheffield City Council has turned into as much of a nursery for future MPs as Oxbridge. Five former members of the city's council, including several chairmen of committees, were MPs after the April 1992 election. These included former leaders such as David Blunkett and Clive Betts, as well as Bill Michie and Helen Jackson. They all sat for Sheffield seats, while James Boyce was the MP for nearby Rotherham. Two, Clive Betts and Helen Jackson, are Oxbridge graduates. This is contrary to the previous tradition of the working-class and non-graduate former aldermen who went on to become Labour back-benchers. David Blunkett recalls (1988) that at one stage he did nothing else but politics. 'I think that's very bad for anyone. I try to make time for other things now, for relaxing.' He had an experience not dissimilar to Ron Leighton's in just missing coming to Westminster several years before he made it. It was the time he was on South Yorkshire County Council.

I had a belief in the mid-1970s that it was very important to get to Westminster, that was where everything would be achieved, and I stood in Sheffield Hallam in February 1974. In 1978 I missed being selected for a by-election in the constituency where I lived by one vote. There's no question in my mind that the person who didn't vote for me did me a very big favour indeed. Had I come into the Commons ten years ago, I would have had only a fraction of the experience of both life and politics that I have now. I would have been extremely green and whatever people think of me now – I would have been very bumptious and even more full of myself.

Instead, he became leader of Sheffield City Council in 1980 and for the following seven years led one of the biggest cities in the country. Because Sheffield had such a high profile, at a time of constant confrontation between central and local government, David Blunkett became the first non-MP to be elected to the constituency section of Labour's National Executive Committee since Harold Laski in the 1940s.

The nearest Tory equivalent in recent years has been Wandsworth Borough Council, which has been in the vanguard of the Thatcherite approach to local government. Both of its leaders in the 1980s, Christopher Chope and Sir Paul Beresford, went on to enter the Commons, though they had to look outside the borough. They were joined by some other members of the council. A more traditional former Tory councillor turned stalwart of the back-benches is Sir John Hunt, who succeeded Harold Macmillan at Bromley in 1964. Sir John tried to get on the Conservative Central Office list of approved candidates when he was just twenty-one. He was told to go away and gain experience of local government and of more public speaking. Sir John (1990) regards that as 'rather funny, because that year I was elected to Bromley Council and won the Conservative Party's national speaking championship'. He was Mayor of Bromley at the age of thirty-four, and an MP at the age of thirty-five, becoming a pillar of the Tory back-benches. He says he always thought of service on the council 'as a stepping stone to politics'.

A new way into the Commons, especially on the Labour side, has been through service as a Member of the European

Parliament. The Westminster Parliament elected in April 1992 included twenty who had served at Strasbourg since the start of direct elections in 1979. This included eleven Labour MPs and seven Tories, as well as two from Northern Ireland. There were no new Tory MEP entrants in April 1992, and service at Strasbourg is increasingly regarded by the Tory leadership as a separate career rather than just a stepping stone to Westminster. But four previous Tory MEPs have become junior or middle-ranking ministers (David Curry, Robert Jackson, Eric Forth and John Mark Taylor). A curiosity on the Labour side is how four of the MEPs from south and west Wales have gone on to Westminster. Outside Northern Ireland, no MEPs seek re-election after they have entered Westminster. This is in contrast to the dual mandates held by several leading French and Italian politicians, which is possible partly because their national parliaments sit for a shorter period each year.

The path to selection is seldom smooth and can be very frustrating, requiring local knowledge and contacts, especially in the Labour Party, where union nominations and backing have been crucial. For a safe seat in particular, getting selected is always likely to be a tough fight with local candidates against any outsiders. The contenders' varying ideological stances have, however, seldom been crucial in selections, provided the prospective candidate is broadly within the party mainstream. But a minority of Labour constituency parties have been strongly right- or left-wing (especially the latter in some inner cities during the late 1970s and early 1980s), and some Tory local parties are likely to reject candidates who oppose capital punishment. The position is still partly as described by Austin Ranney in 1965:

The aspirants' general political ideologies and specific views on the issues of the moment play almost no role in the selection of Conservative and Liberal candidates. Both factors have been somewhat more prominent in Labour selections because of the sharp and persistent factional fight between left and right. But even so, ideological consider-ations have been decisive in only a minority of Labour selections.

That was only partly true at the time, in the mid-1960s, when those on the hard left were kept off many short lists. By the early 1970s, it was a disadvantage to be pro-EC in seeking a Labour candidacy, while in the early 1980s, the height of Bennism, support for unilateral disarmament and constitu-tional change in the party was often required to gain selection, especially in big-city constituencies.

Peter Lilley, generally regarded as one of the most Thatcher-ite members of the first Major Cabinet, found that his involve-ment with the Bow Group meant he was labelled as being on the left by constituency parties (1991): 'It just exposes the meaninglessness of such labels. I found that a great handicap when I was trying to become a Conservative candidate. I would go along to interviews in safe Labour seats where Tory associations are very right-wing and they would imply that a "pinko" like me had nothing in common with blue-blooded Tories like them.' Powellism and immigration were divisive issues in the late 1960s and early 1970s. David Hunt, a leading student Tory and chairman of the Young Conservatives, recalls (1988):

I was very interested in standing for Parliament and in 1968 was adopted as Conservative candidate for Bristol South, which I fought in 1970 against Michael Cocks. Then in 1972 I was selected for Plymouth Drake but it came just before the party conference at which I led the Young Conservatives in an attack on Enoch Powell and his views on immigration. When I went back to Plymouth Drake afterwards, a lot of supporters of Enoch Powell came to the adoption meeting, including some people who were rather upset that a local candidate had not been considered, and by a narrow majority they referred back my selection.

David Hunt fought and lost Kingswood in 1974 before his local seat, the Wirral, came up in 1976 when Selwyn Lloyd stepped down as Speaker and went to the Lords.

The most important influence on selections is the personality of the candidate in fitting in with the activists' idea of what they want their MP to be. Austin Ranney (1965) argues: 'Some of the specific qualities mentioned are common to all the parties: skill at public speaking, ability to get on well with people (especially with local party workers), a willingness to serve the local organization as well as the national party, and so on.' There are differences between the parties, and some of the comments made by people interviewed by Ranney now sound rather dated:

Most Conservatives speak of wanting a man of character – solid, loyal, dependable in a tight spot, not flashy or brilliant. Most Socialists, on the other hand, speak of wanting a dedicated servant of the movement. But to most trade unionists this means a man who has worked with his hands, served his union faithfully, and accumulated the seniority that entitles him to parliamentary candidature. To most CLP members it means an intellectual who has proved his devotion to certain causes – nationalization, racial equality, nuclear disarmament, equal educational opportunities, or whatever.

Nowadays, service on a local council would be more important and experience as a manual worker would be a rarity.

When Arundel and Shoreham, a rock-solid Tory seat, was looking for a candidate in 1971 after the death of the previous member, more than 170 people applied. According to a rare detailed insight in a BBC documentary (King and Sloman, 1973), Noel Barker, chairman of the local association, said he had pretty clear ideas of what the party was looking for: 'Firstly, someone in an age group which was not too old. Secondly, we wanted a very good constituency member, because many of our constituents are old people; they need looking after. And thirdly, we wanted a man who we thought would go a long way in politics – in other words a high-flyer.' In the end, Richard Luce was chosen. He rose to become a middle-ranking minister just outside the Cabinet.

Local, and at times even chance, contacts can be important. Robert Key, a schoolmaster, had an advantage worthy of a Trollope novel when the tightly fought selection in Salisbury came up in 1982. He was a bishop's son. As he said (1991): 'If ever there was one seat I would have wished to represent it was Salisbury, and I was very lucky to get it. I tried not to play the local card but it was perfectly obvious I was local and also a fact of life that half the selection committee had been confirmed by my father.' All four finalists, Robert Key, Michael Howard, Peter Lilley and Charles Goodson-Weekes, became MPs. Tam Dalyell had an even stranger advantage (1988). He had been a teacher at a school about 4 miles from the family home of the Binns and he was responsible for a lot of the football as coach and referee. One team was particularly successful and he took them all over Europe and to Leningrad, as it was then.

The upshot of it was that the grandfather of one of the boys thought I had to be rewarded for services to his difficult grandson and the form of the reward was to give me the nomination of his union for West Lothian. There was a bit of a row. I was only twenty-nine at the time, but people decided I must be a man of substance to have enraged some of the characters involved. There was a selection conference and I made a speech – I often make bad speeches – and they wanted someone who would stay in Scotland and they chose me.

Chance can work against a candidate. George Younger had already fought a hopeless seat before the chance of getting into Parliament came again when the member for Kinross and West Perthshire dropped dead. The constituency was a few miles from his home and he remembers (1985) thinking:

This is it. I've got to try and get adopted or else I'm never going to be a politician. Well, I eventually was, and in the middle of the by-election Harold Macmillan resigned and Alec Home needed a seat, like yesterday. I handed it over to him. That was a colossal political experience; in three weeks I had about ten years' worth. When the time came, I applied for Ayr, perfectly naturally because it happened to be the seat my grandfather – also called George Younger – held for many years at the beginning of the century.

In other cases, chance, or rather mistakes by politicians themselves, intervene. Boundary changes present a particular trap, upsetting an apparently lifelong parliamentary career. Susan Crosland (1982) recalls how, as the 1955 general election approached,

the heavyweights at Westminster judged that South Gloucestershire [Tony Crosland's then seat], its boundaries lately redrawn in favour of the Conservatives, would inevitably change parties. The local Labour Party believed the seat could be held by a personal vote for their member, a view he dismissed as sentimentality. He decided to stand instead for Southampton Test, a new constituency that Hugh Dalton and Co. believed he had a good chance of winning for Labour, despite the foregone conclusion that a Conservative Government would be swept back to office ... When the election results came in, the Conservative majority at Southampton Test was nearly 4,000 larger than at South Gloucestershire, where it was a near thing. Tony felt he'd made a bad mistake in not taking local advice, saw it as a salutary lesson that those 'in the know' at Westminster may have antennae less sensitive than people on the spot.

He used his years away from Westminster to complete his classic work, *The Future of Socialism* (1956), undoubtedly a more valuable use of his time than another stint on the back-benches. Iain Sproat made an even more unfortunate decision. A rising junior minister in the early 1980s, one of the advance guard of Thatcherism, he decided that the Aberdeen South seat he had held since 1970 was too risky after the boundary changes and opted for the new seat of Roxburgh and Berwickshire. In the event, Gerry Malone held Aberdeen South for the Tories, though he lost it in 1987, while Iain Sproat was defeated in his new seat by Archy Kirkwood, a Liberal. It took Mr Sproat nine years to return to the Commons, not in Scotland but south of the border, representing Harwich.

The selection of candidates is not, of course, just a measure of relative talents. Much energy is devoted to nobbling the right people at the right time. The first instinct of many MPs, and political journalists, when they hear that a sitting MP is seriously ill, let alone dead, is to look up his or her majority. The Liberal Democrats have been known to carry out preliminary investigations of seats even before the current member is dead. The old SDP geared up for a campaign in Dundee West in the early 1980s when it learned that Ernie Ross, the Labour MP, was seriously ill. Party officials were almost monitoring his temperature. Ten years later he was still a vigorous member for the seat, long after the SDP had died.

Little has changed since the days of George III. Peter Paterson records (1967) how the King was

informed on the morning of 31 October 1773 of the death of Sir Robert Ladbroke, one of the members for the City of London. With an expedition that revealed his anxiety that so important a decision as the choice of a Member of Parliament should not be left to chance, particularly since it affected the strength of his own support in the House, the King wrote about the vacancy to Lord North, his Prime Minister, at 6.42 p.m. the same day.

Such alacrity would be regarded as tasteless today, at least if it were publicly known. But once the decencies are over, potential candidates operate like George III and friends are contacted. In the Labour Party especially, contenders are careful to line up nominations from both wards and unions. Where a sitting MP is old and known to be considering retirement, this preparatory work can last several years, particularly when a prominent local figure, like the leader of the council, wants the succession.

Many subsequently successful politicians have been aided in their careers by a helpful party official. Jean Lucas was a highly successful Tory agent in south London for the generation up to 1990. Bruce Anderson describes (1991) how, 'over the years, she helped to train a large number of young politicians, including Chris Chope, the late Ian Gow, David Mellor, Dick Tracey – and John Major. She has a claim to being the Alf Gover of Tory politics.' Later, after he had unsuccessfully contested Holborn and St Pancras North in the two 1974 elections, John Major consulted Jean Lucas to ask her what he had been doing wrong to be rejected out of hand for the first half-dozen seats to which he had applied. It turned out that the CV of another John Major had mistakenly been sent round the country. Once the mistake was rectified, he was interviewed in a number of seats – South Dorset, Ruislip Northwood and Portsmouth North – though none of them picked him. When the then Labour-held marginal of Putney came up in early 1976, Jean Lucas suggested that he apply, which he did, before withdrawing because he was doing well in the preliminary stages of selection for Carshalton, where a by-election had arisen. The selection there was won by Nigel Forman, whom John Major appointed to a junior ministerial job in April 1992, while David Mellor won Putney. John Major did not have to wait long, since within a few months Huntingdon came up. There he had to compete against four future members of his Cabinet – Peter Brooke, Michael Howard, Peter Lilley and Chris Patten – as well as several former MPs defeated in 1974, including Jock Bruce-Gardyne and Alan Haslehurst, who were on the final short list. John Major received advice from Peter Golds, an old south London friend and then party agent in Brent North, about the social changes in the area and he struck the right note about trying to unify the constituency in his speech at the final conference.

It often helps to have a local supporter working on your behalf. After the ailing Stafford Cripps stepped down from the Commons in October 1950, Mervyn Stockwood, later Bishop of Southwark and then a local vicar, suggested the name of Tony Benn to the executive of the Bristol South East party. His name arose from talks Stockwood had had with Roy Jenkins and Tony Crosland, both of whom were – in a delightful political irony – anxious to see him in the House of Commons. The party's National Executive was keen to see the return of Arthur Creech-Jones, a former Secretary of State for the Colonies, who had lost his seat at the general election earlier that year. Tony Benn was helped by the support of Herbert Rogers, a local political fixer who had admired his father. Rogers advised him on the tone to adopt. Benn's fluent speech, emphasizing his passion, vigour and ideas, apparently swept the selection conference, according to Jad Adams (1992). There was also, apparently, some resentment at the National Executive's clumsy promotion of Creech-Jones. A year later, when the South East Leeds seat came up at the end of 1951 after the sitting Labour member had become a peer, the main claimant was a local councillor who, Denis Healey (1989) says,

had as many enemies as friends. His enemies looked for an outsider to run against him. Solly Pearce, the editor of the *Leeds Weekly Citizen*, who had immense influence behind the scenes, liked the articles I had written for him from time to time, and knew I had done well in the nearby seat of Pudsey and Otley in 1945. Since I had no personal friends in the constituency, he got a member of my trade union to persaude the Leeds branch of the Jewish Labour Party, Poale Zion, to nominate me.

Again here, the National Executive's promotion of a former MP also backfired.

Because local parties guard their autonomy in the selection of a candidate in this way, there is less scope for national groups to place their candidates, as in the days of patronage before the second and third Reform Acts. There have been a number of exceptions. In the early 1960s the Campaign for Democratic Socialism was set up to combat the influence of left-wing activists in the Labour Party. Discussions about the formation of the campaign started in the months before Hugh Gaitskell's defeat over unilateralism at the 1960 party conference at Scarborough. This vote stimulated the campaign's work in constituencies and in the unions. Many supporters were active in local union branches and the CDS claimed that over one-third of its grass-roots backers held office in local party organizations (according to an analysis in Haseler, 1969). Haseler notes that the CDS was 'extremely successful in its promotion of parliamentary candidates, for in the majority of by-elections in the 1961–3 period there was a large influx of the type of MPs that a moderate and revisionist party would call forth. These new MPs, in practice, and also in public-image terms, had little in common with unilateralism or fundamentalism.' Of the twenty-nine Labour MPs returned in by-elections in the 1959–64 Parliament, as many as fourteen had a close association with the CDS including its first secretary, Bill Rodgers, Dick Taverne, Tom Bradley, Jeremy Bray and Tam Dalyell, as well as two returning ex-MPs, Denis Howell and Niall MacDermot. A further nine new MPs were loyalist right-wingers. Trade union and Labour Party regional organizers were helpful to CDS candidates, especially in the east Midlands and the north-east. Contacts at the top level of the Labour Party also helped. Hugh Gaitskell had noticed Dick Taverne because he made a good party conference speech and Transport House was told to get him a seat. Bill Rodgers was selected for Stockton because Hugh Dalton knew a prominent local activist.

The closest later parallel was the Campaign for Labour Party Democracy and similar loosely Bennite groups. The CLPD itself was concerned with changing the Labour Party's constitution to ensure greater accountability through changes in the method of electing the leader and in requiring mandatory procedures for reselecting MPs in each parliamentary constituency. These changes were approved during the two years of bitter recriminations and charges of betrayal following Labour's defeat in 1979. Supporters of CLPD were involved in putting pressure on a number of older right-wing MPs, some of whom left to join the newly formed SDP either after or in anticipation of being dumped, while a few others were rejected and dropped out of politics. The impact was muddied by the boundary changes ahead of the 1983 general election, which would anyway have forced local parties to choose candidates afresh. The direct effects were less significant than predicted, apart from the defections to the SDP, though there may, initially, have been indirect effects as MPs sought to avoid saying or doing anything which might offend local party members. A safety-first conformity may have been one result in the 1980s. One or two right-wing Labour members took left-wing public stands to appease their local parties. Some were left-wing in their constituency and right-wing in the House of Commons. There were some conflicts between allegedly moderate Labour MPs, often championed by the press, and extremist local activists. This produced some long-running sagas, notably involving Frank Field, whose persistence rewarded him with several lives in Birkenhead. There was evidence of organization by far-left groups, not just Militant but some similar quasi-Trotskyist groups in London, taking advantage of the low memberships of inner-city parties.

The overall number of casualties was small, about half a dozen MPs in each of the 1983–7 and 1987–92 Parliaments, partly thanks to the greater willingness of the National Executive to intervene. In most cases it was not a clash over ideology but a feeling that the sitting MP was too old and had grown out of touch. Indeed, left-wingers such as Ernie Roberts and Norman Atkinson lost out as well as right-wingers. In the 1983–7 Parliament barely a quarter of those seeking reselection had to face a ballot. In general, Denis Healey's remarks in his memoirs (1989) still hold true: 'A Member of Parliament who works hard in his constituency and is trusted as a human being by the active members of his local party can normally count on personal loyalty to override differences about policy.' That has not always been true. Several assiduous Labour members with good records did run into trouble when their local constituency parties moved to the hard left, including George Cunningham and John Grant in Islington and Ron Brown in Hackney (contributing to their decisions to join the SDP), as well as Reg Freeson in Brent.

The people who survive these hurdles are in the main those who passionately want to get selected – those who are willing to devote the time and go through the necessary apprenticeship. There are still some accidental selections, but they are now rare. The survivors are the career politicians. But who are they? Most are male, middle class and white, in spite of the record total of sixty women MPs elected in April 1992 and six non-white MPs. There are now fewer upper-class Old Etonians on the Tory benches and fewer Labour MPs who have been manual workers than in the early 1950s. The number of graduates has increased, to 73 per cent among Tory MPs and 61 per cent on the Labour benches. But suggestions that members of different parties are gradually growing more alike are exaggerated. You just have to look down from the press gallery at the Commons chamber: with few exceptions (including, curiously, both John Major and John Smith), comparatively few MPs can, at least by external appearance, easily be imagined on the opposite side. More than three-fifths of Tory MPs are still public-school products (down only a little from the peak of three-quarters in the 1945–74 period), while only one in seven Labour MPs has been educated in this way. Similarly, more than two-fifths of Tory MPs are graduates of Oxford and Cambridge, down slightly from an average of half in the pre-1974 period. By contrast, only one in six Labour MPs is a graduate of these two universities, down slightly from a peak of more than a fifth during the 1970s. Using broader educational measures, and just focusing on new Tory

MPs, David Baker *et al.* (1992) argue that any broadening of the social base among these new members, suggested by the large 1983 intake, was halted in 1987 and 1992. The meritocrats have not yet pushed out the public schoolboys in the Tory parliamentary party.

More significant has been the contrast in the occupations of MPs before their election. Andrew Adonis notes (1990): 'The major difference between the parties' MPs lies not in class distinctions but in the type of middle-class professional they recruit; a quarter of all Tory MPs are private-sector professionals (mainly lawyers and accountants), while 40 per cent of Labour members come from the public-sector professions (mainly teaching and lecturing).' Three times more Tory than Labour MPs are barristers and solicitors, while three times more Labour than Tory MPs are teachers and lecturers.

In the late 1970s, around half of Labour MPs were the children of manual workers and had moved up the social/ occupational scale, thanks mainly to the state secondary and higher education systems. More than a fifth of Labour MPs can still be defined as manual workers, reflecting the impact of trade union nomination on the selection of candidates. Trade union involvement ensures that Labour MPs are more socially representative than they otherwise would be.

The Commons remains a predominantly male institution, even though the number of women MPs has risen steadily in the past decade from twenty-three at the 1983 general election to forty-one in 1987 and sixty in 1992. There have been similarly few women ministers, just ten at Cabinet level since women first entered the Commons in 1919. That has partly reflected the reluctance of local parties to select women, especially in winnable seats; the female success rate is roughly half that of men. But, until recently, fewer women had sought to stand for Parliament, even though women have traditionally played a large part at a local level, particularly in the Conservative Party. Much of the approach to political careers discussed in this book – the style of speaking and the manoeuvring for position, whether learned at the Oxford and Cambridge Unions or at a union branch meeting – reflects a male rather than a female approach. Women have also found it more difficult to go through the apprenticeship of local involvement and fighting a hopeless seat in their twenties normally required to win selection for a safe seat. Women with young children also have to face the obstacle that they may have to keep up two homes – one in London and one in their constituencies.

However, in the past decade a more deliberate attempt has been made to increase the number of female candidates and MPs. The number of women candidates rose by 30 per cent between the 1987 and 1992 elections. The effort has been spearheaded by networking and campaigning organizations such as the 300 Group. In early 1993 a British version of Emily's List, the highly successful American fund-raising organization for women candidates, was founded to help elect more women Labour MPs. Emily stands for Early Money is Like Yeast (it makes the dough rise) and the American Emily's political action committee raised $6.2 million for forty-four women candidates in the 1992 elections. The Tories picked women for six safe seats before the 1992 election, while Labour's policy of requiring one woman to be on every short list may have contributed to the sharp increase in the number of women fighting marginal seats and in the total of women Labour MPs. But, as in many other professions, there is a long way to go to redress the overall imbalance and the disadvantages which women face when competing in a career structure favouring men.

For the purpose of this book a more detailed look at occupations is necessary. There has been a marked rise in the number of MPs working in jobs directly linked to politics, whether as a political researcher or adviser, a public affairs consultant, a lobbyist, a full-time councillor or a trade union official (rather than as a voluntary branch officer). There are three broad categories: full-time politicians (as defined above); those in an intermediate position, in jobs which are not regarded as long-term careers but are intended to facilitate political activity; and those in 'proper' jobs, wholly independent of politics. These judgements are inevitably subjective, partly because of the absence of sufficient data and partly because people move from one category to another at various stages of their lives. The clear conclusion is that there has been a marked shift away from those in 'proper' jobs over the past forty years. Among the new MPs elected at the 1951 election, this was 80 per cent, falling slightly to 71 per cent in 1964 among new MPs. The share dropped to just 41 per cent among the 140 new members elected in April 1992. However, 53 per cent of existing MPs had 'proper' jobs before first being elected to the Commons.

There has been a corresponding rise in the proportion of new MPs who are already full-time politicians – from 11 per cent in 1951, and a similar percentage in 1964, up to 31 per cent in 1992 – though only 19 per cent of existing MPs re-elected then came into this group. This is still a minority of new MPs. But, together with the intermediate group, it reflects a marked change in the background of MPs. There is a sharp difference between the parties: some 52 per cent of new Tory MPs in 1992 came from 'proper' jobs, while just 30 per cent of new Labour ones did. Similarly, while just 24 per cent of new Tory MPs in April 1992 were already full-time politicians, 38 per cent of new Labour members were.

Similar trends have been shown by other research using slightly different definitions. For instance, the Industry and Parliament Trust, which seeks to bring members of the Commons and Lords and business closer together, estimated that 29 per cent of the new intake after the 1992 election had been involved in specifically political careers (political public relations, political consultancy, full-time local government and full-time trade union work). This is only two percentage points different from my own estimate. It compares with the Trust's estimate of 14.5 per cent of all MPs in the Commons coming into this category, which points to the recent sharp growth in political occupations. By contrast, the number of newly elected MPs with business experience has declined to just over a fifth in recent general elections, compared with a third in 1979. More than a half of new MPs come from the worlds of law, education and professional politics. This has led the Trust to propose an initiative to reverse these trends, as discussed in Chapter 10.

A supporting indicator of a growing commitment to politics is the increasing number of MPs who have been local council-lors. The proportion has risen from less than a fifth of Tory MPs in the late 1940s and early 1950s to nearly two-fifths in the 1980s. On the Labour side, the rise has been from a higher base, around two-fifths, to more than half. In the last few elections more than three-fifths of new Labour MPs have been councillors. The April 1992 intake included thirteen former leaders of local authorities and twelve others who had chaired council committees.

The rise of the career politician, though undoubted, should not be regarded as universal. There are still many MPs – whether provincial Tory solicitors or Glaswegian local council-lors – who regard reaching the Commons as the pinnacle of their careers, rather than as a step on the lower rungs of the ladder. They do not dream of red boxes. As noted above, this remains truer on the Tory than the Labour benches. It is still possible for lawyers and businessmen to switch in mid-career to become Tory MPs. But these are mainly solicitors in small, often family, practices, or small businessmen, rather than executives in large national organizations. None the less, the Tories can claim, at least in part, to represent a broader spectrum of the professional and business middle classes. By contrast, Labour has become more narrowly the party of public-sector white-collar workers and career politicians.

The contrast partly reflects upheavals in the Labour Party during the early 1980s. These had an impact on both the ideological position of MPs and their social backgrounds. One result was that the old Labour right, as represented by the Manifesto and Solidarity groups, failed to recruit many new MPs from the late 1970s onwards. Instead, most new MPs were broadly on the left, mostly in the mainstream – what became known as the soft left during the 1980s. They appeared less left-wing than in the past because the mainstream left had abandoned a confrontational approach. Mandatory reselection posed little threat to most sitting MPs after the mid-1980s. Of the 205 sitting MPs seeking reselection before the 1987 general election, only fifty-nine faced contests and a mere fourteen polled less than 60 per cent of the votes cast. Just four were defeated in these ballots. Othewise, the changes in Labour during the 1980s, including the departure of thirty Labour MPs to the SDP, as well as the changes to parliamentary boundaries in 1983, favoured full-time politicians, especially local candidates and activists.

The increasing bias towards locally known candidates has been reinforced by Labour's decision to broaden its selection procedures. The change in rules after 1987, allowing all party members a vote (though still alongside the trade unions), was intended to mobilize local party members to offset allegedly atypical activists. This is favoured by critics of the traditional narrowly based caucus method of selection. However, in the early 1990s Labour had little more than 250,000 individual members, or fewer than 500 per constituency. So it was a highly qualified system of mass involvement, prompting efforts to involve union members paying the political levy. The effect has been to narrow the type of candidate chosen. Local aspirants already known to the broader local electorate of party members have been favoured, though a further broadening in the electorate to party supporters might also help nationally known figures. The impact of the changes so far has been shown by the sharp increase in local councillors in the 1992 intake. Many of the replacements for Labour MPs who retired from safe seats were such local figures, including council leaders. The continuation, at least up to the 1992 election, of the separate involvement of unions in selection has reinforced this localizing trend as local trade union officials have often secured selection in safe Labour seats. In his chapter in Butler and Kavanagh (1992), Byron Criddle concludes: 'Interest, more than ideology, coloured the new Parliamentary Labour Party, whose membership suggested deep roots in the public sector. Increasingly, however, on both sides, the House comprised career politicians for whom office counted as much as interest and where dogma became the servant of ambition.'

A further result has been a decline in the number of London-based, Oxbridge-educated Labour candidates, such as barristers, lecturers, consultants and journalists. After the formation of the SDP, these people have been suspect as possible defectors and have suffered from a decline in deference paid to them in local constituency parties. None the less, the drop in the number of Oxbridge-educated new Labour MPs has been surprisingly small – and there was a slight pick-up in the numbers at the 1992 election. That partly reflects the adaptation by these candidates to the new circumstances. Several have returned after university to their home towns and have built careers there, rather than, as often in the past, living in London. Eight of the thirteen Oxbridge-educated new Labour MPs in April 1992 were based in or near the constituency for which they were selected, often their home town, like Clive Betts and Helen Jackson in Sheffield, Geoffrey Hoon in Ashfield and Anne Campbell in Cambridge. The route for the ambitious aspiring politician educated at Oxbridge is to build a career in a provincial city or town with several safe Labour seats in the vicinity. Up to the early 1970s, a friendly union organizer would assist in the placing of the bright middle-class candidate from London. But since then, the London-based

Oxbridge-educated professional sitting for a northern seat has been a rarity; exceptions include Tony Blair, Peter Mandelson and Angela Eagle.

Similarly, there are now just a handful of non-Scots representing Scottish constituencies. It is a long time since the days when Asquith represented East Fife and Augustine Birrell sat for the other part of the County of Fife. As Roy Jenkins recounts (1964):

On one occasion in about 1900, when he [Birrell] and Asquith and Haldane had climbed to the top of a hill near the Firth of Forth which commanded a wide view over both Fife and East Lothian, he turned to the others and exclaimed: 'What a grateful thought that there is not an acre in this vast and varied landscape which is not represented at Westminster by a London barrister!'

Being selected as a parliamentary candidate remains the key event in the lives of career politicians, opening the door to the world of Westminster. But even with the broadening of Labour's procedures to include all party members, decisions are still taken by a tiny minority of the electorate. Peter Paterson's criticisms of a generation ago of a selectorate producing unrepresentative candidates and MPs remain valid. The decline in membership in all parties makes the selectorate even narrower. Successful candidates emerge from a process of political Darwinism in which the fittest, or rather the most committed, survive. It is far from certain that the qualities required to cultivate a local Labour Party and gain sufficient support to become a candidate – or to impress a Tory selection conference – are the right ones for future MPs and ministers. A combination of fluency, even glibness, a willingness to utter the political platitudes of the day and not to challenge the prejudices of party activists, and a dedication to politics above all else are required. Many people with successful careers of their own are in practice excluded by the requirements needed to gain selection. Those who have devoted their energies to being selected have to readjust completely when they are elected and arrive in the Commons.

5
ENTERING THE COMMONS

'I found being an MP in the late 1940s an easy life. There was still an enormous Labour majority, which had been elected in 1945, so that whipping was mostly light. Southwark was undemanding. I went there often – it was only a ten-minute and one-penny tramcar ride away – and tried to find non- or quasi-political organizations to address. But no one seemed to expect this. Neither of the other members did it, nor had my predecessor. Constituency correspondence was negligible. Advice bureaux were more popular, but not much. It was one of the last of the pocket boroughs.'

Roy Jenkins, *A Life at the Centre*, 1991

'The MP's job has two core elements – participation in Parliament and assisting constituents in difficulty. It is evident that, in both these areas, pressures have increased over the last five years – and in our 1986 report we suggested that the level of correspondence and so on had risen in the years preceding that. Constituents write to their MPs more often and have become more demanding.'

Hay Management Consultants report for the Review
Body on Top Salaries, on House of Commons office cost
allowance, July 1992

'As a journalist for twenty years, I've always regarded Westminster as an unhealthy place full of very marginal characters and I'm only slowly being converted.'

Dudley Fishburn, former *Economist* journalist, after two
years as a Tory MP, interview in *House Magazine*,
19 June 1990

When newly elected MPs arrive at Westminster – generally elated, overawed and confused – they enjoy a brief moment of equality. Whatever they have achieved in their past careers, whether as obscure local councillors or as advisers to a Prime Minister, does not seem to matter. They are all the same and have, in theory, the same opportunities. But that moment does not last. In practice, some have a head start, while others will flounder. Their differing previous experiences, talents, aspirations and interests soon surface in their new environment, and some will begin ascending the greasy pole, while others remain as back-benchers.

The first days at Westminster can be a strange and unsettling experience. Teddy Taylor was elected a Tory MP at the age of twenty-six in 1964. He remembers (1988):

I'd never been to the Commons before then. I'd only been in London once in my life before, and that was on a school trip. After the result was announced, I assumed that someone would hand me a bulky envelope saying that I would have to attend Parliament at a certain day, at a certain time, and here were the tickets and here were the instructions, and of course nothing happened at all. I came down on the night sleeper and found myself in Parliament at seven o'clock in the morning, trying to find the way in. It was a very strange start; I always thought you'd be told lots of things, and you're told nothing at all. Wages then were very low . . . It was rather a lonely, miserable life, with very long hours, but I soon got stuck into it and enjoyed it thoroughly.

Ten years later, Peter Snape, a former railwayman, had similar feelings (1988):

It is like everyone says, your first day at school and you don't know your way round or who anybody is. Public speaking in local government and the trade union field was a help, although, even after fourteen years, I still get butterflies when I speak in the chamber. You never know what's round the corner at Westminster.

Willie Whitelaw (1989) had a more traditional introduction:

I was enormously fortunate in an old friend who looked after me. Charles MacAndrew, the Deputy Speaker, later Lord MacAndrew, was a great House of Commons figure and enormously respected. I had played golf with him at Prestwick and St Andrews and knew him well. He set out to ensure that I was properly educated in House of Commons procedures, which I found valuable later on when I became a whip.

As John Biffen, that shrewdest of observers of the moods of the Commons, said during a debate in the House on MPs' conditions, 'There is no such thing as an average Member of Parliament. That is an abstract concept. We have 650 people who adopt completely different approaches to work.' The point was made with typical pith by Clement Attlee. Richard Marsh (1978) recalls how the then retired Labour leader visited the writer's Greenwich constituency shortly after he was elected in 1959 and asked how he liked the Commons. Marsh said it was fascinating meeting the people there, meaning that he was now mixing with household names and involved at the top. Attlee saw it quite differently. 'He puffed his pipe a couple of times, nodded his head and said, "Quite right, my boy. Very profound remark; 635 of them, all peculiar one way or an-other."'

Peculiar they may be, but increasingly the now 651 members regard being an MP as a job – if not full-time, then at least their primary occupation. MPs may find different outlets for their energies and interests, but most now regard being in the Commons as a career, not as an interlude or something to be fitted in alongside a full-time job in the City or business. Even barristers, traditionally seen as part-time MPs, have found it increasingly hard to combine more than the occasional short case with being a member. This has applied especially to those with practices in the more demanding and time-consuming areas, like commercial law. Only lawyers with a criminal practice can manage a few short-lived cases, and then generally only in the recess. Sir Ivan Lawrence, a successful barrister with a criminal practice, became a QC seven years after entering the Commons and then became a Crown Court recorder. He has said he loves both jobs, but politics the more, so that if he ever had to choose between politics and the law, he would not even have to think about it.

The trend towards full-time legislators has developed even more dramatically in America. William Schneider (1992) has noted how at the national level Congress has been redesigned to fit the career aspirations of its members: 'Professionalism creates the perception of a governing class of elected officials who treat themselves as privileged experts.' This change has also spread at the state level. Instead of legislatures consisting of amateur citizen politicians meeting infrequently, usually every other year for two months, they now have more frequent and longer sessions. All but seven of the fifty state legislatures meet every year. State legislators have become more professional, with higher salaries and better staff support. More than 33,000 people work on the staff in state legislatures, 40 per cent of them full-time professionals. Instead of citizen legislators, who were representative of the population, nearly one in five legislators views the legislature as a career, a full-time occupation with a reasonable income of its own and ample outlets for his or her energies in committee work and service to constituents. As William Schneider points out:

There's only one problem with this. The voters hate it. They hate the idea that people go into the legislature as a career. And they hate the fact that state legislatures are becoming more and more like Congress – full-time professional bodies where members have become independent entrepreneurs who require elaborate fund-raising activities to mount expensive re-election campaigns.

This is similar to the views of Alan Ehrenhalt, whom I quoted in the first chapter. He argues (1991) that full-time jobs in Congress and in legislatures attract people who want to devote most of their waking hours to politics. It is now much harder to combine politics and a career in private life. Moreover, politics offers a route to prestige and social acceptance that is often unavailable in the private world.

Even though, as in America, more MPs treat the Commons as a career, many also have outside incomes, as shown by the increasing controversy over the disclosure of members' financial interests (required to be registered since 1975). More than two-thirds of members have outside earnings or another part-time occupation. There is an argument for such outside interests as a means of keeping in touch with the business and other worlds, but the question is whether some of these interests go beyond maintaining contact and stray into lobbying and other activities which might compromise an MP's independence. There are charges that MPs misuse their privileged access to Westminster in asking parliamentary questions and in arranging meetings with fellow members and with ministers. Many, especially Tory, back-benchers act as consultants and public affairs advisers to private companies.

The edition of the register of members' interests which appeared in January 1993, the first of the new Parliament, showed the extent of outside interests, particularly on the Tory side. Excluding the quarter of the 336 Tory MPs who are ministers and whips and cannot have such interests, 60 per cent of the rest are paid consultants to outside bodies, a handful having as many as five or six consultancies. The habit starts early: twenty-five of the sixty-three new Tory MPs elected in April 1992 held consultancies. There is a sharp contrast between the parties. None of the new Labour MPs was a paid consultant to an outside business, and only nineteen of the total 261 Labour members were. Roughly half of Tory back-bench MPs were directors of companies, while just twelve Labour MPs were, according to the register. Many Labour MPs have links to trade unions which sponsor their candidacies and support their local constituency parties, though they only very rarely receive any direct financial benefit. It is doubtful whether these consultancies and directorships make much difference in practice to decisions taken by civil servants and ministers, who know well which MP represents which interest. There is a distinction between MPs who act as political advisers to some company and those who are, in effect, working in public relations, hiring themselves out. However, the safeguards are weaker than in other countries since, while the register has been tightened up in respect of links with lobbyists, MPs are not required to specify how much they receive from consultancies and directorships. But, whatever the ethics of these activities as semi-lobbyists, they are mainly a lucrative addition to the members' principal work in the Commons. Most MPs still concentrate on developing their careers as politicians. Since the early 1980s, there has also been a sharp growth in the number of former MPs becoming lobbyists, either with public affairs or consultancy firms, or as retained consultants to companies.

The result, however, is that the burden of work is borne unevenly, as the late David Penhaligon observed (quoted in Mitchell, 1982):

I've always said you could divide the House into three categories for how hard they work. About a third work very hard, really very hard, a fifteen-hour day would be the norm and they're workaholics really, but the other 200 probably do a reasonable day's work, and there's 200 if you can discover anything they do, let me know.

The rise of the career politician, discussed in earlier chapters, has meant that new MPs arrive in the Commons eager to play an active role. They do not want to be largely passive bystanders, as many of their predecessors used to be. Henry McLeish, a Scottish Labour MP, commented (1991) that most of the 1983 and 1987 intake brought a 'managerial ethos to what we are doing'. An increasing number arrive having spent a long time in preparation, often much of their adult lives, working in related occupations or with their main focus on getting into the Commons. Since the Second World War, the number of MPs first elected under thirty, usually Tory aristocrats or squires, has dropped sharply. None of the 140 new MPs elected in April 1992 was in their twenties. Now, most members have served the type of apprenticeship described in the last chapter and enter the Commons in what used quaintly to be described as the prime of life. Around three-quarters of the 1992 new intake were aged between thirty and forty-five. Thus, whether or not they were previously full-time politicians by my definition, they became MPs at an age still eager to develop a career.

Dudley Fishburn, a long-serving journalist quoted at the beginning of this chapter who became an MP at the upper end of this age range, claims (1990) that while 'one knows that one achieves in between little and very little here in the Commons, there are some advantages to coming into this place at the advanced age of forty-two, and also to coming in after a prolonged period of government'. But Terry Dicks, who became an MP at the age of forty-six, was sceptical (1988):

I came into the House too late to have a political career. I have no ambitions at all, and I don't think it's ambition that makes people get on here. It's who you know and whether you keep your nose clean. I've got about as much chance of getting a place in the Government as I have of taking off and flying from Tower Bridge.

Lord Chesterfield's famous observation that no member enters the Commons without secretly believing he will end up as Prime Minister was, of course, a gross exaggeration when made two centuries ago, and is so even today. While a majority of new MPs would probably like to become ministers (and some even have the fantasy/hope of becoming Prime Minister), many do not. For many MPs, merely being elected is the pinnacle of their ambitions. They find fulfilment, and often a full and lengthy career on the back-benches. There are probably more ministerial aspirants than in the past but there are also more ministerial posts than eighty, or even fifty, years ago. As discussed in the following two chapters, the interactions of supply and demand in balancing the number of ministerial posts and the number of office-seekers are subtle and complicated. It is a mistake automatically to regard career politicians as being synonymous with ministerial aspirants. There is, of course, a large overlap, but many perpetual back-benchers are as much career politicians as members of the Cabinet, even if in some cases their hopes of becoming ministers have been frustrated.

In a survey of more than half the Commons, Donald Searing (1985) found members divided in their self-assessments: 40 per cent believed their primary role lay in supporting and criticizing the executive, while 25 per cent believed it lay in constituency service and 25 per cent put ministerial aspirations at the top of their list (the remaining 10 per cent referred to other factors). A survey of newly elected MPs conducted shortly after the 1992 election by Michael Rush of Exeter University, for the Study of Parliament Group, showed sharp contrasts in expectations between members of different parties. More than two out of three Tories expected their parliamentary careers to last twenty or more years, while little more than a fifth of Labour MPs did. This partly reflects the contrast between the large number of new Tories elected for what have been considered safe seats, and the large number of new Labour MPs elected for marginal seats, often winning them from the Tories. More than half the MPs replying (in turn over three-fifths of those elected) hoped to become ministers. Some 60 per cent of Tories had that hope, but only 43 per cent of Labour MPs did. Moreover, while no Tories denied ministerial ambitions, nearly a fifth of Labour MPs did. George Jones (1984) has argued:

'MPs seem uncertain of their role. Confused by a babble of conflicting interpretations and envious of foreign models, some have totally misunderstood what they should be doing.' He maintains that they should mainly be supporting their party either as Government or as Opposition, and checking the national bureaucracy rather than debating policy with ministers on select committees or trespassing on the responsibilities of local government. 'There are too many MPs, with the result that many MPs have really no satisfying role to perform.' Professor Jones has a point, though only retiring MPs ever advocate a reduction in the size of the Commons. In the Commons as it is, career politicians eagerly look round for roles to perform.

Their ambitions express themselves in various ways. One of the clearest indications of MPs' own view of themselves as full-time professionals is their campaign for better pay and conditions. Michael Rush (in Ryle and Richards, 1988) notes:

How much the professionalization of MPs is related to the socio-economic composition of the House of Commons is unclear, except that it is unlikely that generally well-educated individuals with experience of the professions or business or as trade union officials or journalists would have been satisfied with the salaries and facilities available to MPs as recently as the 1960s.

The growing number of MPs with local government experience, especially the many former leaders of councils or chairmen of committees, are used to adequate offices, secretaries and proper facilities, if not to high pay. They are therefore often dissatisfied when they arrive in the Commons, as occurred after the 1992 election. Michael Rush's later survey after this election, noted above, shows that more than three-quarters of new Tory MPs earned more than their parliamentary salary before being elected, while two-thirds of Labour MPs earned less. A large majority of MPs of both parties expected, when elected, that office accommodation would be inadequate. Few were later favourably surprised by their actual experience.

John Biffen (1989) points out how, in the Middle Ages and in some constituencies up to the mid-seventeenth century, boroughs and shires paid wages to their representatives in the Commons and there was a system of fining MPs who did not attend the House. Samuel Pepys complained in his diary entry for 30 March 1668 that: 'At dinner all concluded that the bane of Parliament hath been the leaving off the old custom of the places allowing wages to those that served them in Parliament, by which they chose men that understood their business and would attend it, and they could expect an account from, which now they cannot.' It was not until the rise of the Labour Party and the entry of working men into the Commons in the early years of this century that payments to MPs from taxpayers' funds were introduced in 1911. Lloyd George, then Chancellor of the Exchequer, argued in the Commons:

When we offer £400 a year as payment for Members of Parliament it is not a recognition of the magnitude of the service, it is not a remuneration, it is not a recompense, it is not even a salary. It is just an allowance, to enable men to come here, men who would render incalculable service to the State, and whom it would be an incalculable loss to the State not to have here, but who cannot be here because their means do not allow it. It is purely an allowance to enable us to open the door to great and honourable public service to these men, for whom this country will be all the richer, all the greater, and all the stronger for the unknown vicissitudes which it has to face by having them there to aid us by their counsel, by their courage, and by their resource.

The pay of MPs has increased in often uneven stages since then. But it was not until 1971 that the whole system was thoroughly investigated and put on a more professional basis, when MPs' pay, allowances and pensions were referred to the Review Body on Top Salaries, as these issues have subsequently been. The body's recommendations have occasionally been scaled down by the Government, and frozen at times of general pay restraint – though in rare, but highly significant, demonstrations of back-bench independence, MPs have twice successfully revolted, in 1987 and 1992, to secure a larger increase in pay and office allowances. The debates on these matters are generally held early on in the life of a Parliament, so they will be long forgotten by the time of the next general election. But almost any increase in MPs' salaries or allowances attracts criticism in the tabloids, especially during difficult economic times. MPs are fortunate that party ties and loyalties protect them. Unlike in the 1900s, it is now accepted that an MP should receive a salary; at the time of writing it is nearly £31,000 a year and is increased annually in line with the senior principal scale of the Civil Service. Ministers receive about 75 per cent of their MPs' salary in addition to their ministerial pay.

MPs also receive allowances to cover some of the costs of living both in London and in their constituencies, as well as an office allowance for research and secretarial help and for office equipment (an increasingly expensive item with the almost universal spread of the word processor). While the overall levels of remuneration are often criticized, few MPs who have previously enjoyed a successful career benefit financially from being in the House. There are stories of MPs supplementing their salaries by padding out their expenses, notably their travel allowances. The scale of such fiddling is hard to assess, but in most cases it does not appear to be very large. A few MPs probably do abuse the system, rather like those who regularly take up free trips paid for by outside companies. Even so, the total of remuneration and perks for the majority of MPs is less than that for many middle-ranking business executives. And though a number of MPs employ their wives as secretaries, the vast majority seem to work hard for their husbands as genuine members of their offices. An MP's pay does not increase with the length of service, but the introduction of a contributory pension scheme from the mid-1960s means that a parliamentary career has conformed more to a normal working life. Fewer MPs are now staying on well into their seventies. Previously, many less well-off Labour MPs could not afford to leave the Commons and so continued to seek re-election after the age of sixty-five. Now, most, though not all, retire at the election nearest their sixty-fifth birthday.

More significant is the continued campaign for improved facilities in buildings originally intended to be offices. The Palace of Westminster has, as a result, gradually expanded from the New Scotland Yard buildings, now known as Norman Shaw North and South, and the following redevelopment of the Bridge Street site on the edge of Whitehall. At the start of each parliament there are always stories about new MPs spending weeks looking for desks and a room for themselves and their secretaries. Many former leaders of councils and successful businessmen experience a big down-grading in their working environment.

MPs argue that they need improved facilities and increased allowances to run their offices because of the greater demands being made upon them. It is an open question how far MPs are responding to, or are themselves creating, such demands. A study by Ashley Weinberg, a research pyschologist at Manchester University, reported that two-fifths of MPs said they worked more than a seventy-hour week and four-fifths said they put in at least fifty-five hours. He concluded that one in six MPs displayed 'quite poor psychological health'. The change in MPs' views of their job towards a greater emphasis on the constituency social-worker aspect is partly linked with shifts in the character of local campaigning. The 'pavement' politics approach, which highlights local grievances, was pioneered by the Liberals but has been taken up by the other parties. Most serious candidates, particularly those challenging an incumbent in a marginal seat, are now active in taking up local concerns. By proclaiming their role as welfare officers for constituents (a responsibility which most claim to find satisfying), as well as being party activists, they generate an influx of correspondence. The introduction of mandatory reselection for Labour MPs in each Parliament has meant that such local activity has become more important, and Labour MPs have been keener on having constituency offices.

Enoch Powell was always a sceptic about calls for greater resources, wondering whether a version of Parkinson's Law was operating in which if the money is there, MPs will always find ways of spending it. In a debate on MPs' salaries in 1978, he said:

During the first eighteen years that I was a member of this House, I had no secretary. In those years many complaints were made of me, but one complaint that was not made was that I neglected my correspondence or my duties to my constituents; nor was it urged against me that I was failing in diligence in applying my mind to the matters which successively were put before this House.

Even at the time Mr Powell's views were unusual; by the early 1990s they would be generally seen as a quaint anachronism. Sir Robert Rhodes James (1991), a former clerk as well as a back-bencher for sixteen years up to 1992, and a historian, has noted the change in the MP's relationship to his or her constituents. The vast majority of MPs, he suggests, are far closer to their constituents' concerns than they used to be. Before becoming an MP he had thought that serving constituents would be 'a necessary chore, but actually being able to help people large and small has been a source of real pleasure and satisfaction'. Commenting during the 1987 general election campaign in an article for the *Daily Telegraph*, and nearly five years before he lost his Bath seat, Chris Patten wrote, 'when you've looked after a constituency for a few years, you can't walk down a street without finding old friends or a regular correspondent'.

The increase in the constituency workload has been real. It has reflected the impact of the recession and the associated rise in long-term unemployment, cutbacks in local authority services and changes in the social security system. The shift to a more discretionary system has produced more complaints about, for example, disability benefits. The report of the Review Body on Top Salaries of July 1992, quoted at the beginning of this chapter, concluded:

Whilst the basic elements of an MP's job have changed little, the nature of the pressures and demands upon MPs have altered significantly. This is due to a variety of factors, chief of which is increased awareness on the part of the public of the role of the MP and how the MP may be approached for help or support. TV coverage of Parliament, the impact of local radio and increasingly sophisticated lobbying techniques by interest groups have all been elements in this development, as has the use of diverse forms of media presentation by MPs to publicize their activities or promote causes. At the same time, the trend within Parliament appears to have been towards heavier involvement in select committee work, requiring more research and greater commitment of time.

Among the evidence to support the call for more resources was a survey by Hay Management Consultants. This showed that in 1992 MPs were often receiving an average of 300 letters a week, up from the average of 200 letters a week indicated by a similar survey in 1986. The report noted evidence of an increasing complexity of individual constituent cases and, at the same time, higher expectations on the part of constituents about the help they would receive from MPs. It is, of course, arguable that some of the work being carried out by MPs should be referred to other agencies, such as local authorities, but the significant point for this book is that MPs themselves feel they should undertake this work. It is part of their role as career politicians. The proportion of MPs with at least one full-time member of staff, either as a secretary or a research assistant, rose from 68 per cent in 1981–2 to 82 per cent in 1985–6, and up to 87 per cent in 1990–91. Indeed, all the report recommended was that MPs should be able to employ the equivalent of two full-time staff, rather than 1.5 as previously. In addition, the costs of some researchers are paid by outside groups, while students, particularly from American universities, are employed as interns for periods of a few months to help with research.

Michael Rush did a note for the Review Body on the experience in other countries. This showed that, while the position of British MPs, in terms of salaries, allowances, services and facilities generally, has been transformed since the late 1960s,

the important fact remains that British members are not as well provided for as their counterparts in two of the three EC countries to which Britain could be said to be closest in terms of population and size of economy: French deputies and German MPs are clearly better-off than British members, who in turn are better off than Italian MPs.

This leaves out of account the superior support provided for members of the American Congress and the legislatures in Australia and Canada.

The extent of the change in the workload and life of an MP has been brought out vividly by Paul Tyler, who was briefly in the Commons as Liberal MP for Bodmin between the February and October 1974 elections, and only returned to the House as Liberal Democrat member for Cornwall North in April 1992. He notes (1992) how in 1974 there was no television coverage, limited radio interest through the BBC, no (departmental) select committees, no word processors, PCs, databases or POLIS, and precious few offices for members.

I dictated to my assistant in a subterranean corridor, and she then had to produce perfect individual letters (without the benefit of toned Tippex) in cramped cupboard conditions. On the other hand, the mailbag was, if my memory is correct, appreciably smaller. My electorate was admittedly some 20,000 less then, but I am sure that it is not just the numerical change that has transformed the scale and substance of correspondence.

He suggests that broadcasting has perhaps made the MP seem more accessible. The elector is also more alert to his or her rights, while the scope of personal problems has increased as a result of the sharp rise in unemployment.

If increased work for constituents is one outlet for the energies of career politicians – also safeguarding their home political base – another is sitting on committees. Few MPs are now satisfied with just watching, and very occasionally participating in, set-piece debates on the floor of the Commons. Many now find more satisfaction in work on the select committees monitoring the work of individual government departments. The system was reorganized in 1979 with the specific aim of providing an alternative career path for MPs. In practice, the committees, whatever else they may have achieved in strengthening the scrutiny of the legislature over the executive, have provided such an alternative, offering those who want to be full-time MPs a time-consuming job to do. But the appeal has been more diverse than originally envisaged. Some MPs have made their names as members of select committees, or at any rate have become best known for this side of their lives as MPs. Some have been back-benchers pure and simple, who have never been on the front-bench, like Sir John Wheeler on the Home Affairs Committee or Nicholas Winterton at Health before the 1992 election. Frank Field, although briefly a front-bench spokesman, also comes into this category of the back-bench champion of committees.

Other successful committee men have been former ministers who have been dropped, or who have resigned, while still in their late forties or fifties with a lengthy parliamentary career ahead of them. David Howell has probably gained more influence and respect in the Commons as chairman of the Foreign Affairs Select Committe than as an at times uneasy member of the Thatcher Cabinet from 1979 until 1983. Sir Terence Higgins, a Treasury minister in the Heath administration from 1970 until 1974, became one of the leading lights of the select committees during the 1980s. He served on the Treasury and Civil Service Select Committee from 1979 until 1992, being its chairman for nine years. He was also chairman of the liaison committee representing all the select committees. Among other former ministers or whips active on committees have been Sir Jerry Wiggin, Sir Richard Luce and Nicholas Budgen. There is, however, some suspicion among MPs of too much participation by recent ex-ministers for fear that it might endanger the independence of committees and might limit opportunities for younger members. Suggestions that a former minister might become chairman of the Treasury and Civil Service Select Committee were successfully rebuffed in the summer of 1992.

The select committees have also been training grounds for several future ministers and Opposition front-benchers. Among the first members of the Treasury and Civil Service Select Committee in 1979 was Tim Eggar. He has acknowledged that the experience gave him 'a unique insight into the fundamentals of economic policy, about which I did not have strong views when I first came in'. Other future ministers who have served on select committees include Gillian Shephard, Kenneth Baker (before he was brought into the Government in January 1981), Nigel Forman, Roger Freeman, Tim Yeo, David Curry, Eric Forth, Michael Mates and Charles Wardle, among a list of more than twenty. This trend has been less true on the Labour side, where new MPs of promise tend to be appointed to the front-bench very quickly and therefore cannot serve on select committees. It is significant that MPs willing give up a place on a select committee even to take on the lowly and unrewarded post of parliamentary private secretary to a minister – commonly known as bag-carriers – since, as discussed in the following chapter, this has become the first step on the ladder of preferment.

MPs also find occupation, if not stimulation, in working on standing committees which consider the details of bills. These are generally frustrating for Government back-benchers, who are mainly required to attend, keep silent and vote. But on the Opposition side such committees provide a training ground for younger members. For instance, in the long session after the June 1983 general election, Gordon Brown and Tony Blair both learned about the ways of the Commons and showed their parliamentary skills when they were enlisted by John Smith, then Labour's employment spokesman, to serve on the committee considering a further instalment of the Tories' industrial relations legislation. That, incidentally, not only showed John Smith's shrewdness in picking out two of Labour's brightest new MPs of that intake but also increased their liking and respect for him. Similarly, after the 1992 election, Labour deliberately chose a number of its brightest younger members – John Hutton, Geoffrey Hoon, Peter Mandelson, Alan Millburn and Barbara Roche – to serve on the committee scrutinizing the Finance Bill. This was to show them both how the Commons worked and that the Opposition still had some life in it, even after a fourth successive defeat.

The expansion of committee work may occasionally be a nuisance for departmental ministers, but it serves the purposes of the whips in giving back-benchers something to do to keep them out of even more disruptive mischief. It is a means of spotting talent – permitting future ministers to learn about the work of government – while allowing MPs to let off steam. But the committees have had only a limited impact because they have been seen in this light by the party leaderships. Their reports have often been brushed aside by ministers, and when trouble has been threatened – over, for instance, the Westland

affair or the health service before the 1992 election – the whips
have intervened to enlist the support of sympathetic back-
benchers. And after an election the whips have sought to
influence the membership of committees to keep out vocal
critics. None the less, the departmental select committees have
provided an alternative career path for more than 150 back-
benchers, with more serving on other permanent select committees like the Public Accounts Committee. For some MPs,
service on a committee has been a continuing alternative
career; for others, a preparation for a period on the front-
bench, or an interesting aftermath. But while the select committees have provided such an alternative, they have not been a
substitute for a ministerial career. They have been more a
consolation prize.

The majority of MPs find a role as ministerial and front-
bench aspirants or on committee work of various kinds (both
the departmental select committees and those dealing with the
procedure of the House and broadcasting its proceedings).
Some long-serving back-benchers also join the panel appointed
by the Speaker or chairmen of standing committees on bills.
This at least creates an opportunity to be treated with outward
respect and to observe the foibles of your parliamentary colleagues. Only a minority become resigned to, or enjoy, life as
perpetual back-benchers with no more formal outlet. Some
like being well-known mavericks (such as Dennis Skinner on
the Labour side or Bill Walker on the Tory benches); some
become elder statesmen (former Cabinet ministers like Edward
Heath, John Biffen and Tony Benn); some become absorbed in
constituency work and are little noticed at Westminster; and
some devote more time to outside consultancies and similar
work. Some are obviously out of their depth and are content
to be loyalists, jogging along from one election to the next.
Some foot-soldiers are necessary in any army. Some never
expected to be any more, while others have had, painfully, to
realize the limits of their likely achievements.

A number of MPs have always been regarded as maverick or independent-minded (it rather depends on whether you are on the receiving end). Ministers of both parties had learned to be wary of Tam Dalyell when he adopted a campaign, long before he became nationally known for his criticism of the Government's account of the sinking of the Argentine cruiser *Belgrano* in the Falklands war. Many find Mr Dalyell's interests obsessive, and sometimes wrong, but no one disputes his ability – this was especially so during the 1960s and 1970s – to attract attention to an issue and put ministers under pressure. Most effective is his short question, sometimes just a blunt, 'Why?' George Cunningham, the Labour MP who became a Social Democrat, had a similar ability to fight lone campaigns. On the Tory side, Nicholas Winterton has become anathema to successive Tory Chief Whips for his rebellious attitude. Mr Winterton himself is unrepentant. He accepts (1990):

Since I've been in the House of Commons, I've never conformed. I have been a thorn in the side of the Conservative whips for years. I have been summoned into the office many times over the years and am always happy to talk to them, but they won't make me change my mind. There was a short period after I had been part of the team that helped Margaret Thatcher win the leadership of the party when I thought I might get some recognition of that. I didn't and was briefly disappointed and frustrated. But I came through it very quickly and re-established myself as a back-bencher and a House of Commons man.

Mr Winterton's chairmanship of the Health Select Committee before the 1992 election so annoyed the Tory whips that they used every device to keep him off the committee afterwards. In the process, the whips and their associates invented a wholly new precedent that MPs cannot serve on such a committee for more than three Parliaments.

An intriguing, but still unresolved, issue is how far the rise of the career politician has made MPs more ideological, and rebellious. It turns on the balance between their pursuit of preferment and the strongly held views of more articulate MPs. Whatever the precise cause, there is clear evidence that back-benchers have become more independent-minded since the late 1960s. Philip Norton has recorded in various books (1975, 1978 and 1980) the marked change in parliamentary behaviour after 1970. The previous, virtually unanimous, party cohesion on votes ended; two-thirds of all Tory back-benchers voted against the official whip during the Heath Government on one or more occasions. The Government was defeated six times in spite of having a clear working majority and on three occasions the defeat was despite the strict summons of a three-line whip. That period also marked the start of cross-party voting on European issues. The legislation taking Britain into the European Economic Community was only carried thanks to Liberal votes and some Labour abstentions since fifteen to twenty Tory MPs repeatedly voted against the bill. This pattern of dissent continued during the Wilson and Callaghan Governments of the 1974–9 period. These administrations lost twenty-three divisions as a result of Labour back-benchers voting with the Opposition. That is even before taking into account the Government's minority position in the Commons from 1976 onwards.

Tory MPs continued to rebel after their party was returned to office in May 1979, and from 1983 to 1992 when the Government had huge majorities in the Commons. However, the continuation of sizeable rebellions by Tory MPs even after the April 1992 election, when their party's majority fell to twenty-one, suggests that a deeper change in behaviour was under way. Most of the big revolts concerned Europe, underlining how Tory leaders could not count on loyalty when dealing with such a deeply divisive issue. When the Tories had a large majority, small rebellions were tolerated because they could easily be brushed aside. Half a dozen Tory MPs abstaining or voting against a bill hardly made a headline in the second half of the 1980s. But the Government was defeated on a few occasions, notably over new immigration rules in 1982 and on the second reading of the bill liberalizing Sunday trading in 1986. Moreover, the threat of defeat, or at least serious unrest, forced a number of changes of policy and the withdrawal of bills throughout the decade. While defeats, or, more frequent and significant, the threat of defeat, forced changes of policy several times during the 1980s, this was mainly on second-rank issues. Governments normally faced down rebellions on first-rank questions, such as the poll tax, which was approved by Parliament in the 1987–8 session with no significant amendments to the original bill.

The bluff of the whips had been called. They could no longer pretend that every vote on every measure was a matter of confidence in the Government as a whole. MPs were not willing to be loyal on every issue, irrespective of its merits. The previous attitude of unquestioning loyalty disappeared as MPs demanded a greater say. Professor Norton has argued that the increased dissent primarily reflected mistakes of leadership by the Heath administration. The Prime Minister's failure to consult and his insistence on pushing through measures encouraged disagreement and revolt, providing a precedent for later Parliaments and giving momentum to greater independence of behaviour. But that does not seem a sufficient explanation. It is possible that the growing numbers of career politicians have been less deferential by temperament and inclination. Not only are some more ideological but some are also not going to risk their seats, and careers, by taking an unpopular stand on an issue like, say, student grants. The greater degree of independence by back-benchers might appear to conflict with an image of careerist politicians determined to secure preferment at all costs. But that is to underrate the importance of ideology and to make the mistake, highlighted earlier, of assuming that all MPs, even all career politicians, are necessarily ministerial aspirants. Many of the regular dissenters do not come into this category but are better seen as career Commons politicians.

But how do MPs sort themselves out into these various categories of loyalists, ministerial aspirants, pillars of the back-benches, etc. – as they do within a year or two of arriving in the Commons? Most MPs realize they have to make their mark fairly quickly. Adam Ingram, a Scottish Labour MP, acknowledged his ambitions. Talking (1990) two and half years after he had entered the Commons and when he had become parliamentary private secretary to Neil Kinnock, he said: 'For the moment I am just going to throw myself into life here. I believe that if you have ambitions you have to make it in your first Parliament and consolidate your position in the first half of the second Parliament.' Most MPs do after all want to do something, as Gerald Kaufman (1980) observed:

Generally – though not always, for some of the most attractive politicians are genuinely unambitious even though they sometimes obtain office – they will hope at least mildly to obtain advancement within their party. For them the first and most important rule is: be noticed. There are some MPs who go through a long and hard-working parliamentary career without the leader of their party being very sure who they are.

Some MPs, even those who later rise to heights, can arrive both ignorant and naïve about the process of politics. David Owen was a busy doctor when he was elected in 1966. He was soon invited to join the 1963 Club, a dining group for people closely identified with Hugh Gaitskell. He records (1991):

At my first dinner the conversation kept referring to CDS, and eventually I asked my next-door neighbour Jack Diamond what the initials meant. He was amazed to discover that I had not been involved in the Campaign for Democratic Socialism [discussed in the previous chapter] ... Thus within months of becoming an MP, I was pitched into the inner circle of people who, at their mildest, were highly suspicious of Harold Wilson and, at their strongest, loathed his guts. I was totally ignorant of all the tensions and bitterness of the past . . . The dinners themselves and the friendships that were opened up were a revelation. For a young back-bencher, listening as we went round the table, each contributing to the discussion, it was fascinating, particularly hearing Tony and Roy talk, often indiscreetly, about what was going on in Cabinet. It is impossible to exaggerate how ignorant and innocent I was about so much of the internal politics of the Labour Party.

The sense of equality among new MPs described at the start of this chapter is in part artificial. Some new MPs are better known than others; prominent council leaders like Ken Livingstone or David Blunkett or close advisers to a Prime Minister like John Redwood. There is in practice a distinction between those well known politically before they arrive in the Commons and those who have to make their mark from scratch. People with outside reputations do have a head start, but they still have to prove themselves anew in the Commons. They have to demonstrate that their previous reputations were justified. If they have made an impact in some previous activity, they may do so again, but only in terms of the standards of the Commons itself. Nigel Lawson (1992) has underlined the predicament of this group:

I had entered the House of Commons rather later and rather better known than most new members. This meant, to those on the Labour benches, and some on the Conservative benches, too, that I needed to be taken down a peg. I was soon made aware that the House of Commons is like a school, in which the new boys are expected to show all the humility of new boys, irrespective of whether or not they have achieved anything before passing through its portals. In other words, I had to establish myself in parliamentary terms from scratch. It clearly made sense to specialize in economic policy, but I felt I needed to do more than that. The obvious answer was to specialize in Prime Minister's Questions, too.

Nigel Lawson made a success of his jousts with Harold Wilson at Prime Minister's Questions and was soon on the Opposition front-bench. He became a middle-ranking minister within just over five years of entering the Commons and a member of the Cabinet two and a quarter years later.

The nature of outside reputations has, however, changed. Almost echoing the words of his father, Leo Amery, quoted in the first chapter, Julian Amery reflected (1992), in an interview shortly after he retired from the Commons, on the shift since he was first elected in 1950:

In those days Parliament used to be dominated by people who had a position outside the Commons. It wasn't just that most of the young men had fought in the war, and achieved something. It was simply that the importance of most MPs didn't depend on their membership of the House. You had people who had made a reputation for themselves elsewhere, in other fields, not just politics. You had people with an independent standing, a personal power base outside Parliament, for one reason or another ... Now, even the Conservative Party is composed entirely of people who depend wholly on their position in Parliament for any importance they may have. Now the Commons has become like the Roman Senate in the time of Augustus; its privileges have increased as its powers have been weakened. Members have no independent status. It's part of the professionalization of politics.

Julian Amery, typically, romanticized the earlier generation in the Commons. But he had a point in that few MPs now have an importance separate from their membership of the House, while those who do come in with a reputation made elsewhere have normally made it in political activities.

Not all the well-known newcomers make a mark. For all his fame as a high-profile leader of the Greater London Council in the first half of the 1980s, confronting the Thatcher Government, Ken Livingstone has never made an equivalent impact in the Commons. He has always been rather a loner there. His dislike for many of the trappings of the Commons has been matched by the dislike of him by many of his fellow Labour MPs, particularly those from the north and Scotland. By contrast, both Tony Banks, an ally of Ken Livingstone in GLC days, and David Blunkett, the leader of Sheffield City Council, have thrived in the Commons. Mr Blunkett has managed to surmount the handicap of his blindness and has earned the respect of fellow Labour MPs for his patient hard work, being elected to the Shadow Cabinet in July 1992. The difference between Ken Livingstone and David Blunkett is in part the classic outside left/inside left contrast – as existed between Tom Driberg and Harold Wilson in the 1950s. It is a difference based on political stance rather than on House of Commons performance. But Ken Livingstone and David Blunkett are exceptions among former council leaders on both sides of the House. While many more MPs, including John Major, have experience of a spell on a local council, few who have made their careers there have become leading Westminster politicians, as Herbert Morrison, for example, was in an earlier generation. There are several cases on both sides of the House of people who arrive with high reputations but do not make an equivalent mark in the Commons. The list includes, for instance, Geoffrey Robinson, a senior motor industry executive before becoming a Labour MP, and George Walden, a high-rising diplomat who was briefly a junior education minister before returning to the back-benches at his own request. In general, Julian Amery's view of the contemporary House as being composed of people dependent on their position there for any importance they may have is upheld.

Similarly, people completely unknown nationally before they arrive at Westminster often carve out a niche for themselves there. They become House of Commons figures, typically as whips or committee men. John Wakeham, the former Chief Whip and Leader of the Commons, is a classic example of someone, already in fact a succesful businessman, who found fulfilment in the House, like two of his protégés, John Major and Tristan Garel-Jones. On the Labour side, Don Dixon was a shipyard worker in Jarrow before being elected to the Commons in 1979. Ten years later, he said (1989):

I've enjoyed every minute I've been in the House of Commons; that's why I spend so much time here. I always refer to it as the word factory – you never use one word when six will do. I'm not at all ambitious. It was never my ambition to go on the council, and it was never my ambition to be an MP. When I was working in the Whips Office, I was nominated for Deputy Chief Whip, so I stood. I didn't expect to get as many votes, but it's one of those things. It's a job I can cope with, and if you can cope with a job with an elementary education, it's not particularly hard, is it?

The Commons is above all a place with its own institutional character, changing and developing with each Parliament. Reflecting before his departure from the Commons, Sir Robert Rhodes James (1991) noted that the charm of the House, and also its most fearful aspect, was its total unpredictability. He was puzzled by colleagues who neglected the chamber and wondered why they went to all the trouble to get elected. He regretted the very real danger that MPs might become too constituency-oriented and spend too much time on committee work rather than in the chamber. The result was that MPs did not know each other very well. The House, he felt, needed characters: 'In the age of the ambitious professional politician it needs them more than ever.' The Commons takes a collective view of a member, whether they are a star, a well-meaning plodder, a charlatan, a publicity seeker, a hard-working defender of constituency interests, a drunk, a crook, etc. These judgements can vary. Disraeli is not the only member to have to live down a bad first performance, though his was a spectacular disaster. The diarist Greville noted (Fulford, 1993): 'D'Israeli made his first exhibition this night, beginning with florid assurance, speedily disintegrating into ludicrous absurdity, and being at last put down with inextinguishable shouts of laughter.' The less extreme assessments of most new members are formed in varying ways – through speeches, questions, interventions in debates, performances in committees, on television and on radio, through conversations around the corridors and bars of the House, and the general courtesies of a collective assembly. The judgement of the whips of an MP's own party may differ from the opinion of fellow backbenchers or of the other side. But it is in this way that reputations are made.

Within a party, many MPs soon become identified with a particular faction, which may advance or retard their careers. On the Tory side, new MPs seem to have a compulsive tendency to form themselves into dining clubs of various kinds. The most durable is the One Nation group, founded in the early 1950s by the highly talented Tory intake of that era to develop new economic and social policies. It has now become very much a mainstream group of the respectable and the responsible. More significant during the early 1980s was the Blue Chip group, predominantly public-school- and Oxbridge-educated MPs who mainly entered the Commons in 1979. Its leaders expressed elegantly phrased dissent from Thatcherite economic policies. They published a pamphlet in September 1981 entitled 'Changing Gear', which urged a shift of emphasis in economic policy (in fact already occurring). It became a manifesto for the moderate 'wets', as the dissenters of the time became known. The group's most prominent members were Chris Patten, William Waldegrave, Ian Lang, Nick Lyell, Richard Needham, Tristan Garel-Jones, Robert Cranborne and Michael Ancram. John Major joined the Blue Chips after this pamphlet appeared and when he was already a rising figure. In time all of its members accommodated themselves to Thatcherism and its leader. Ten of the signatories of the pamphlet subsequently joined the Government and three became Cabinet ministers.

In the second half of the 1980s the highest profile was taken by the No Turning Back group, most of whom entered the Commons in 1983. Their unifying belief was the need for the Government to press ahead with radical free-market reforms in areas such as the health service, education, housing and employment. Among the group's leaders were Michael Portillo, Peter Lilley, Francis Maude, Michael Fallon and Michael Forsyth. In 1985 they jointly wrote a pamphlet entitled 'No Turning Back', which set out a series of further reforms and became a manifesto for the so-called 'drys', even though these terms were by then starting to cease to have much meaning. Nine of the signatories of the pamphlet became ministers, with two in time joining the Cabinet. However, four of them lost their seats at the 1992 general election. The group, which refreshed itself with some of the brightest new members after both the 1987 and the 1992 elections, continued to meet together regularly to discuss the political situation and to press in a free-market and Euro-sceptical direction.

A group of prospective Tory candidates, all from safe seats, even sought to jump the gun in September 1991 by issuing a pamphlet even before they were elected to the Commons. Entitled 'Raising the Standard', it marked some of the complacency of a generation used to seeing the Tories in power apparently for ever. It noted:

The old labels of wet and dry are now just misleading. All of us were too young to have taken part in those ancient battles. We were, at most, spear-carriers rather than leading players. Now, we see ourselves as in the mainstream of a party which is committed both to free enterprise and to national cohesion, to liberty and to responsibility alike.

And, the pamphlet did not need to say, to advancing their careers under whoever happened to be leading the Tory Party at the time. On the back cover of the pamphlet was a photograph of the authors looking rather pleased with themselves. All were duly elected in April 1992. However, the rather too obvious ambitions of some – waiting impatiently for office – irritated not only a number of their contemporaries but also their seniors. Some ran into trouble with the whips when they signed an early-day motion sponsored by Euro-sceptic critics of the Government.

The significance of these groups is not that they change policy – though the No Turning Back group may have had some influence – but that they foster a sense of cohesion. These exercises in, predominantly male, bonding and networking allow rising politicians to express themselves and to gain the ear of party leaders. Those with like views tend to coalesce and to reinforce each other's career ambitions. Like the select committees, they provide a safety valve for back-benchers' opinions, which are only seldom a nuisance to the whips. Most factional groupings within the Tory parliamentary party arise on a particular issue – such as the poll tax or, more persistent Europe. In addition, every year right and left groups organize slates for the elections of the officers of the back-bench specialist committees. These are of no wider significance, although the officers are regularly interviewed on television and radio, and treated as if they are serious figures somehow representative of Tory opinion. Many are not, though becoming secretary of a party committee is a useful addition to an ambitious MP's curriculum vitae. The right-wing ticket has been organized by the 92 Group, named after the address in Cheyne Walk, Chelsea, of Sir Patrick Wall, its founder, while the left-wing ticket is run by the Lollards, named after the residence in Lambeth Palace of Sir William van Straubenzee, its founder.

On the Labour side, MPs have defined themselves more by whether they belong to larger organizations such as the Tribune Group, established in 1966; or the right-wing Manifesto Group, set up in the 1974–9 Parliament; or the hard-left Campaign Group, in the second half of the 1980s (later retitled the Socialist Campaign Group). The latter, which emerged after a sizeable number of Tribune Group MPs, including Neil Kinnock, abstained on the key vote between Tony Benn and Denis Healey in the deputy leadership contest in 1981. These groups not only discussed the political issues of the moment ahead of the weekly meetings of the Parliamentary Labour Party but also organized tickets for the annual elections to the Shadow Cabinet when Labour was in opposition. Gradually, however, the formal left versus right ticket system disappeared, though the hard left with the support of around forty Labour MPs, continued to organize a slate. This reflected the disappearance of the old right and the splintering of the left into two: a large, soft-left group loyal to Neil Kinnock after he became leader in 1983, and a hard-left group led by Tony Benn and Dennis Skinner. In practice, the old right and the soft left worked together, and on many issues they became indistinguishable. Most of the new members of the 1983 and 1987 intakes became associated with the soft-left Tribune Group, which grew so large, at well over a hundred, as to lose any ideological identity. It came to be seen as a vehicle for preferment. Attempts were made to bridge the soft-left and hard-left split, notably via the Supper Club, which, unlike Tory equivalents, held modest buffet meals in pubs near Westminster. Its membership included shadow spokesmen who still saw themselves as on the left. But tickets survived, some involving complex deals of regional loyalty (Scots, Welsh and northern MPs); in other cases, deals were arranged between candidates on personal grounds. It was a murky and devious process each year, with allegations that some MPs gave blank ballot papers to secure favours. Success has also reflected individual performances and reputations, though some talented MPs outside the soft-left mainstream, such as George Robertson, have found it hard to get elected to the Shadow Cabinet because of their right-wing, pro-European histories.

If you look at the end result in each of the main parties – why one member is rated highly and another is not – it is normally possible to point to obvious personal characteristics or performances. Not everyone manages a startling speech like Iain Macleod did in 1952 which propelled him to become Minister of Health without ever being a junior minister. In most cases, it is more a question of hard work plus an occasional display of independence. In conversations with MPs in 1973, Anthony King (1974) records the comments of MPs themselves about what impresses. Among the qualities noted are attending the House (notably the chamber); speaking, but not too often; not becoming known as a publicity seeker (capturing headlines for oneself rather than for one's point of view); an ability to articulate views and be listened to; some knowledge of, and authority about, what he or she is talking about, either from first-hand experience or from a legitimate claim to speak on behalf of some interest or group outside; and sincerity. 'The man who does worst is the chap who gets up on every single occasion, on every different subject, and makes a speech which he thinks will go down well with his own side, or, if he's a member of some rebel group, with his own group.' Being a rebel once or twice seldom hurts anyone long-term, provided it does not become a habit. As Kenneth Baker once remarked in the House, a back-bencher has to tread 'a fine line between sycophancy and rebellion'.

The qualities needed to make an impact in the Commons, and in internal party manoeuvring, are not necessarily those required to be a successful minister or front-bench spokesman. Richard Rose (1988) has argued persuasively:

Experience in the Commons does not lead naturally to the work of a minister – as primary school leads to secondary school. The MP's chief business is dealing with people and talking about ideas. A minister must have other skills too; knowing how to analyse policy options and relate political generalization to technical problems; mastering complex arguments for use in Cabinet committees; and digesting large masses of information. A minister may find the transition from the back-benches to government greater than the shift from being a constituency activist to becoming a back-bench MP.

It is, however, questionable whether experience as a constituency activist prepares potential MPs for their diverse and complex roles in the Commons itself, either for the welfare work or for scrutinizing ministers and officials on a select committee. That is, in a sense, where a new MP who has already been a full-time politician has an advantage. He or she knows how the system works and how to operate and monitor it.

The filtering process not only divides MPs into the ministerial aspirants and the perpetual back-benchers, it also in the process forces members to come to terms with what being a career politician means. Some never adjust to the frustration of their ambitions; others take it stoically as part of the lowering of horizons of middle age. A committee chairmanship, a consultancy, the occasional trip abroad, an appearance from time to time on television and radio, even the odd gin and tonic and, on the Tory side, an eventual knighthood are compensations. A minority take it badly, or rather they take it out on their fellow MPs in tedious ways. Austin Mitchell (1982) notes:

Some learn the lesson that while MPs have little positive influence they have enormous nuisance value. In a soured middle-age they can make a career of this and exploit it to the full . . . Some tortoises take pleasure in tripping up the hares as opportunity arises. They become 'House of Commons man', outwardly pompous, inwardly soured, obstinately attached to the dignity and privileges of the House because these are useful weapons against men who have outdistanced them and because their life offers nothing else.

Anyone who knows the Commons well has a little list of half a dozen such people on either side of the House.

Yet, the striking feature of the Commons is that it is not

seething with frustration. There are obviously young back-benchers eager for promotion and bitter middle-aged ones who have been passed over or who have been dropped. But most seem to find a degree of satisfaction in the myriad opportunities available to them. The next reshuffle might bring promotion and the next election might always bring their party to power. Alistair Darling, a Scottish lawyer and one of Labour's rising stars, was more detached than most in his comments after nearly four years in the Commons. He noted (1991) that his Edinburgh Central seat was a marginal so he had to be realistic:

I think we will hold it this time round but I am not even sure that if it was rock solid I would want to spend the rest of my life here. I regarded this as a job. I don't really go along with the idea that it is an honour and a privilege. I will carry on doing it as long as I can contribute something and when the time comes that I can't contribute, if the electorate haven't dealt with it before, then I will go.

Most of his fellow MPs remain committed to staying for as long as they can. That may, in part, be because former MPs, particularly back-benchers defeated at an election, are not necessarily immediately employable elsewhere – at any rate, not in jobs they find satisfying. Among the seventy-five MPs voluntarily stepping down at the April 1992 general election (excluding those forced out through reselection or expulsion from their party) only fifteen were aged under sixty. Just nine were aged under fifty-five, most of whom, for varying personal reasons, had expressed disillusion with their life at Westminster. The majority of MPs want to hold on to what they have fought so hard to achieve.

6

JOINING THE PAYROLL

'It is a fine opening for a young man of talent and ambition and places him in the way to the highest distinction.'

Lord Aberdeen, Colonial Secretary, on the appointment of Gladstone in 1835 to be an under-secretary in his department

'On the morning of Thursday, 7 March, my telephone rang and a Downing Street private secretary said that the Prime Minister would like to see me. I walked into the Cabinet Room – and our relationship had changed completely. I was now a very new, very inexperienced, very junior colleague, and a great distance opened up between myself and my old friend, now my awesomely remote boss. Very rightly, he allowed me no greater familiarity with him than any other junior minister. And very rightly he made me a very junior minister indeed ... At the time, though I readily accepted the post, I was not sure that I liked being at the very foot of the tree. But in requiring me to learn the job from the bottom Harold Wilson did me an inestimable kindness. He helped me to acquire the most precious commodity for anyone who holds ministerial office: experience.'

Gerald Kaufman, on being appointed a junior minister in 1974 by Harold Wilson, whom he had served as political press adviser in the late 1960s, in *How to be a Minister*, 1980

'Monday, 26 August 1929. I am forty-two! Many happy returns as a Minister of the Crown! We've never said that before.'

Hugh Dalton, two months after being appointed an under-secretary at the Foreign Office, in his political diary

Most MPs have a good chance of becoming front-benchers provided they avoid scandal, do not have extreme views and demonstrate a modest level of competence and speaking ability. The standards required to reach the bottom rung of the ladder are not high. The front-benches of both the Government and the Opposition are a good deal larger than just a glance at the Cabinet or the Shadow Cabinet might suggest. Governments nowadays have about eighty-five paid posts in the Commons, including whips. In addition, there can be up to forty unpaid parliamentary private secretaries to ministers. That means not only that the Government Chief Whip can count on unswerving support from around a third of the MPs of the governing party, but, as important, a similar proportion have been given some kind of office to keep them happy, and hungry for preferment. In practice, a much higher proportion are likely to be content.

Richard Rose has estimated (in Herman and Alt, 1975) that the total number of MPs in the majority party who are *de facto* ineligible for a ministerial appointment ranges from one-third to two-fifths. Among those defined as ineligible on that basis are those newly elected to the Commons; those aged over seventy or under thirty (the latter only very rarely appointed); those with extreme political views; those with unsuitable personal characteristics, such as poor health, drinking problems, questionable business associations and sexual delinquencies; those reckoned unable to handle administrative tasks. There are also those who desire not to hold office because of a preference for the freedom of the back-benches or for personal and business reasons. This process of selection is far from infallible, to judge by the regular number of ministers who run into trouble for one or other of the reasons which might seemingly have disqualifed them from office at the start.

Prime Ministers therefore have a more limited pool of MPs available than their total number of supporters in the House. Professor Rose estimates that ministerial appointments or the

status of parliamentary private secretaries must be given to
half or more of all MPs who are not unsuited to receive such
appointments. The exact proportion depends on the size of the
majority party in the Commons. So, talk of intense competition
for office is misleading at the junior ranks of government.
That is partly because British Government is a closed shop
largely restricted to members of the House of Commons. This
is so taken for granted in Britain that its significance is often
ignored. Until the late nineteenth century, a small number of
junior ministers were neither peers nor MPs at the time of
their appointment. They generally worked in the military
departments or the Foreign Office. (This point and several
others in this chapter are drawn from Kevin Theakston's book
Junior Ministers in British Government, 1987.) Moreover, as
discussed later, overseas governments recruit their ministers
from much wider groups than is the case in Britain. This
applies not only to countries, notably America, where there is a
formal separation of executive and legislature but also in
Western European parliamentary systems such as France and
Germany, where there is a greater blurring of the line between
elected politicians and appointed officials.

The extent of the competition for office has been affected by
changes on both the demand and the supply sides. As argued
earlier, the proportion of MPs who want office has grown in
the past half-century with the rise of the career/full-time politician. Harold Macmillan (1975) wrote than when he first entered the Commons in 1924, 'many members of the Conservative Party, perhaps the majority, had no desire at all for
political advancement. A large number, young and old, had
come into the House of Commons as their fathers and grand-
fathers had done, from a feeling that it was the right way to
serve their country and especially the localities in which they
lived.' Just before he left the Commons in 1987, Francis Pym
said that when he was first elected in 1961, 'a comparatively
small proportion either wanted to become, or expected to

become, a minister. Today it is the legitimate ambition of everybody.' A pardonable exaggeration perhaps; the legitimate ambition of a majority would be nearer the mark.

Very few MPs refuse office, though three successive leaders of the Labour Party have done so, for a variety of ideological and tactical reasons. Michael Foot, along with Eric Heffer, refused to join Harold Wilson's Government in the 1960s on policy grounds. But they both joined after the February 1974 election. Michael Foot entered the Cabinet as his first post, though Eric Heffer left the Government just over a year later because of disagreement about its policy towards the EC. After the February 1974 election, John Smith, then a thirty-five-year-old MP with less than four years' experience of the Commons, turned down the post of Solicitor-General for Scotland, a ministerial backwater and for most a cul-de-sac of ambitions. Even the most avid enthusiasts for political trivia would be hard put to name more than a couple of Solicitors-General for Scotland. Instead, John Smith became parliamentary private secretary to the Secretary of State for Scotland, where he learned far more. However, he was complimented for his shrewd judgement by Harold Wilson and that autumn he became an under-secretary at the Department of Energy, joining the cabinet four years later when just aged forty. A couple of years later, Neil Kinnock turned down a junior job at the Department of Prices and Consumer Protection, since he was then a strong critic of many of the Labour Government's policies. But such actions did not harm any of the three, though it was perhaps only the exceptional circumstances of the early 1980s that permitted Neil Kinnock to become Labour leader with no previous ministerial experience. In the other two cases, Michael Foot and John Smith, the initial rejection of office was completely overshadowed by experience in office.

On the Tory side, there are fewer cases of back-benchers turning down office for ideological reasons, though some with outside business interests have done so on financial grounds, since they cannot afford the drop in income involved in becoming a minister. But that is much less true than it was, say, in the 1950s or early 1960s in view of the growth of career politicians for whom service in the Commons, and preferably on the front-bench, is their top priority. A number of ministers voluntarily give up office in mid-career for family and financial reasons, though again they are exceptions.

Most MPs, then, are keen to accept office, while, at the same time, the number of posts available to be given out has also risen. That is partly because of the growth in the size of government itself as the welfare state and Whitehall's relations with industry have expanded. As in so many other aspects of British life, the two world wars produced big changes which were not subsequently reversed. The total number of paid posts – that is, excluding parliamentary private secretaries – rose from about sixty at the beginning of this century to nearly 110 from the Wilson Government onwards. But that total includes peers. The other big change this century has been the decline, both in the absolute number and in the proportion, of peers in any Cabinet. For instance, Lord Salisbury's Cabinet in 1900 contained nine peers and ten members of the House of Commons; only thirty-three MPs held paid posts. Only two peers are now members of the Cabinet as of right, the Lord Chancellor and the Leader of the Lords. Another peer occasionally serves, though generally as a personal adviser to the Prime Minister of the day or out of personal patronage. Another ten or so serve as junior and middle-ranking ministers dotted around departments, but very few have any political importance or influence. This is unlike Lord Salisbury's day, when peers occupied several of the most important posts.

The overall result is that there are many more ministerial posts for MPs at all levels of Government than there used to be, so ambition can at least be partly satisfied. Looked at in terms of the MPs' own careers, rather than the jobs a Prime

Minister has to fill, it is clear that a member who manages to get elected three times has at least an even chance of becoming a minister or a whip. That is, of course, provided his or her party wins office. Over the 1945–74 period, when the Tories were in power for only slightly longer than Labour, nearly a third of all MPs held some kind of office. That proportion rises for MPs with longer service. Take, for example, the eighty-seven Tory MPs newly elected to the Commons in 1979. By the time of the ministerial changes after the April 1992 election, some thirty-three had received office, seven at Cabinet level, including John Major himself. But even after the 1987 election, nineteen of the eighty-seven had left the House, through defeat, death or voluntary departure. That means that roughly half the 1979 intake who managed to stay in the Commons for eight years received office. Of the rest, it is hard to say that more than one or two potential ministers were overlooked, that a large number of hidden talents were un-tapped. The perpetual back-benchers were mainly people with-out obvious abilities for office, for the familiar reasons of age, preference for back-bench life, lack of any obvious ability and often just plain personal unsuitability. Only a Chief Whip with a taste for masochism or the bizarre would have put Geoffrey Dickens, Harry Greenway or Bill Walker into even the most junior ministerial job, though they might regard that as a tribute to their independent-mindedness.

While being a shadow spokesman offers few of the rewards of office, it is at least a mark of recognition. The Opposition front-bench announced by John Smith at the end of July 1992 totalled seventy-six MPs, which, when whips are included, is as large as the number of paid posts on the Government. Of the sixty-eight Labour MPs newly elected in 1987, nearly two-thirds were serving, or had served, on the Labour front-bench by the summer of 1992. Three were members of the Shadow Cabinet elected in July 1992, a further thirty-one were spokesmen, two were parliamentary private secretaries (to Neil

Kinnock and John Smith), and three had worked in the Labour Whips Office. A further four, mainly former MPs re-elected in 1987, served for a time as spokesmen during the 1987–92 Parliament. That left just twenty-five who had no place on the Opposition front-bench. With a handful of exceptions, these were mainly hard-left irreconcilables, such as Ken Livingstone and Bernie Grant; Glasgow machine politicians; and the occasional maverick or eccentric. So, in practice, almost any new Labour MP who has shown the slightest trace of ability has been given the chance to prove himself or herself on the front-bench. This comprehensive principle has been applied, of necessity, even more fully by the Liberal Democrats. There is no selectivity. Every new MP immediately becomes a spokesman, though that brings little glory and, in most cases, little attention.

If political careers are shaped like a pyramid – with the Sphinx looking on to warn of hubris – then the lower tiers of government are the last level where the structure is broad, before it starts narrowing out. None of this makes the job of a Prime Minister any easier in picking a government or shuffling the pack every couple of years. Even a number of the obviously unsuitable will think that they have been unfairly overlooked, while others will feel they have not got the job they wanted or deserved. Prime Ministers have to balance a number of factors, of which the apparent ability of ministerial aspirants is only one. Prime Ministers never start from scratch. They inherit teams of ministers or spokesmen left by their predecessors and even the most strong-willed leader cannot dispense with all the previous top team, especially given the limited number of experienced people available. The formation of Cabinets is discussed in more detail in the next chapter.

In his strange but revealing book *The Governance of Britain* (1976), Harold Wilson argues that a Prime Minister

should take as much trouble with his second team [ministers of state] and his third, the parliamentary secretaries, as with his Cabinet. With the heavy load on a modern government they have to be in the firing line, not only for parliamentary questions, but in evidence before the new range of select committees, as well as in handling difficult deputations and meetings. More important still, they are the raw material for the future.

That does not, however, make ministerial changes any easier:

A redisposition affecting a substantial number of ministers at all levels is like a nightmarish multidimensional jigsaw puzzle, with an almost unlimited number of possible permutations and combinations – including the complementary qualities between the senior and junior ministers in a given department. Sometimes, after hours of juggling with the pieces, the Prime Minister finds that the last consequential piece will not fit, as when I was once left with a Yorkshire lady minister and a vacancy as minister of state in the Welsh office, and had to go back to the drawing-board.

Prime Ministers also like to reward personal loyalty: John Major included several of his close supporters in the November 1990 leadership election in his first Government. They also want to maintain a balance within the party. Even Margaret Thatcher, the most single-minded of Prime Ministers, always included several 'wets' in her Government, too many for the liking of her fervent supporters, who at times felt their claims had been ignored by the dampish Tory Whips Office. Indeed, the presence of a number of former 'wets' in her Cabinet, all promoted by her, proved to be fatal to her in November 1990. Harold Wilson was a master at this exercise of political balance, in ensuring that a left-wing Cabinet minister was matched by right-wing ministers of state and under-secretaries, and vice versa, though the most senior ministers, like Roy Jenkins and James Callaghan, could normally pick their own teams. However, Attlee was typically careful in this respect (interview in King, 1969):

You must take care over junior ministers too. It's generally best to have a talk with the minister concerned in choosing an under-secretary, not just foist someone on him. But you can't necessarily accept the man a minister wants. He's the only one who doesn't know his own deficiencies. You may have picked a minister who is awfully good but, although he doesn't know it, rather weak on certain sides, so you must give him an under-secretary who fills in the gaps.

Margaret Thatcher also ensured that one or two sympathizers were included at a junior level to keep an eye on a notably 'wet' Cabinet minister like James Prior in the early 1980s.

Personal likes and dislikes also matter. Ambitious politicians who have almost given up hope of office under one leader may suddenly find their prospects transformed if there is a change at the top. Richard Crossman would almost certainly not have held a top Cabinet post in any government formed by Hugh Gaitskell. But, as he immediately recognized, that changed when Gaitskell died and was succeeded by Harold Wilson in February 1963. Anthony Howard has noted (1990):

In his introduction to the first volume of his *Cabinet Diaries*, having dwelt on his own bleak prospects under the old regime, Dick could not resist adding: 'But as Harold Laski used to remind us, in British politics where there is death there is hope.' Nor could he be accused of inventing such a reaction retrospectively. His own contemporary *Backbench Diaries* reveal all too clearly the sense of excitement, almost of elation, he felt as the realization dawned upon him that Wilson stood the best chance of being elected as Gaitskell's successor.

Regional factors also play a part, though this has become more difficult for the Tories as they have increasingly become the party of the southern half of England, with few MPs in Scotland, Wales and northern industrial cities. Moreover, the need to find ministers for the Welsh and Scottish Offices has meant that MPs from Wales and Scotland have had a better chance than their English counterparts of becoming ministers. So hard pressed have the Tories been in Scotland that two ministers who had left the Government in the early 1980s had to be recalled to join the Scottish Office team – in the case of Sir Hector Munro after an interval of nearly eleven years. Four out of the five Conservative Welsh Secretaries have represented English constituencies. Modern Prime Ministers are also conscious of the need to include women in their governments, or in a team of shadow spokesmen. However, women have tended to go to social departments, like Health, Education and Social Security, and very few have served in central economic ministries, like the Treasury or Trade and Industry.

Given all these constraints, what makes one MP rather than another ministerial material? It is not just a matter of excluding the unsuitable; it is also an act of inclusion: Prime ministers do have a choice. Being a Scot, a woman or having a safe seat is not enough. Like so much else in British politics, the qualities so widely recognized by Westminster insiders are hard to define for outsiders. Terms such as a 'safe pair of hands' and 'sound' are used to define potential ministers by the party whips, the talent-spotters closest to the ground. Some new MPs stand out because of their intellectual ability and past record and reputation. So, provided they do not make an obvious error when they arrive in the Commons, they are promoted at the first opportunity – usually a couple of years after they are first elected. This applied to William Waldegrave in 1981, Michael Howard in 1985 and John Redwood in 1989. Others prove themselves quietly behind the scenes, occasionally making what the whips would define as a 'helpful' speech or intervention here or there, being active in the other work of the House and, above all, being loyal.

However, a touch of outspokenness does not always do any harm. In the early hours of 2 July 1968, his thirtieth birthday,

David Owen had been dining with Robert Maclennan, later his opponent in the bitter break-up of the SDP in 1987. 'The main topic we discussed was how to get rid of Harold Wilson, when a message was brought to me by one of the badge-holders who circulate all around the House of Commons asking me to go over to No. 10 Downing Street immediately to see the Prime Minister.' He was offered, and accepted, the post of under-secretary in the Ministry of Defence for the Royal Navy. As he wrote (1991) to his future wife Debbie:

I thought as deeply as I could if I should serve but everyone I spoke to was insistent that I should, even though my view of the Prime Minister has not changed. It's part of the political game that you operate inside. I know all this. I know my friends would have taken the job if offered. I know that to refuse would have been jejune and revealed a disdain for politics. But I really did question whether I should have done it. Of course the Prime Minister knows what I feel – he knows that I'm potentially dangerous on the back-benches so he has in effect bought me off – all this is true and it worries me that I have allowed myself in effect to be a pawn on his cynical chessboard, but for all this it offers me a real job, a position in which I can really try to influence events and to start on the ladder of political office.

The offer of the job came only two months after David Owen had spoken sharp words to Harold Wilson in a lift in the Commons. But such exchanges are no bar to preferment, as John Major discovered seventeen years later.

It is a common feature of most promotions that what matters is what is said, notably on the floor of the House of Commons, where whips are often the only people actually listening to a speech apart from the *Hansard* reporters. Britain is unusual in the appointment of ministers in that such a premium is put on parliamentary performances rather than any potential executive abilities as a decision-maker or adminis-trator. Whips have seldom been heard to say of a potential junior minister that he knows how to run an organization or to make decisions. Ambitious MPs can also impress by their activities on standing committees, or often by their lack of them. Silence by Government back-benchers can be as, if not more, valuable than participation. But it is essentially the floor of the House that is crucial and there it is the judgement of fellow MPs, as interpreted by the whips, that matters. In the summer of 1981, Michael Jopling, then Tory Chief Whip, wanted to promote a couple of the 1979 new intake in the forthcoming reshuffle. One was the obviously bright William Waldegrave. For the other, he looked at the reports from his whips and read through *Hansard* reports to see which back-benchers had understood the Government's point of view and made the most effective speech on its behalf, especially under pressure. The result was the selection of David Mellor. A similar process led to the appointment of Edwina Currie to a junior post in 1986. The results might be described as patchy.

One factor rarely mentioned is specialist knowledge or experience. The qualities described above are essentially those of the generalist, who can lend his or her hand in a debate or on a committee to almost any subject. There is some evidence that MPs specialize more than they did, though often in a very diffuse way. This is partly associated with the growth of the select committee system. But it also reflects the recognition that a back-bencher is only likely to be listened to with authority if he or she knows something about a subject. Given the complexity of modern government, that is usually only possible in two or three areas. Prime Ministers pick the top levels of their first governments from the spokesmen who have been shadowing the relevant department before the election when they won office. But there are many shifts made further down a government, and Prime Ministers often do not take too much notice of a back-bencher's specialist knowledge when appointing him or her – apart from a desire to have at least one Roman Catholic at the Northern Ireland Office, an MP from a farming constituency at the Ministry of Agriculture and a doctor at the Department of Health. It is general abilities that mainly count, though no one is likely to go to the Treasury unless they have shown an interest in economic and financial matters. Edmund Dell, Joel Barnett and Robert Sheldon, all old friends from the north-west, were obvious choices to go to the Treasury under Denis Healey after the February and October elections in 1974. Similarly, Nigel Lawson, a former financial journalist, was a natural Financial Secretary to the Treasury in 1979.

The common tendency to regard ministers as generalists is also reflected in the habit of moving junior ministers from department to department to gain experience as they climb the ministerial ladder. Bill Rodgers moved around a series of Whitehall jobs under Harold Wilson – from the Department of Economic Affairs, to the Foreign Office, to the Board of Trade, to the Treasury, to the Ministry of Defence, before being promoted to the Cabinet in 1976 as Transport Secretary by James Callaghan after more than nine years as a junior and middle-ranking minister. Norman Lamont, a merchant banker, served at the departments of Energy, Trade and Industry and Defence before moving to the Treasury in 1986 and rising from Financial Secretary, via Chief Secretary, to, finally, Chancellor. Similarly, John Patten, a university lecturer in geography, was successively a minister at the Northern Ireland Office, then for Health, for Housing, Urban Affairs and Construction, and at the Home Office before entering the Cabinet as Education Secretary more than eleven years after first joining the Government.

The selection of Nicholas Soames, a well-known diner about town, as Minister for Food after the 1992 general election was an exception to the preference for generalists. In that series of changes, John Major appointed a number of ministers with specialist knowledge, such as Michael Mates, a former regular Army colonel with experience in Northern Ireland, to be minister in charge of security in the province, and Anthony

Nelson, who had taken a close interest in City matters, as minister responsible for financial services in the Treasury. But, in general, the attitude of most Prime Ministers remains the same as a century ago when Sir Edward Grey, later to be Britain's longest-serving Foreign Secretary of modern times, was appointed an under-secretary in the Foreign Office in 1892: 'I had had no special training for Foreign Office work, nor had I till then paid special attention to foreign affairs. But special knowledge is not a necessary qualification in a young man appointed to a parliamentary under-secretaryship.'

The first step up from the back-benches is often appointment as a parliamentary private secretary. The position of a PPS is anomalous. He or she is appointed by ministers personally, though only after consultation with the Chief Whip and subject to approval by the Prime Minister. The Cabinet Office's document 'Questions of Procedure for Ministers', officially released by John Major in May 1992, states that parliamentary private secretaries

are not members of the Government, and should be careful to avoid being spoken of as such ... Official information given to them should generally be limited to what is necessary to the discharge of their parliamentary and political duties. This need not preclude them from being brought into departmental discussions or conferences where appropriate, but they should not have access to secret establishments, or information graded secret or above, except on the personal authority of the Prime Minister.

Moreover, 'their special position in relation to the Government imposes an additional obligation which means that no parliamentary private secretary who votes against the Government may retain his or her position. Parliamentary private secretaries should not make statements in the House or put questions on matters affecting the department with which they are connected.'

So there is little gain or glory, and no pay, in return for

surrendering independence. In practice, the role varies enormously. Some parliamentary private secretaries are clearly being groomed for promotion to the Government proper within a year or two; others are solid loyalists who, partly because of age, are never likely to become ministers. Similarly, what is involved can vary enormously from arranging a pair for a minister with an opposition member, so that he or she does not have to attend a particular vote, via organizing deputations of back-bench MPs, to being a fully-fledged political adviser, in effect an extra junior minister who attends meetings and sees official papers. The relationship depends both on the minister and on the parliamentary private secretary. In the early 1980s, Richard Needham became closely associated as an adviser to, and spokesman for, James Prior, while Stephen Dorrell performed the same function for Peter Walker. Others are less identified with a particular minister. Nigel Forman, for instance, served as parliamentary private secretary both to Douglas Hurd, when he was a minister of state, and to Nigel Lawson, when he was Chancellor of the Exchequer. The attraction for the ambitious MP of being a parliamentary private secretary is that it illuminates the workings of Whitehall. Tim Yeo, for instance, a former businessman and director of the Spastics Society, was parliamentary private secretary to Douglas Hurd when he was Home Secretary and then Foreign Secretary before himself becoming a junior minister in November 1990. He found (1990) that the role of parliamentary private secretary 'allows me to be quite closely involved in what he is doing and I have learned a lot from his diplomatic and ministerial skills. He is very adept at ensuring that all areas in his department are advancing at the same time.' Talking nine months before he became a minister, he said:

As far as ambition goes, I am enjoying this job very much, but in due course I would like to make progress. I don't regard myself as a great success, but there's time. If I had carried on with my career in business, I would probably have established myself in a senior position by now. Coming into politics is a bit of a gamble, but I think I will stick with it – it's much more interesting than the City.

Not all new appointees, however, have quite the enthusiasm of Chips Channon in 1938 at the prospect of becoming a parliamentary private secretary to R. A. Butler, the under-secretary at the Foreign Office. His diary (1967) records his growing excitement. On 2 March, hopes rose high: 'Of course, I cannot believe it. I, Chips, at the Foreign Office. Will my star lead me there? It cannot happen. But what a romance my life would have been.' Two days later, he was unsure: 'As I was leaving the House, rather discouraged – politics bring one these exalted hopes, only to have them dashed – I was caught up by a [whip's] runner who told me the "chief" wanted to see me, and once again I was ushered into David Margesson's sanctum.' He records, more in the language of a shy maiden in a Victoran novel getting engaged, how Rab asked him whether he would consider being his PPS. 'My heart throbbed, and I felt exhilarated, as I said he was voicing my life's dream. I, Chips, PPS – how lovely – but to the Foreign Office is beyond belief exciting.' A few weeks later, Chips notes how he 'held almost a court in the House of Commons lobby . . . I am on the crest of the wave.' His career never advanced further, and his main political legacies were to leave his diaries and a son, Paul, who became a long-serving minister under Edward Heath and Margaret Thatcher, eventually reaching the Cabinet.

Kevin Theakston (1987) notes that, between 1945 and 1983, 43 per cent of all junior ministers in the Commons had previously been parliamentary private secretaries. But that understates the significance of the role. Since shadow spokes-men, apart from the leader and deputy leader, do not appoint parliamentary private secretaries, many MPs who become junior ministers after their party wins power at an election have not had the opportunity to serve in that role. Thus many

Tory ministers appointed either at the 1970 or 1979 elections had previously been in the House only in a period of opposition, since 1966 and 1974 respectively, and had not been parliamentary private secretaries. However, since the Tories came to power in 1979 service as a parliamentary private secretary has become an almost automatic part of the promotion route.

Service as parliamentary private secretary to a Prime Minister has been a sure way to secure office, going back to the days of Lord Dunglass, later the Earl of Home, Sir Alec Douglas-Home and Lord Home, who served Neville Chamberlain in that capacity during his premiership from 1937 to 1940. Anthony Barber, later Chancellor of the Exchequer under Edward Heath, served briefly as parliamentary private secretary to Harold Macmillan in 1958–9. James Prior served Edward Heath when he was Leader of the Opposition in the late 1960s and was immediately appointed to the Cabinet in 1970. Peter Shore briefly served as joint PPS to Harold Wilson in the 1964–6 period, as did Eric Varley in 1968–9. More recent parliamentary private secretaries have had less successful later careers, though Jack Cunningham served James Callaghan as Foreign Secretary, and then for a few months when he became Prime Minister in 1976, before he became a junior minister. Ian Gow was a notably assiduous PPS to Margaret Thatcher in her first term, but his subsequent ministerial career was derailed by his decision to resign in 1985 over the Government's policy towards Northern Ireland. He remained a prominent back-bencher until his assassination by the IRA in the summer of 1990.

On the Tory side, the Whips Office has also become a Sandhurst or Dartmouth for future ministers, after they have, with hardly any exceptions, served as parliamentary private secretaries. This has applied much less on the Labour side. While, in the 1945–83 period, 21.6 per cent of Conservative junior ministers had experience of the Whips Office, just 12.4

per cent of Labour junior ministers had. The proportion on the Tory side rose during the 1980s. Nine members of John Major's Cabinet after the April 1992 election, including the Prime Minister himself, were former whips. They included some of the sharpest and cleverest political operators in the Cabinet, such as Kenneth Clarke.

John Major is himself the classic example of the whip who has prospered. When he entered the Commons, he did not at first join the fashionable Blue Chip group – though he did in the mid-1980s. He became involved in the less glittering Guy Fawkes group, whose members included solid new members, rather than obvious stars, such as Graham Bright (later Mr Major's own PPS), John Butcher, Stephen Dorrell, John Lee, Peter Lloyd, Brian Mawhinney, David Trippier and Gary Waller. Most of them later became ministers. John Major was then seen as a non-ideological member. Bruce Anderson recounts (1991):

He was happy to progress in characteristic Major style, gradually and steadily. There was no dramatic breakthrough to fame, or notoriety – but by 1980–81 his name would crop up regularly in those endless Westminster conversations in which parliamentary reputations are traded like an active share on the Stock Exchange. I began to find that an increasing number of his colleagues would say: 'Have you met John Major?' Around this time, Lord Cranborne contacted a firm of bookmakers, and said that he wanted to stake a bet on the first member of the 1979 intake to reach the Cabinet. 'You'll be thinking in terms of one of the Pattens, or William Waldegrave,' said the bookies. 'No,' replied Robert Cranborne, 'John Major.' 'Who he?' inquired the bookies – and quoted odds of 25–1. Lord Cranborne took them.

Earlier, not long after the 1979 election, Robin Oakley, a leading political journalist, wrote a piece saying that the 1979 intake themselves thought that John Major was the one among them with the makings of a Prime Minister.

John Major impressed by his assiduity around the Commons. This led to his first appointment in early 1981 as parliamentary private secretary to Sir Patrick Mayhew, then a minister of state at the Home Office, whom John Major in turn promoted to the Cabinet more than eleven years later. He was also noticed then by Willie Whitelaw. In January 1983 he was appointed an assistant whip and quickly made a mark with his feel for the Commons and his fellow members. His judgement was respected, both by the other whips and by political journalists who wanted to assess the mood of the Tory Party on a particular issue. He demonstrated his shrewd understanding of what motivates politicians. The whips move round each year from one government department to another, dealing with any legislation it has. His key role was as Treasury whip, where his assessment of the back-bench mood and his handling of the often difficult passage of the Finance Bill during the summer was noted by senior ministers. So he was in line for promotion to a ministerial job in spite of a heated exchange with Margaret Thatcher about party worries over the economy during a dinner for the whips in July 1985. But this did not prevent him from being appointed under-secretary for social security in September 1985, where again he impressed with his thoroughness and ability to handle the heavy legislation of that department. But it was the Whips Office that established him as a rising star.

The development of the Tory Whips Office as the fast-stream for promotion candidates reflects a deliberate decision. As John Wakeham explained (in Riddell, 1986a); 'Whips have to be more intelligent and articulate people, both because of the complexity of the issues and because of better informed back-benchers, who require a more rational explanation and will not respond just to a "loyalty to the regiment" approach.' That is in contrast with the 1930s, when David Margesson, mentioned above by Chips Channon, was described by one MP as treating 'dissenters personally as defaulters on parade'.

Even in the early 1950s, Patrick Buchan-Hepburn was regarded as autocratic, with a schoolmasterly approach. There was more than a touch of a stuffy regimental mess, not surprisingly since many, at times most, of the whips up to the late 1970s had had military service. Julian Critchley has recalled (1985) being reproved after he was shown in the early 1960s modelling a suit especially designed for an MP in *Town* magazine, jointly owned by Michael Heseltine, not then himself a member of the Commons. After complaints at the weekly meeting of the 1922 Committee, Critchley was summoned to see Martin Redmayne, the Chief Whip.

I was asked to sit down. A copy of *Town* lay upon his otherwise empty desk. Redmayne picked it up between finger and thumb and asked, 'Are ye hard up?' I said I wasn't. Had I admitted to being so I might well have been paid a monthly remittance from party funds, provided I lived in Alice Springs. The suit, which was black and pompous, with a white waistcoat, lasted me for years, but it was no substitute for promotion.

A more persuasive approach is now needed with the more independent-minded career politicians less used to appeals to regimental loyalty, though the Tory Whips Office still retains some traditional bruisers like the physically imposing David Lightbown.

The Labour Whips Office has never had the role of being an apprenticeship to ministerial office. Only two of John Smith's Shadow Cabinet elected in July 1992 had had experience there. Unusually, these were both women, Margaret Beckett and Ann Taylor, who served as whips during the 1974–9 Labour Government. None of Labour's leading lights who have entered Parliament in the elections from 1979 onwards has served in the Whips Office. The Labour Whips Office has mainly consisted of not very bright party loyalists whose job has been solely to enforce discipline. Derek Foster, Labour Chief Whip since 1985, regrets this reputation and has sought to secure the promotion of some of his whips to shadow spokesmen, as well as to recruit potential high-fliers to the Whips Office.

David Hunt, who served twice in the Tory Whips Office, including a spell as Deputy Chief Whip on his way up to becoming Welsh Secretary in 1990, said (1988) the office was 'a unique training group for learning the procedures of the House. I was delighted to come back last year, renewing former friendships and taking on the challenging task of Deputy Chief Whip at a time when there is so much important legislation going through the House.' Mr Hunt is not unusual in spending time as a junior whip, before becoming an under-secretary, and then moving back to take a senior position in the Whips Office. The same route was taken by David Heathcoat-Amory (1990), who also stressed its virtues: 'The Whips Office is a totally loyal organization where everyone helps each other out. Politics is a very competitive system and it's rare to come across a completely loyal group.' From an earlier generation, Willie Whitelaw (1989) has written of how, at the beginning of 1959, Edward Heath, then the Chief Whip, asked him to become an assistant whip: 'I found the duties of a whip fascinating. They certainly provide an excellent insight into the workings of the parliamentary party and its relation-ship with the Government. They also ensure an appreciation of human reactions and of the various personalities in one's own party.'

Becoming a junior minister is the first visible step up the ladder, where an ambitious politican has his or her first chance to show what they can do. There is the private office with attendant civil servants, the ministerial car and the respect from outsiders usually given to a minister of the crown. This is apart from the sense of being at, or near, the centre of power and possibly having some influence on decisions. As noted above, few can resist its appeal. Chris Patten had been one of the most articulate Tory critics of aspects of the Government's policy during the 1979–83 Parliament. He never dissented to the point of an open breach, but was sufficiently eloquent, and noticed, to irritate Margaret Thatcher, with whom he had worked closely as head of the Conservative Research Department during the late 1970s. He reflected (1982):

I'm not particularly ambitious to be parliamentary secretary at the Department of the Environment, although I would be kidding if I didn't say I would like to hold office one day. I think people very rarely define power when they talk about it in politics. I suppose they mean office if they mean anything, but it is, of course, the case that some of the most influential people in contemporary politics don't hold office.

However, within seven months, Chris Patten was in the Government, at the instigation of his friend James Prior, under whom he served at the Northern Ireland Office.

The role of the junior minister can vary enormously, depending on the department and on the secretary of state. Some Cabinet ministers are reluctant to delegate, preferring to keep the spotlight on themselves. In the 1930s Duff Cooper found time to write a two-volume biography of Douglas Haig when he was a junior minister. And, more recently, one junior minister spent some time learning classical Greek. The Cabinet Office's 'Questions of Procedure' is typically imprecise:

The minister in charge of a department is alone answerable to Parliament for the exercise of the powers on which the administration of that department depends. The minister's authority may, however, be delegated to a minister of state, a parliamentary secretary or to an official; and it is desirable that ministers should devolve on their junior ministers responsibility for a defined range of departmental work, particularly in connection with Parliament.

The point was put more elegantly by Richard Crossman (1958), who defined some of the qualities involved when reviewing the autobiography of Sir Geoffrey Shakespeare, who served as a junior minister during the 1930s and early 1940s in five departments under seven ministers. Crossman writes: 'Every prime minister requires for the majority of the posts in his administration honest, unassuming career politicians who can read a departmental brief almost as though they had composed it; put a questioner off the scent without actually saying what is untrue; and accept without frustration the unimportance of their own activities.'

In the main, as Crossman implies, junior ministers live obscure lives. Their function is to assist their secretaries of state in answering MPs' letters and parliamentary questions, in taking legislation through the Commons, in seeing outside interest groups and in contributing to the formulation of policy. In some cases junior ministers are looked down upon by civil servants, and they are often patronized as being suitable just for regional tours and minor decisions – 'We are lucky, for once we have a good under-secretary.' But some can have a greater say. When Nigel Lawson was Financial Secretary to the Treasury, from May 1979 until September 1981, he had a considerable influence on the creation of the medium-term financial strategy in discussions on monetary policy, much to the irritation of the Bank of England. Some individual junior ministers now have courtesy titles – Minister for Public Transport, for Disabled People, for Consumer Affairs, etc. Such ministers become the focus for outside lobbying groups, but invariably the big decisions are taken by the secretary of state concerned.

In departments where there is a heavy legislative load, such as Environment and the Home Office, the secretary of state will speak on the floor of the Commons on the second reading of a bill, leaving his or her ministers of state and under-secretaries to handle the detailed work in standing committee. Michael Howard made his name guiding through the highly complicated Financial Services Act in 1985–6, following that with the legislation on the poll tax and on water privatization. He impressed with his fluency, skill and experience as a barrister arguing his brief, even though later the financial services legislation was regarded as flawed and the poll tax was abandoned. But by using his advocate's skills Mr Howard achieved the Government's immediate objectives of securing passage of the bills.

Roughly half of under-secretaries never move higher. They hold one or possibly two posts and then are dropped to make way for new, younger MPs. In some cases, the process can be brutal. Attlee always believed in coming to the point in explaining why a minister was not up to the mark. Ministers are not given a second chance if their performances are inadequate. Dick Tracey had less than two years as Minister for Sport in the mid-1980s and Marion Roe lasted only thirteen months in the Department of the Environment, largely because she was unable to hold her own in standing committee.

Of the roughly half of all junior ministers who do advance beyond the level of parliamentary under-secretary, just over a third become ministers of state and ministers outside the Cabinet – and less than a fifth reach Cabinet rank. Almost all ministers move up by moving around from department to department to broaden their experience. The primary way for a junior minister to impress is by his or her performance in the Commons, mainly on the floor but also in committee. A senior minister takes particular note of what happens when a junior colleague is under pressure. Has he or she cultivated friends who will rally round and support him or her? Or has he or she remained aloof, buried in his or her department, and is therefore friendless? There are few more cruel sights than when a minister is left to dangle in the wind alone, in a packed chamber, as happened to Sir Nicholas Fairbairn over a Scottish legal incident in January 1982. He resigned within a few hours. Gerald Kaufman cautions: (1980)

If you think administration is the be all and end all of ministerial life, and regard the Commons as an irritating distraction that has somehow to be coped with, the Commons will make you miserable when they have it in their power to do so. If you regard Parliament as your highest priority, and take the trouble to let it know that you do, you will experience in it the most fulfilling moments in your ministerial life.

Performances in the Commons are only the most public of conditions for preferment. Prime Ministers also notice if they are told a minister shows qualities of competence and can handle people well. Politics is, after all, about persuasion. It is noticed at Westminster if a minister spends time talking to interested MPs and to the officers of the relevant back-bench committees. Prime Ministers are impressed both by these public performances and by contributions at Cabinet committees and private meetings. In May 1992, the Cabinet Office made publicly available, for the first time, the membership of the permanent ministerial committees of the Cabinet. The main committees are attended just by members of the Cabinet, though their ministers of state sometimes attend as substitutes. But the ministerial subcommittee on health strategy is attended as of right not just by several Cabinet ministers but also by the Paymaster-General from the Treasury, the Ministers of State at the Department of Health and the Department of Employment, and the parliamentary under-secretary at the Department of National Heritage. The ministerial subcommittee on London, chaired by the Environment Secretary, otherwise consists entirely of ministers of state and under-secretaries. Gerald Kaufman records how, on the basis of his experience from 1974 to 1979, 'in Cabinet committee your reputation is at stake every time you open your mouth. Colleagues will judge your quality by your performance there more than by your achievements on the floor of the House.' The right way to impress most Prime Ministers is by keeping quiet and intervening only occasionally and with skill. This involves asking the right question in the right way to show a breadth of vision and understanding beyond the departmental brief.

Performances within a department are more difficult to assess. Civil servants have clear views on the merits of their ministers. These are not necessarily the same as those of politicians. These assessments of whether a minister is 'good' – generally defined as handling his or her red boxes expeditiously and competently, and standing up for the department in the Commons and in Cabinet committees – are quickly conveyed around the private office network. They then filter their way upwards to the Prime Minister via his or her principal private secretary and the Cabinet Secretary.

The most striking feature remains how the key skills of a junior minister are to operate in the worlds of Parliament and party politics. Kevin Theakston (1987) argues: 'Recruiting junior ministers on the basis of parliamentary ability, promoting them from department to department, and rewarding those who demonstrate talent in collective fora would seem a good way of training the type of Cabinet leaders needed for a party to govern and survive politically.' But it is less clear whether such a career pattern helps ministers to understand decision-making and to gain executive and other policy-making experience. Richard Rose has argued (in Herman and Alt, 1975). 'The fact that service in such a post [as a junior minister] is today virtually a *sine qua non* for Cabinet office does not assure that the time spent in these qualifying posts necessarily imparts skills useful in higher offices.' Theakston argues that policy formulation and managerial control 'would seem to call for qualities and styles rather different from those stressed and developed by the generalist model'. There is, however, a danger of exaggerating the importance of administrative abilities compared with skills of political persuasion in the work of ministers.

As noted earlier, junior ministers in Germany and France are much more likely to have specialist knowledge and executive experience than in Britain. Although parliamentary state secretaries in Germany are professional party politicians, many are former public servants, including several who worked in the civil service, as well as a large number of teachers and lecturers. There is also a greater preference for appointing ministers with specialist knowledge. In France, roughly half the junior ministers, or secretaries of state, have a civil service background, as do up to two-fifths of members of the National Assembly. That includes teachers, but a number of senior civil servants are appointed directly as ministers with no, or very little, parliamentary experience. Civil servants in France can be active members of parties and in Germany they are often party appointees in the first place. So it is not just that politics is open to civil servants, but also that the civil service is open to those with a party allegiance, in direct contrast to the British tradition. If British rules had applied, some French and German politicians might have gone straight into politics, possibly via a time as a political adviser. In practice, however, an increasing number of British MPs do have direct experience of the workings of government, not as civil servants but as political or special advisers. That is like the young aristocrats in the nineteenth century whose first political experience was as private secretary to a leading minister, often a relative, as Arthur Balfour was to Salisbury at the Congress of Berlin in 1878. In Britain, there have always been a number of new MPs who know the inside of a Whitehall department.

In America, the separation between the executive and the legislature is set out in the constitution. In Washington, many senior administrative posts which would be held in Britain by a senior civil servant are taken by political appointees of the president. Often, a British permanent civil servant will be dealing with a political appointee of an American president. But that does not mean that the political appointees have legislative experience. Most do not. There are always a number of former Congressmen in top jobs in any administration – as well as a number of ex-Congressmen defeated in an attempt to win another office – but they are a minority. Many political appointees, especially when one party is in office for a long time, move between working in the administration and in the private sector, as lawyers, lobbyists and consultants. But they seldom move along Pennsylvania Avenue to Capitol Hill. Congress has its own career structure, in which ambitious legislators aim for leadership positions and committee chairmanships, often turning down the offer of posts in the administration.

In Britain, the virtual closed shop of promotion from the House of Commons is peculiarly attuned to the supposed supremacy of Parliament. Outsiders who are brought in, mainly as peers, like C.P. Snow in 1964 or Irwin Bellwin, a former leader of Leeds City Council, in 1979, are seldom successes. They have had no experience of the Commons. But there remain deficiencies in the development of junior ministers. Even in the mid-1950s, Herbert Morrison (1954) suggested a 'Charter for Parliamentary Secretaries' to avoid their lives being 'uninteresting and rather empty'. William Rodgers, a veteran undersecretary and minister of state, has argued (1982):

To talk of a career framework for ministers may sound like heresy. Politics is too precarious and prime ministerial skill remains a matter of handling a restless team of individualists and preserving a delicate balance within his or her party. But there is much to be said for using the office of parliamentary secretary as a probationary one with no dishonour in moving out as well as up. The minister of state would then become the 'career grade' helping to ensure a combination of traditional Cabinet authority with real responsibilities for junior ministers down the line. Many ministers come into office with virtually no experience of administration and some have little natural aptitude for it. Their political weight and competition in the House of Commons are the factors that lead to their appointment. A little on-the-job training will do them no harm.

But, for the moment, the skills that matter for promotion are handling the House of Commons.

7

CLIMBING THE MINISTERIAL LADDER

'I suppose, as you say, I ought to feel satisfied and happy. When I was a boy I used to think that to get into the Cabinet before one was forty was, for an Englishman who had to start on the level of the crowd, the highest height of achievement. I shall not be forty until September so the odds are (between you and me) that I shall have the chance at any rate, of bringing off this dream of young ambition.'

> Asquith writing to a friend on 1 August 1892, in
> anticipation of his appointment by Gladstone to the
> Cabinet, quoted in Roy Jenkins, *Asquith*, 1964

'The need for widespread consultations [on forming a Cabinet] varies inversely with the degree of unity the prime minister can count on. A bewildered or divided party means an unsure prime minister. Above all, it denotes cliques, factions and fights for protégés. He may not be able to count on senior minister A's continuing support if protégé B is not in a given job; senior minister C will resign if B is. It is an unhappy Cabinet with an unsure parliamentary base if the Prime Minister has, to any real degree, to put his Cabinet-making function in pawn, or get involved in bargaining.'

> Harold Wilson, *The Governance of Britain*, 1976

'"David," she started, "I have made up my mind that I would like you in my Cabinet. You will come into the Lords, well you have nearly earned it anyway, but you will not have a department. I would like you to take a special interest in job creation. Unemployment must be dealt with." I have often read the expression the "floor opened up" and discounted it as pure hyperbole, but this time it actually happened. I am not too sure that I heard the rest of the conversation . . . All that was running through my mind was "cabinet – cabinet", and wondering what that would entail.'

> Lord Young, on being invited in 1984 to join the Cabinet
> by Margaret Thatcher, in *The Enterprise Years*, 1990

Membership of the Cabinet is the pinnacle of most politicians' careers. It is highly public recognition that you have succeeded – that you are one of the elect at the centre of decision-making. Not only are you the head of a department but you also, of right, attend the weekly meetings of the Cabinet, smiling a trifle smugly or trying to look serious as you go in and out of 10 Downing Street.

Political scientists from Bagehot onwards have debated the relative power of a Prime Minister in relation to his or her Cabinet and the balance of influence between a secretary of state in relation to his or her permanent civil servants. In practice, there is no definitive answer, whether supplied by Richard Crossman or by Sir Humphrey in *Yes, Minister*. The relative balance of power and influence largely depends on the personality of the Prime Minister of the day. Some, like James Callaghan or John Major, favour a collective approach, involving the whole Cabinet. Others, most recently Margaret Thatcher, develop – though she did not start with – a more dominant style, often bypassing the formal Cabinet structure.

But what matters for this book is that entry into the Cabinet is regarded by the public, by the media and by fellow MPs as the moment when a politician has reached the top. In such a hierarchical and status-conscious society as Britain, it is the equivalent of being capped for your country at sport, or, equally telling for most male MPs, becoming a prefect at school. Only a few ever captain their country, head their school or become Prime Minister (just nineteen so far this century), but many more have served in the top team, or as prefects, and they know, or have reluctantly come to accept, that this is the peak of their careers. At any time, roughly one in eight MPs are current, former or future Cabinet ministers. In 1970, just after the Tories had defeated Labour at that year's general election, some ninety-three MPs came into this category. In 1979, after a similar change of government, the total was eighty-two. On both occasions there were just five past, present and future occupants of 10 Downing Street sitting in the Commons – in 1970, Home, Wilson, Heath, Callaghan and Thatcher, and in 1979, this group minus Home but plus Major.

As the last chapter showed, the selection and promotion of ministers follows a common pattern in which most have served a lengthy apprenticeship before entering the Cabinet. The median period for a minister to have served in the Commons before becoming a member of the Cabinet was about fourteen years in the late nineteenth century and the first half of the twentieth century. The median period for members of the first Wilson Cabinet in 1964 was nineteen years (partly reflecting Labour's long period in opposition), while for the Heath Cabinet in 1970 the median time was seventeen years. The gap was thirteen years for Margaret Thatcher's first Cabinet in May 1979. The steady turnover of ministers, especially towards the end of the Thatcher era, and the Tories' unbroken period in office during the 1980s meant that the median period before entry to the Cabinet dropped to around eleven and a half years in the Cabinet which John Major formed after the April 1992 election. Indeed, of the five newcomers to the Cabinet then, their periods in the Commons ranged from the eighteen years of Sir Patrick Mayhew, via the thirteen years of John Patten, the nearly eight years of Virginia Bottomley, the seven and a half years of Michael Portillo to the just under five years of Gillian Shephard.

The rapid advance of some women MPs has been matched on the Labour side, especially since the introduction in 1989 of reserved places for women in the Shadow Cabinet. Paradoxically, therefore, once women have overcome the obstacles of initial political involvement and selection for a winnable constituency (much more difficult than for men), they nowadays have a better chance of promotion up the ministerial or shadow ladder. Such was the volume of protests when there were no women in John Major's first Cabinet in November 1990 – for the first time since the Home Cabinet in 1963–64 – that he virtually had to include at least one woman after the 1992 general election. In the event, two were promoted to the Cabinet: Virginia Bottomley and Gillian Shephard. It is now probable that all future Cabinets will include women as a matter of deliberate policy, rather as President Bill Clinton has sought to give women prominent positions in his administration.

In general, new entrants to the Cabinet have served an apprenticeship of at least three Parliaments on the backbenches and in junior and middle-ranking posts. Even a century ago Gladstone preferred what he called the 'old rule' of not putting men into the Cabinet until they had first served in junior office. In the spring of 1892 Gladstone had told Rosebery that he was 'averse to giving Asquith Cabinet office'. But he did in the event make an exception in Asquith's case, appointing him Home Secretary, or, as he put it, 'I find myself able to offer this just and I think signal tribute to your character, abilities and eloquence.' Asquith regarded it as 'the highest height of achievement' to be in the Cabinet by the time he was forty. In those days it was more difficult than now for a member of the Commons, especially one not from the aristocracy, to enter the Cabinet, since half the members were peers. Now, it is not unrealistic for someone of talent who has entered the Commons in his or her early thirties, and whose party stays in power, to expect to be in the Cabinet by his or her mid-forties, if not by forty. The most recent entrants to the Cabinet under the age of forty have been Malcolm Rifkind and Michael Portillo.

Later Prime Ministers have almost invariably stuck to Gladstone's 'old rule', so potential Cabinet ministers have had to prove themselves at a lower level. Even a conviction leader such as Margaret Thatcher operated like the headmistress of an old-fashioned grammar school, promoting boys, and a few girls, on the basis of hard work and merit, so that ministers gradually moved up the promotion ladder until it was their 'turn'. Administrative competence, ability in Cabinet committees and smooth overseeing of bills in committee are all important, but the key is often a minister of state's skill in handling the Commons. Prime Ministers also balance regional and ideological factors. Most often, ministers' reputations rise, fall or stagnate on a cumulative basis. They establish themselves as worthy of entry to the Cabinet on the strength of competent handling of a succession of jobs. For some, a particular incident or issue may accelerate their rise. The sudden promotion from the back-benches of Iain Macleod was a rarity. In early 1990 David Hunt, then a minister of state at the Department of the Environment, was widely reckoned to have made his promotion to the Cabinet certain after a Commons speech without notes replying to widespread Tory back-bench unease over the level of central government grants to local authorities. John Smith proved himself not only as an efficient energy minister dealing with North Sea oil (he was praised by Tony Benn, his secretary of state) but also in his painstaking work in handling the devolution legislation on the floor of the Commons from 1976 to 1978. His work there was valued not only by Michael Foot, the Leader of the Commons, but also by James Callaghan. So, when a vacancy came up at the Department of Trade in November 1978 following Edmund Dell's decision to leave politics, John Smith, though largely unknown outside the inner circles at Westminster, was the obvious candidate in the eyes of James Callaghan.

Similarly, John Major looked a likely choice for promotion to the top level after the June 1987 general election. Although he had been a minister for less than two years, he had earned widespread praise for his handling of potentially explosive issues, particularly cold weather payments for the elderly during the severe winter of 1986–7. He then hoped he might become Chief Whip after the election, and Willie Whitelaw and John Wakeham backed him for the post. However, Nigel Lawson was looking round for a new Chief Secretary to handle public spending. His first choice was John Wakeham, or, as he put it in his memoirs (1992), 'failing him, John Major, who had seemed to me the pick of the 1979 intake'. After sounding out John Wakeham before the election, and learning that he was not interested, Nigel Lawson pressed the claims of John Major, who had impressed him as a result of his work as whip responsible for Treasury matters and as a social security minister. 'The relatively unusual combination of a mastery of detail and likeable manner would, I felt, make him an excellent Chief Secretary.' He was also recommended by Mr Lawson's special advisers, who admired his work in both roles. Initially, Margaret Thatcher wanted John Major to become Chief Whip, but Nigel Lawson countered with the suggestion of David Waddington. After Willie Whitelaw, himself a former Chief Whip, had been persuaded to change his view and support the Chancellor's case, the Prime Minister also came round. Lawson notes: 'It is ironic that, had he instead become Chief Whip, as Margaret had intended, he could never have been a candidate to succeed her when she stepped down in 1990.' It is also possible that as Chief Whip he might have defused some of the tensions which contributed to her downfall.

That is a reminder of the importance of chance at the top of politics. Whether one particular minister is picked for one particular post or another – the inspired last-minute decision by Attlee in 1945 to switch Ernest Bevin to the Foreign Office and Hugh Dalton to the Treasury – can affect the development both of policy and of later careers. Similarly, some MPs only enter the Cabinet thanks to the misfortunes of others. David Owen might never have served in the Cabinet but for the death of Anthony Crosland in February 1977. Owen was Minister of State at the Foreign Office at the time and recalls (1991) his conversation with James Callaghan:

He asked me to sit down and said simply, 'David, I am going to make you Foreign Secretary.' I was stunned. Jim says in his autobiography that I went white as a sheet. It took me a few seconds to reply and then he said that this was not going to be a temporary appointment. He had discussed the situation with Denis Healey and Denis really did not quite know what he wanted to do. So, as Jim put it, he had decided the issue for him – he would stay at the Treasury.

Otherwise, David Owen might have had to wait until after the 1979 election before he had a chance of entering the Cabinet, an opportunity which might, therefore, never have come since Labour, of course, went into opposition then. David Owen's subsequent prominence, during the rise and fall of the SDP, was based on his period as Foreign Secretary. During the Thatcher years, Paul Channon had largely given up hope of ever getting into the Cabinet after nine years as a minister of state, starting in 1972. But Leon Brittan's resignation in January 1986 during the Westland crisis gave him the opportunity to take over as Trade and Industry Secretary. He served in the Cabinet for three and a half years. Like David Owen, Paul Channon had the advantage of already being in the department where a vacancy had arisen, so his promotion from minister of state to secretary of state minimized the need for a wider Cabinet reshuffle, which Prime Ministers always dislike, especially in the middle of a parliamentary session.

Chance and timing can also work in the other direction. Many of the younger ministers in the Callaghan Government, including some who subsequently joined the SDP, would have enjoyed a much longer Cabinet career but for the Tories being in government continuously after May 1979. Roy Hattersley, Eric Varley, Peter Shore, Bill Rodgers, Shirley Williams and David Owen would all presumably have spent a long time in the Cabinet during the 1980s. Denis Healey would have occupied the one post, Foreign Secretary, for which he had spent most of his career preparing. Some middle-ranking ministers in the Callaghan Government who might have entered the Cabinet after the May 1979 election have been denied the chance, notably Gerald Kaufman and perhaps Denzil Davies, a promising Treasury minister before May 1979. Only John Smith may now have the chance of picking up the threads following a gap of seventeen to eighteen years after his six months in the Cabinet over the winter of 1978–9.

Prime Ministers usually follow some ground rules in making appointments. Harold Wilson prided himself on close attention to Cabinet-making, and frequent remaking in a regular series of reshuffles. However, both at the time and subsequently, his tendency to undertake changes in his team for no obvious reason created bitter resentment and instability. These shuffles fuelled, rather than dampened, the atmosphere of conspiracy in the Wilson years. He has argued (1976): 'There has to be a central strategy in Cabinet formation, which must reflect the Prime Minister's broader political and policy strategy. He should be prepared to listen to advice, especially that of the Leader of the House and the Chief Whip, who are in closest touch with back-benchers, then to keep his counsel, and make his own decisions.' Wilson lists several factors to be taken into account by a Prime Minister:

First, he needs a good memory of his colleagues' specializations and past experience, or any tendencies to weakness in a crisis. Even more, he needs a good 'forgettory'. Forming a Cabinet is no time for settling old scores, or bearing grudges or associating a first-class potential minister with some groupings during some best-forgotten party argument . . . Second, the Prime Minister must pay full regard to preserving a real balance in the party in Parliament, and in the country . . . No government should be based on a faction, still less a clique. It should embrace and reflect the whole party, though the Prime Minister can be forgiven if he disregards a few idiosyncratic extremists at the margins . . . Third, he must concentrate on the doctrine of horses for courses, not only in using the specialist

knowledge of individual ministers, but also in reflecting the changing
priorities of national and international relationships ... Horses for
courses includes the great and unteachable quality of being able to
handle the House of Commons. In the first resort, as in the last, a
government survives, and deserves to survive, in proportion to its
success in understanding Parliament, in reflecting, and sometimes
knowing when to resist, its changing moods ... Fourth, Cabinet and
other ministerial appointments should reflect a real rapport with the
party nationally, and above all in the country. Every member of his
administration – regardless of which party is in office – must remember that he is not where he is, not even in Parliament, as a result of
his own transcendent qualities: he is there because people believe in
him, work for him, not primarily as an individual but as a standard-
bearer.

Even on the basis of these criteria, no Prime Minister has a
free hand in picking his or her Cabinet. He or she has to make
do with what is available, and that is strictly limited by the
convention that the vast majority of all governments are chosen
from current members of the House of the Commons. This is
in marked contrast to the experience overseas. Jean Blondel
and Jean-Louis Thiebault (1991) show that, for the 1945–84
period, 95 per cent of British Cabinet ministers had previous
parliamentary experience – the exceptions were mainly those
appointed to the Cabinet and made peers. But the proportion
was only 74 per cent in Germany, 69 per cent in France and
just 53 per cent in the Netherlands. This means not only that
the values and attitudes of most British ministers are set by
their lengthy apprenticeships in the Commons, but also that
they are much less likely to have had direct experience of the
Civil Service or the executive agencies of central government
than their counterparts on the Continent. Many French and
Scandinavian politicians were previously civil servants, and
indeed members of political parties while holding such posts.
However, an increasing number of British MPs, and therefore
in time ministers, including John Major himself, have had

experience of local government as elected councillors. This is similar to many of their counterparts in the rest of Europe. In marked contrast to the emphasis on parliamentary experience and skills in Britain, in France, the Netherlands and Norway MPs are required to resign their parliamentary seats as a condition to becoming ministers.

Given these constraints, incoming Prime Ministers can dispense with only a handful of ministers whom they do not like or value; they cannot remake the whole team. They have to make do with what is available on the basis of those who have shown their abilities in Westminster and Whitehall. Margaret Thatcher's first Cabinet in May 1979 – more than four years after she had become Leader of the Conservative Party – was still dominated by former close allies of Edward Heath. The old Heathites, later generally known as 'wets', such as Sir Ian Gilmour, Lord Soames, Mark Carlisle, Norman St John-Stevas, Francis Pym, etc., were dropped in a series of reshuffles. They were replaced by strong supporters of her views (at least at the time of their appointment, if not subsequently), such as Leon Brittan, Norman Tebbit, Cecil Parkinson and Nigel Lawson. But no Thatcher Cabinet, even at the height of her powers in the mid-1980s, was entirely 'one of us', just as the Tory Party in the Commons was itself never entirely Thatcherite. By the mid- to late 1980s she was promoting to the Cabinet a number of middle-ranking ministers who were far from Thacherite, such as Kenneth Clarke, Malcolm Rifkind, Chris Patten, David Hunt and William Waldegrave, many of whom opposed her in the final battle of November 1990. They were put in the Cabinet because they had proved themselves in a series of junior- and middle-level ministerial posts and because similar talent was not available on the Thatcherite wing of the party.

Prime Ministers also do not want to leave too many angry and frustrated opponents on the back-benches. James Callaghan, for instance, put up with the increasingly open dissent of Tony Benn, thinking that he could probably do more harm outside than inside the Cabinet. And since he was unwilling to resign, his ability to stir revolt within the Labour Party was to some extent limited until after Labour was defeated in May 1979. Similarly, Margaret Thatcher always reckoned it was better to have Peter Walker inside her Cabinet as a licensed, though largely impotent, dissident than outside as a potential rebel, even if he had lost most of his fire by the mid-1980s.

Labour leaders now have the additional constraint that they have to pick their initial Cabinets from those who formed the Shadow Cabinet before the general election (provided they have been elected to the Commons). When, as up to 1981, this was the leader, his deputy and the twelve members of the Shadow Cabinet elected by Labour, there was still some freedom of manoeuvre for an incoming Prime Minister, not just in shifting people between portfolios but also in bringing in some potentially good ministers outside the Shadow Cabinet. For instance, Harold Wilson in 1964 brought into his first Cabinet Richard Crossman and Anthony Greenwood, neither of whom had been in the previous Shadow Cabinet. But the Shadow Cabinet was increased in size to fifteen members in 1981 and to eighteen in 1989. When the leader and deputy leader are included, this has removed virtually all flexibility in forming a first Cabinet. This can be remedied over time in reshuffles, but Attlee (as quoted in King, 1969) felt: 'The responsibility of choosing the members of the Government must rest solely with the Prime Minister, though in practice he will consult with his colleagues. If he cannot be trusted to exercise this power in the best interests of the nation and the party without fear, favour or affection, he is not fit to be Prime Minister.'

The criteria by which people are elected to the Shadow Cabinet are only loosely to do with their ability as potential Cabinet ministers. Success or failure in the annual elections reflects personal and regional alliances and ideology, as well as his or her record as a junior spokesman. Most newcomers to the Shadow Cabinet from the mid-1980s were members of the broad Tribunite left. But winning still depends at least in part on performance. For instance, Bryan Gould's success in the Commons in harrying the Government over the relatively obscure area of City affairs ensured his election to the Shadow Cabinet in autumn 1986, in time to achieve national prominence as campaigns coordinator in the 1987 election. His subsequent failure to sustain his rise reflected MPs' doubts about his judgement on policy, notably over his handling of the party's alternative to the poll tax. In the damning Westminster phrase, he was regarded as 'unsound'. His deep hostility to the European Community and his support for devaluation led to an increasing personal detachment from party leaders. His very poor result in the 1992 leadership elections aggravated his disillusionment, so his resignation from the Shadow Cabinet on the eve of the party conference in September 1992 and defeat in the annual ballot for the party's National Executive Committee the following day were the culmination of a process almost of self-destruction.

While most Cabinet ministers and shadow spokesmen have to serve lengthy apprenticeships, there have been a few cases of accelerated promotion after only a few years' service in the Commons. This has applied especially in opposition, where there is more scope for new faces to make an impact. For instance, Gordon Brown and Tony Blair were elected to the Shadow Cabinet within four and five years respectively of becoming MPs, and in July 1992 David Blunkett and Marjorie Mowlam were elected just over five years after first entering the Commons. On the Government benches, Gillian Shephard is highly unusual in having been an MP for less than five years before her promotion. Twenty years earlier, Sir Geoffrey Howe joined the Heath Cabinet as Trade and Consumer Affairs Minister after less than four years as an MP, though his service was interrupted. He was briefly an MP between the October 1964 and March 1966 elections before returning to the Commons in June 1970. In earlier times, Asquith became Home Secretary within six years of entering the Commons and

Winston Churchill joined the Asquith Cabinet after eight years as an MP, though he had already changed his party once in the meantime. Harold Wilson and Hugh Gaitskell joined the Attlee Cabinet within just over two and five years respectively of becoming MPs.

One of the most widely remembered cases of rapid promotion is that of Iain Macleod, who became Minister of Health in May 1952 without ever having served as a junior minister. Frequent telling has embellished the story. Macleod had been an MP for more than two years, since the February 1950 general election. And, unlike his predecessor as Minister of Health, he did not enter the Cabinet itself. He had to wait until he was shifted to become Minister of Labour in December 1955. The legend relates as much to the manner as to the speed of his rise. Macleod made his name by a sharp attack in the Commons on Aneurin Bevan, the main architect of the National Health Service, who had spoken previously. Winston Churchill was in the chamber. Nigel Fisher, Macleod's biographer, records (1973):

When Bevan sat down, the Prime Minister was rising slowly to leave the chamber, but his attention was caught by the opening sentence of Macleod's speech: 'I want to deal closely and with relish with the vulgar, crude and intemperate speech to which the House of Commons has just listened.' It was an arresting start and, instead of leaving at once, Churchill remained, perched on the edge of the bench, waiting to hear if the next few sentences would be as good as the first.

They were. Nigel Fisher was sitting on the parliamentary private secretaries' bench, immediately behind the Government front-bench, and overheard the exchange between Churchill and Patrick Buchan-Hepburn, the Chief Whip. After being told who the MP speaking was, Fisher notes: 'There was a pause, then: "Ministerial material?" suggested the Prime Minister. Buchan-Hepburn had learned to be watchful of Winston's enthusiasms and replied cautiously: "He's still quite young" – to which Churchill, who had himself been in the Cabinet at the age of thirty-three, snapped back: "What's that got to do with it?"' Within a few weeks Macleod was Minister of Health, thanks both to the speech and to the recommendation of James Stuart, a former Chief Whip and then Secretary of State for Scotland, on whom Churchill relied for political advice.

The exceptions to the general selection of senior ministers from the Commons closed shop are very rare and, in general, underline the main argument. After a long and distinguished career as a public servant, Sir John Anderson entered the Commons early in 1938 as an independent member for the Scottish Universities supporting the National Government. By that October he had been asked to join the Cabinet as Lord Privy Seal with responsibility for civil defence. Over the following nearly seven years he was successively Home Secretary and Minister of Home Security, Lord President of the Council, with wide responsibilities over the home front, and Chancellor of the Exchequer. But that career was only possible because of the national emergency. In peacetime his role disappeared, because of his refusal to align himself with one of the parties and following the abolition of the university seats in 1950.

Ernest Bevin entered the Coalition Government as a senior minister in 1940 and became an MP as a result. But that was in the unusual conditions of wartime. Other cases have been less successful – Frank Cousins, who joined the Cabinet as Minister of Technology after the October 1964 election and had a by-election specially created for him; and John Davies, who entered the Cabinet, also as Minister of Technology, within a few weeks of first becoming an MP in June 1970. Both were seen to represent key industrial interest groups: Cousins as general secretary of Britain's largest trade union and Davies as a former director general of the Confederation of British Industry. Neither had a happy time in Westminster politics.

On becoming Prime Minister in October 1964, Harold Wilson brought in a number of other outsiders to become ministers of state, serving in the Lords, including Lords Caradon (a member of the Foot family and a leading colonial administrator), Chalfont (a former regular Army officer and defence correspondent of *The Times*), Bowden (principal of what became the University of Manchester Institute of Science and Technology) and Snow (the novelist and attempted bridge between science and the arts). The first two served for the whole 1964–70 period in the Foreign Office, Caradon as permanent representative at the United Nations and Chalfont as minister responsible for arms control and disarmament issues, but Lords Bowden (at education and science) and Snow (at technology) left the Government within eighteen months. After the February 1974 election, Harold Wilson brought in Lord Crowther-Hunt, a prominent academic, to become higher education minister and, briefly, minister of state responsible for constitutional matters. At the same time, John Harris, a long-serving Labour Party official and latterly a close associate of Roy Jenkins, was made Lord Harris of Greenwich and minister of state at the Home Office. He served there for nearly five years and had influence over a wide range of criminal justice issues. Apart from Lord Bellwin, mentioned in the previous chapter, there have been relatively few subsequent examples of people with distinguished outside careers being appointed as ministers with real responsibilities and involvement in policy-making, rather than just acting as spokesmen in the Lords for their departments. The main exceptions have been Lord Mackay of Clashfern, a leading Scottish judge and former Scottish law officer, as Lord Chancellor from 1988, and Baroness Blatch, minister of state for education after the April 1992 election, who had been leader of Cambridgeshire Council Council in the first half of the 1980s.

The main direct entrants to the Cabinet without previous political or parliamentary experience have been peers who were personal favourites and allies of the Prime Minister of the day and dependent on their patronage. There are now many fewer of these than before, say, the First World War, though Winston Churchill included a number of his close allies and some wartime military leaders in his 1951–5 Cabinet. Among those who served then were Lords Ismay and Cherwell and Earl Alexander of Tunis. None made much impact and since then there have been at most a couple of peers in the Cabinet apart from the Lord Chancellor and the Leader of the Lords. Lord Young of Graffham was the classic example during the Thatcher years. Previously a successful property developer, he started as a special adviser, served as chairman of the Manpower Services Commission, before joining the Cabinet and becoming a peer in September 1984, first as Minister without Portfolio with special responsibility for enterprise and wealth creation for a year, then as Employment Secretary for just under two years and, finally, as Trade and Industry Secretary for two years before returning, with little regret, to the private sector.

Lord Young was regarded as an outsider who did not really understand Parliament by most MPs, and by many of his Cabinet colleagues. He was undoubtedly an energetic and single-minded minister, especially in devising employment and training schemes, but his lack of knowledge of the Commons did not help him to handle tricky political difficulties, such as the British Aerospace purchase of the Rover Group and the Monopolies and Mergers Commission report on the brewing industry. The Commission's proposals to end the brewers' monopoly provoked fierce opposition in 1989 in both the Commons and the Lords. In his memoirs (1990), Lord Young recalls how he

ran into more trouble with the back-bench committee and again with the 1922 Committee. Too late I realized what had happened. It was nothing to do with public opinion, which was uniformly for the proposals. It had nothing to do with the merits, which were rarely discussed. It had everything to do with the brewers' support for constituency associations up and down the land.

As he points out from reading Trollope's *The Prime Minister*, the Duke of Omnium was also sorely troubled by the brewers.

Lord Carrington, though a far more experienced and astute politician, ultimately foundered in April 1982 after the Argentine invasion of the Falkland Islands because of resentment by Tory MPs, in part dating from his role in the Rhodesia settlement of 1979. In his memoirs (1988), he concedes that, in the initial circumstances of shock and fury after the Argentine invasion, there

must be a resignation. The nation feels that there has been a disgrace. Someone must have been to blame. The disgrace must be purged. The person to purge it should be the minister in charge. That was me. I was also very aware that my membership of the Lords was at that moment an embarrassment to the Prime Minister, and a weakness ... When there's a real political crisis it is in the House of Commons that the life and death of Government is decided and I bitterly regretted that I could not face that House at Margaret Thatcher's side.

The failure of most of the direct entrants to the Cabinet in the Commons and the difficulties faced by those in the Lords underline the central features of any Cabinet career – skill in handling the Commons, and appearing on television, as well as the generalist tradition. Poor parliamentary performances, particularly on big occasions, often prevent a minister from being promoted, especially when these failures are related to a more general lack of touch in handling sensitive issues. The Cabinet careers during the 1980s of a number of ministers, such as John Moore, Peter Rees and Paul Channon, ended not only because they were not giving a firm direction to policy but also because they did not command the respect of the

House. By contrast, Kenneth Clarke, David Hunt and Tony Newton prospered because of their ability to handle any kind of tricky problem in the Commons. They proved to be 'safe pairs of hands'. Similarly, Michael Heseltine's long political career has reflected his ability to make memorable speeches on big occasions, whether in the Commons or at the annual Conservative Party conference. Harold Wilson became a national political figure during the late 1950s and early 1960s by living down his early reputation as a dull, almost bureaucratic member of the Attlee Cabinet. He developed formidable skills as a House of Commons debater.

Parliamentary success is a necessary condition for Cabinet survival, but it is far from the whole story. As a minister, and later as Prime Minister, Edward Heath was seldom an exciting Commons performer (he added public wit in the bitterness of his later years), but he could command the House because of his authority and competence. He was clearly on top of his brief. The same applied to Sir Geoffrey Howe, who was rarely memorable as a speaker, except, ironically, in his resignation speech in November 1990, after he had become a back-bencher following more than twenty-one years on the front-bench. Nigel Lawson became Chancellor of the Exchequer in June 1983 not because of his Commons performances, which were variable, but because of the force of his intellect and his views – with which Margaret Thatcher agreed at the time of his appointment, if not for much longer. In his case, he left the Government not because of any weaknesses in his parliamentary performances, where he appeared to relish sparring with John Smith, but because of his disagreements with Margaret Thatcher.

None the less, in the eyes of MPs and political commentators, performances in the Commons are critical to the reputation of ministers on the Westminster stock market. These can fluctuate considerably from year to year. John Moore enjoyed a short-lived time as a rising star in the mid-1980s in the view of some newspapers, though not that of political insiders. Kenneth Baker was a coming man, particularly in his own eyes, for much of the second half of the 1980s, before his reputation suffered during the downfall of Margaret Thatcher. John Major always sought to avoid being too much the fashionable figure, even turning down Margaret Thatcher's request to deliver the Conservative Political Centre lecture at the party conference in October 1988 for fear that he might attract too much attention too soon. In the end, of course, he got his timing exactly right.

A common feature of most Cabinet careers is that the successful minister is a generalist, not a specialist. Most rising junior and middle-ranking ministers move round a number of departments to gain experience and will not necessarily enter the Cabinet in a department where they previously served. There are exceptions. Both Nigel Lawson and Norman Lamont had served as Financial Secretary to the Treasury before becoming Chancellor, Lamont moving up, via Chief Secretary, to the top post. John Major was also Chief Secretary before becoming Chancellor, though, by contrast, Kenneth Clarke had no links with the Treasury before becoming Chancellor. Douglas Hurd was a minister of state at both the Home Office and the Foreign Office before becoming secretary of state in both departments. Overall, only six of the Cabinet which Mr Major formed after the April 1992 election had previously served in the departments of which they were secretary of state. That is true of past administrations, though following a change of government after an election the main spokesmen have generally been shadowing the departments they are then chosen to head, usually with only a couple of exceptions at Cabinet level. The value of that experience should not be exaggerated, since any shadow spokesman's knowledge is restricted by the lack of resources and knowledge possessed by opposition parties in Britain. Even in the 1990s with the so-called Short money financing research assistants for members of the Shadow

Cabinet, the opposition parties are at a big disadvantage compared with the government. They may have ideas but they seldom have the opportunity to assess their feasibility in practice which the Civil Service has. It is only six months before the final date of a general election that the Leader of the Opposition and his main spokesmen are, by convention, allowed to consult permanent secretaries.

The other feature of British Cabinets is the frequency with which ministers are shifted. In a paper for an Institute of Economic Affairs study (in Vibert, 1991), Professor Richard Rose estimated that the average length of time a politician heads a Whitehall department was just under two and a half years between 1964 and 1991. There has been little variation in this rate of turnover between governments of different parties and even since 1979, when there has been just one party in power. Reshuffles and forced resignations seem to be an inherent feature of British government quite separate from the operation of the electoral system. The greatest stability was for Prime Ministers and Lord Chancellors, who averaged 4.7 years each over twenty-seven years. Chancellors of the Exchequer were above average at three years each, though that would be higher but for the inclusion of Iain Macleod, who served only just over a month in 1970 before his death. The greatest turnover was in the departments dealing with trade and industry, which were merged, demerged and merged again over the period, leaving an average change of once every 1.3 years. However, in the eight years between the merger and the completion of the study, there were seven different secretaries of state – Parkinson, Tebbit, Brittan, Channon, Young, Ridley and Lilley. After the 1992 election, Michael Heseltine became an eighth in nine years. Moreover, secretaries of state in Transport, Employment and Environment held their posts for an average of less than two years over the whole period. The turnover of under-secretaries and ministers of state was even more rapid.

There are many reasons for the relatively short time which
most Cabinet ministers remain in charge of departments.
Some do not measure up to the job and have to be moved,
or sacked. In other cases, ministers make themselves unpopular with the department's client groups. This led, for instance, to the switch of Tony Benn and Eric Varley between
the departments of Industry and Energy in the summer of
1975. In other cases there are policy disagreements. During
Margaret Thatcher's eleven and a half years as Prime Minister, eight ministers resigned, whether because of a dispute
over policy (for instance, Michael Heseltine, Nigel Lawson
and Sir Geoffrey Howe), because of an apparent policy failure (Lord Carrington and Humphrey Atkins over the Falklands), because they had lost the confidence of their colleagues (Leon Brittan over Westland) or because of personal
failings (Cecil Parkinson and Nicholas Ridley). Others decided to retire from the Cabinet voluntarily, and some left
because of ill-health. Margaret Thatcher also sacked a
number of ministers with whom she grew out of sympathy,
like Sir Ian Gilmour, Francis Pym and John Biffen. In other
cases changes were made because she felt a new minister
was needed in an area of greater political priority, such as
Kenneth Baker's shift to become Education Secretary in May
1986 and the splitting of the Department of Health and
Social Security in July 1988, with Kenneth Clarke taking
over the health side. She was also conscious of the need to
promote talented middle-ranking members of the Government. In most of these changes, the impact on the departments concerned seems to have been secondary to the priorities of party management.

As Professor Rose argues:

By the standards of most leading positions in British society, the rate
of turnover of Cabinet ministers is very high. A managing director of
a leading company would expect to spend half a dozen years in the

post, and a bishop often remains in place for a decade or more. In universities, a professor may be a department head for only a few years, but each academic devotes thirty to forty years to mastering a single field of knowledge.

Admittedly, civil servants often move from post to post every two or three years, but that is often within the same ministry, where they spend most of their careers. So they will have learned many of the ways in which a department functions. Moreover, permanent secretaries and deputy secretaries tend to spend a longer time in their posts.

An equally telling comparison is with experience overseas. The Blondel and Thiebault study quoted above shows that the average duration of Cabinet ministers in Britain of 2.5 years from 1945 to 1984 was higher than in Belgium, France since 1958 and Italy, but lower than in Germany, the Netherlands and most of Scandinavia. Professor Rose makes the fair point that 'the lower rate of turnover there [in Sweden and Germany] is a reminder that coalition government is not necessarily a cause of frequent reshuffles between departmental posts. There is a distinction between stable and unstable coalitions, with the former guaranteeing ministers a longer stay in office than is normal in a single-party British government.' Before he retired in 1992, Hans-Dietrich Genscher had served as Foreign Minister in various Bonn Cabinets for half as long again as Margaret Thatcher was British Prime Minister.

The high rate of turnover in Britain raises the central question of how far Cabinet ministers are doing a good job. Of course, it partly depends on how the job is defined. Ministers combine several roles: head of a department making policy; being responsible to Parliament for its operations and decisions (the heavily qualified doctrine of ministerial responsibility); a department's chief spokesman to the public, not only in the Commons but also on television; and the department's leading representative within Whitehall in pressing its viewpoint and arguing for resources. These roles call for different qualities and talents. But the British system, with its concentration on picking ministers almost solely from the pool of talent available in the House of Commons, and judging them heavily by their performances in the Commons, stresses parliamentary rather than managerial abilities. British ministers are good at party management, and have to be if they are to survive, in spite of a number of obvious lapses over the years. British ministers have much less knowledge of the administrative workings of central government than many of their continental counterparts. Moreover, the rapid turnover of ministers means that they often have little chance to develop a detailed knowledge of their departments. John Major appeared to recognize their weakness after the April 1992 general election when he said that he did not intend to have regular reshuffles and expected his main departmental ministers to spend a long time in their posts. In general, British ministers are amateurs in running their departments and professionals primarily as politicians advancing their own careers.

Some political scientists are inclined almost to say, 'So what?' James Alt argues (in Herman and Alt, 1975) that the era of rapid turnover is not something that began in the mid-1950s: 'Lack of continuity has almost always been present, and has remained at its present level since around the turn of the century.' He is therefore sceptical about whether low continuity in ministerial posts has only recently come to have dangerous consequences for British politics. 'The sort of reasons that might be advanced include changes in the party system, the growth of mass electioneering, or the increase in government responsibilities, but each of these arguments would require a great deal of evidence in order to be convincing.' Valentine Herman, in the same study, argues: 'It does not appear to be the case that ministerial instability has a detrimental effect on the policy-making process. By and large government politics are continuous and lasting and are not unduly affected, at least in the short and medium runs, by a high rate of ministerial turnover.' He maintains that innovative policies are

much more likely to be brought about by changing social and environmental conditions than by a particular minister entering or leaving a department. Given the whole variety of political, social and economic restraints on the policy-making process, it appears most unlikely that the formulation and implementation of policies in Britain would be different in nature if ministerial stability were greater.

These conclusions seem too rosy given the record of British governments, especially since the Herman and Alt study appeared in the mid-1970s. The combination of high turnover and the importance of parliamentary performance means that ministers concentrate on the short-term. They respond to immediate problems and issues for the two to three years that they will be running a department, rather than looking ahead to questions which they know they will never have to tackle. Their priority is often to make a short-term reputation. The Confederation of British Industry was not alone in regarding the rapid turnover of ministers in charge of the Department of Trade and Industry as hardly conducive to a consistent approach by central government to business. This applied even though only one party was in office during the 1980s and the Cabinet ministers responsible for trade and industry were generally close allies of Margaret Thatcher. Yet each had his individual approach: one was more interventionist than another; one favoured the department having divisions into individual sectors; another scrapped this policy. It was all a mess. Similarly, the shambles of the Tories' policy towards local government finance in part reflected the succession of ministers at the Department of the Environment, each with their own ideas. Even those ministers proposing some of the Thatcher Government's most far-reaching changes in education, housing and health policy knew they would not be around to implement the legislation they introduced into the House of Commons. And none was. Instead, later ministers generally had to modify and adapt the plans of their predecessors. By the time his star had faded in the early 1990s, a popular Whitehall joke was the question, 'What is the worst Cabinet job?' Answer: 'The one Kenneth Baker last held.' Mr Baker's legacies at the departments of Environment and Education and as Conservative Party chairman did not always endear him to his successors in these posts.

Many of these complaints go back to the way that British ministers emerge – their lengthy apprenticeships in the House of Commons and their lack of experience outside Westminster politics. As Richard Rose has argued (1987):

Most ministers come to office with little or no experience of management in a large organization, such as a business, an educational institution, a hospital or a trade union. A politician is very much in a solo occupation. The skills needed to compete with other egoists in order to rise in a parliamentary party are not the same as those required to provide executive leadership in a large bureaucratic organization.

Looking back on his five years in the Cabinet, and his decade in Whitehall, Lord Young notes (1990) how little company he had from outside Westminster. 'I had come into government because I simply did not know that it was not done!' A few leading businessmen have acted as special advisers, while civil servants have gone on secondment to industry and commerce (though some have not returned, especially from the City). But very, very few have become ministers – which he regrets:

The French, the Americans, many of the other nations in Europe take a different view. There, a minister cannot be a member of their legislative assembly. If they are, then they have to resign before taking up their post. The Cabinet, all ministers, are open to all members of society. They have a full choice of all the talents. We have a closed shop. We say that, as a general rule, all our ministers, irrespective of party, must come from a small sample of some 600 who get elected to the Commons. They all have to serve a long apprenticeship, either as lobby fodder, or as a whip, or both, before they become junior ministers. By the time they are given charge of a department they have become part of a world apart. It does not help the understanding of all the processes of society. It is little wonder that all too many ministers for decades past have believed that they can communicate Government policy merely by making a speech in the House.

Lord Young has a point, but he exaggerates. He never fully appreciated the need to develop Westminster skills in order to persuade people and to deal with their doubts. Indeed, drawing a large number of senior ministers from outside the Commons would undermine one of the main functions of that chamber, as a training ground for ministerial office. That would in turn weaken Parliament and discourage talented people from becoming MPs, since the possibility of becoming a minister is one of the main reasons for becoming a candidate. While there may be some scope to bring in more policy-makers from outside the Westminster closed shop – whether as members of the House of Lords or as special advisers – the real issue is how to improve the quality and range of experience of those in the House of Commons. At present, the British political system is well designed to produce career politicians and Cabinet ministers who know how to operate in the House of Commons. It does not necessarily produce politicians who have a wider understanding of the world outside Westminster.

8

ON TOP OF THE POLE

'"Yes," he said to friends who congratulated him, "I have climbed to the top of the greasy pole."'

Benjamin Disraeli, on becoming Prime Minister,
27 February 1868

'At 3.30 Lord Stamfordham [George V's Private Secretary] was announced. With some embarrassment he explained that the King had decided to send for Mr Baldwin. Curzon insisted that so ludicrous a decision should immediately be reversed. Lord Stamfordham explained that at that very moment Mr Baldwin was being received at Buckingham Palace. Curzon gasped. The dream of his life-time lay shattered at his feet. Lord Stamfordham left him. In an agony of mortification he collapsed into a chair. Lady Curzon tried to console him. He wept like a child. He had forgotten Baldwin. Nobody had ever thought of Baldwin. "Not even a public figure," sobbed Curzon. "A man of no experience. And of the utmost insignificance." He repeated: "Of the utmost insignificance."'

Harold Nicolson, *Curzon: The Last Phase*, 1934

'Attlee held on long enough to make it impossible – well, very difficult – for Morrison to succeed. One of the cruel things in politics in opposition is that you've always got to add three years or four years, or whatever the rest of a Parliament's life is, to any man's age, because that's the time he would have to form, if he won, the Government for five years. You've then got to add nine years to his age. If you're going to judge people by that standard, then Gaitskell was the only possible one, or at any rate the only possible one to beat Nye Bevan. It was that that got Gaitskell the votes. Lots of people wanted to beat Nye Bevan, but weren't quite sure between Gaitskell and Morrison. The age factor was the determining thing.'

Patrick Gordon Walker, in Alan Thompson, *The Day Before Yesterday*, 1971

In August 1988 Market & Opinion Research International conducted a poll for *The Economist*, asking people whether they could name sixteen leading politicians on the basis of their photographs. Some 78 per cent recognized Mrs Edwina Currie, then parliamentary under-secretary for health, shortly before her downfall over eggs. Some 60 per cent or more knew who Michael Heseltine, Nigel Lawson and Cecil Parkinson were. A handful of voters even recognized a number of then ministers of state like David Mellor, John Patten, Angela Rumbold and William Waldegrave. Bottom of the list, recognized by just 2 per cent, was John Major, Chief Secretary to the Treasury, who had then been in the Cabinet for nearly fourteen months. When the sample was asked whether they had previously heard of the same politicians by name, John Major's recognition improved to 14 per cent, but he was still at the bottom of the list by a fair margin. All but three of his other colleagues had been heard of by more than half the sample. But two and a quarter years later John Major was Prime Minister.

Mr Major's rise was less of a surprise to political insiders at Westminster. After Mr Major became Prime Minister, Robert Atkins, an old friend since their days in the Greater London Young Conservatives in the 1960s, recalled (1991) that when the Blue Chip group, formed by some of the new MPs elected in 1979, first started to meet

there was always the thought in our minds that either John Major or Chris Patten might end up as leader of our party. But there was no idea about timing and no question of plotting. They were the bright men of our generation. Both John and Chris stood out as people who had immense ability, had the common touch, were able to articulate in differing ways their views of society and what they wanted to achieve, and had the driving ambition to want to do something, whether it was Prime Minister or not.

These two looked the rising stars of their generation during most of the 1980s, though John Major entered the Cabinet two years before Chris Patten.

The possibility that John Major might one day be a contender for the Tory leadership first crystallized in the summer of 1986, after the Westland crisis, when he was still an undersecretary. According to Robert Shepherd's comprehensive account (1991), John Major, Robert Atkins and their wives were taking a holiday aboard a narrowboat cruising through the English countryside. The two men chatted at the stern, steering and listening to the radio commentary on the test match. 'Atkins recalls that they were talking over their prospects when they suddenly realized that Major was "in the frame" and "John first saw the possibility that he might become the Prime Minister one day."'

John Major began to be treated as a rising star once he entered the Cabinet in June 1987. However, only after he became party leader more than three years later did it become known that Nigel Lawson, one of his patrons at the time, had had doubts. Lawson has written (1992) in his memoirs:

For a time after the 1987 election I was concerned that I might have made the wrong choice of Chief Secretary after all – a view I suspect was shared by John Major himself. He found the job far more difficult than anything he had ever done before, and had to work very hard to try and master it. He would come and see me at Number 11, ashen-faced, to unburden himself of his worries and to seek my advice. Before too long, however, he was thoroughly on top of the job.

None of these doubts surfaced publicly at the time. Typical of the assessments of Mr Major then was a profile I wrote in April 1988 (included in Jenkin, 1990):

After four years as a whip and social security minister, when his abilities were recognized mainly by Westminster insiders, in the last few months Mr Major has become a fashionable figure ... He understands that this year's fashions do not necessarily last, and he still has some way to go to establish himself as one of the Cabinet heavyweights. Talk of him becoming Chancellor after Mr Lawson is premature ... After another year or so at the Treasury his more likely future is running a big spending department – possibly the environment or health and social security. Still aged only forty-five, he has plenty of time on his side and is likely to be at the top of the Conservative Party until well into the next century.

At almost exactly the same time the *Independent* newspaper carried out a survey of 100 Tory MPs about the party's future leadership. Asked who they would support if Margaret Thatcher went then, 40 per cent said she was not going, had no view or regarded the contest as wide open. Some 12.5 per cent mentioned Michael Heseltine, then on the back-benches; 12 per cent backed Sir Geoffrey Howe; 10.5 per cent supported Kenneth Baker; and 9.5 per cent favoured Norman Tebbit. John Major barely registered. When the MPs were asked who they would support if Margaret Thatcher left after the next general election, 45.5 per cent replied that it was too soon to say. Some 14.5 per cent backed Michael Heseltine and 14 per cent favoured Kenneth Baker, while John Major won the support of 9.5 per cent. This struck the author as the most striking finding. He argued that John Major's popularity rested on his working-class, made-it-on-his-own background. 'He is, like Tebbit, wholly untainted with the old patrician Toryism that many newer Tory MPs are dedicated to destroying. Supporters see Mr Major as representative of the new classless Tory Party.'

Events, however, have a habit of moving faster than cautious profile-writers, or even MPs, assume. I remember talking to a senior Tory whip in the committee corridor of the Commons in summer 1988 when John Major joined us briefly after completing a session of the standing committee on the Finance Bill. After he had left, the whip remarked, 'John does not

know how lucky he is. He is in the ideal position to become
our next leader.' He argued that most of the obvious Thatcher-
ites, like Norman Tebbit and Cecil Parkinson, had ruled
themselves out; the time of Nigel Lawson, then Chancellor,
and Sir Geoffrey Howe, then Foreign Secretary, had passed;
Douglas Hurd was too traditional to appeal to the new generation of Tory MPs; and Chris Patten, not yet in the Cabinet,
was seen as too left-wing. That left Mr Major. You would
have got very good odds on Mr Major then and, indeed, right
up to the leadership contest in November 1990. Neither the
shrewd Tory whip nor I then had the slightest idea that
Margaret Thatcher would be deposed during the course of
that Parliament.

John Major's arrival in 10 Downing Street shows that the
key to getting to the top of the greasy pole is timing. This
applies throughout a career, to Mr Major when he became
Chief Secretary rather than Chief Whip in June 1987, as much
as when a leadership election occurs. The successful candidate
is not necessarily inherently better than his defeated rivals –
whatever that may mean – but he, or once she, is in the right
place at the right time. Or, as Jo Grimond put it: 'The trick of
being a "good" leader is to be on stage when the audience is
ready to like your sort of performance.' Clement Attlee would
never have become Labour leader in 1935 but for his success in
holding on to his east London seat during the whirlwind
which hit the party in 1931. He then became deputy leader of
the rump of MPs which survived the election after the formation of the National Government. That in turn made him a
plausible candidate to become leader after many of the party's
stars returned to the Commons following the 1935 general
election and the hapless George Lansbury was brushed aside.
Attlee was able to beat Herbert Morrison and Arthur Greenwood, defeating the former on the second ballot by eighty-
eight votes to forty-eight. He remained Labour leader for
twenty years, the longest span of any party leader this century.

Little is predictable in the final ascent of the pole, especially when the previous leader is forced out of office. Only when a long-standing Prime Minister steps down, more or less voluntarily, does the obvious heir apparent usually take over. But when there is a fierce contest for the succession, the winning candidates have often not been those initially favoured by the public in opinion polls. In October 1963 the then Lord Home was the least popular of eight candidates listed in a Gallup poll. Two years later Reginald Maudling was clearly favoured over Edward Heath even just before Tory MPs voted on the leadership. In November 1990 John Major came fifth out of six possible successors to Margaret Thatcher in a poll taken just before the first ballot. As R. M. Punnett (1992) points out, 'like Heath in 1965 and Mrs Thatcher in 1975 (and, indeed, like Home in 1963, Macmillan in 1957 and Baldwin in 1923), Major triumphed over candidates who initially seemed to be much more likely winners. To that extent the Conservatives played to form in 1990.'

Chance and luck both play large parts. Death or fatal illness led to Asquith taking over from Campbell-Bannerman, Baldwin from Bonar Law, and Harold Wilson from Hugh Gaitskell. For instance, one of the dominant Tory figures of the 1940s was Oliver Stanley, who had had Cabinet experience from the mid-1930s onwards, was a formidable debater and was as highly regarded at the time as either Butler or Macmillan. In the view of his contemporaries he might well have become Tory leader. But he died in 1950 aged fifty-four.

There is no common pattern to the battles for the party leadership and 10 Downing Street. About the only general rule is that those who have been heirs apparent for many years subsequently fail in office. Arthur Balfour, Neville Chamberlain and Anthony Eden succeeded to the premiership by virtual acclamation, but they all showed fatal flaws as leaders and were forced out of office in humiliating circumstances. Perhaps waiting so long under their distinguished predecessors,

Salisbury, Baldwin and Churchill, had dulled their edge and made them less effective. Perhaps also the underlying tensions within their parties which had been previously suppressed were bound to come to the surface after a change. Whatever the reasons. Balfour was the longest-serving with three and a half years in Downing Street, plus another five and a half years as party leader. Chamberlain managed just under three years as Prime Minister, while Eden, who never settled, was out of office in twenty-one months. By contrast, those who succeeded after bitter leadership contests often served for a long time – Baldwin, Macmillan, Wilson and Thatcher. But there are exceptions – Asquith succeeding the dying Campbell-Bannerman with no dissent.

The main formal requirement to become Prime Minister is to be in a position to assure the monarch that your government can command a majority in the House of Commons. That normally means that you are already a leader of a party, usually the one with a majority of seats in the Commons, or at any rate the largest number. There have been a handful of unusual exceptions. Since 1923, and the rejection of Curzon, it has also been accepted that a peer cannot become Prime Minister. Lord Home only entered 10 Downing Street in October 1963 once he had announced his intention to disclaim his peerage and to seek early election to the Commons. Fortunately, a convenient by-election was available and George Younger, the selected candidate, stood down. So, in practice, the key procedures are those of the individual parties despite all the mumbo-jumbo of the Royal prerogative. That is so much nonsense which was generally invoked in the past to cloak political manoeuvrings by one group in the Cabinet against others, as Harold Macmillan used with advantage in October 1963. Even that no longer applies. Since 1965 all the main parties have relied on varying methods of election to produce their party leaders, even if a vacancy occurs when the party is in government.

These formal procedures matter since they affect the relative positions of incumbents and challengers. The rules have changed considerably in the past thirty years, leading certainly to greater openness and perhaps to greater competitiveness. The Conservatives had traditionally relied on consultations among party leaders to produce their leader, or, before the First World War, their leaders, since they tended to have one in the Lords and one in the Commons. In 1957 the views of the Cabinet were formally sought on the choice between Harold Macmillan and R. A. Butler. This was sometimes, as in 1963, buttressed by unscientific consultations among MPs, peers and leaders of the voluntary party outside Parliament. These procedures were ideally suited to manipulation by the 'Magic Circle', as Iain Macleod vividly dubbed it. The very public row over the 1963 leadership contest led to the introduction of a system of election by MPs, used in 1965, 1975, 1989 (with Sir Anthony Meyer's unsuccessful challenge) and 1990.

Labour MPs elected their leader until the 1981 change to the party's constitution. Indeed, until 1978 the leader was described as the Leader of the Parliamentary Party. The title was then changed as a foretaste of the later alteration in the method of election. After much complicated manoeuvring, which triggered the formation of the SDP in early 1981, Labour introduced an electoral college with the MPs having only 30 per cent of the votes, the same proportion as local constituency parties, as against 40 per cent for trade unions. This system was used for the deputy leadership contest in September 1981 (when Denis Healey narrowly defeated Tony Benn), for the leadership elections of 1983 (when Neil Kinnock succeeded Michael Foot), for the unsuccessful challenge of 1988, and in July 1992 (when John Smith took over). During the late 1980s the Labour leadership required local parties to conduct ballots of their members and encouraged unions similarly to consult widely on the views of members. The Liberals moved in 1976 from election by MPs to a weighted system of voting by members of the party (the weights in part reflecting the success of a local constituency party in elections). Under this system, David Steel defeated John Pardoe for leader. After much debate, the SDP decided to elect its leader by a ballot of party members, leading to the election of Roy Jenkins over David Owen in the summer of 1982. This system was then adopted by the merged party, the Liberal Democrats.

The size of the electorate involved in picking party leaders has increased as a result of each of these changes. But ignoring indirect participation via the trade union block vote, at maximum only about 1 to $1\frac{1}{2}$ per cent of the total adult electorate was even involved in Labour's July 1992 leadership contest, when there was the widest consultation among party and union members so far. It is, of course, merely a tiny fraction when just MPs are involved, as is still the case with elections for the Conservative leadership. This is much smaller than in, say, America, where all voters registered as supporters of a party and even some independents, depending on the law of the individual state, can vote in a primary election to choose a candidate. Turnout can be very low – 30 per cent or less – but the total involvement in the choice is still much larger than under the British system.

The broadening of the selectorate might have resulted in different leaders being elected. Punnett argues that the details of the method of selection have often been decisive in determining who achieves success. For instance, Lord Home would probably not have emerged under any system other than the 'Magic Circle' process of consultation used in 1963. By contrast, Margaret Thatcher would almost certainly never have become leader under the old system, since the vast majority of the Shadow Cabinet believed that Edward Heath should remain as party leader, as did party activists in the country. But Mr Heath had lost the confidence of Tory MPs.

The Tory Party's rules have been seen as loaded against incumbents, since on the first ballot a winning candidate needs to win both an overall majority and also 15 per cent more of the total number of votes cast than any other candidate. If these quite tight conditions are not satisfied then a second ballot is held, when other candidates are allowed to enter. An incumbent leader therefore has to win the backing of a clear majority of the party's MPs if he or she is not to be forced into a second ballot. Failure to surmount the 15 per cent would be seen as a major, and possibly fatal, blow to the existing leader's standing, as proved to the case in November 1990, when Margaret Thatcher was persuaded to withdraw after narrowly failing to win outright on the first ballot. Moreover, the provision allowing other candidates to enter on the second ballot provides a freedom of manoeuvre, both to the electorate of Tory MPs and to potential challengers. Tory MPs wanting to get rid of the existing leader can vote for the challenger on the first round, hoping that their favoured standard-bearer will enter on the second round.

In the 1975 contest, some of Margaret Thatcher's campaign team persuaded MPs to vote for her on the first ballot to ensure that there would be a second ballot, when someone like Willie Whitelaw would be able to enter. This ruse worked spectacularly. She not only knocked Edward Heath out of the contest on the first ballot, winning 130 votes against 119 for him, but built up such a strong position that she had the momentum to brush aside the previously much better known candidates on the second ballot, when she won an outright majority. She turned a protest vote into a victory margin. In 1990 Tory MPs managed to avoid that trap. Mrs Thatcher was denied victory on the first ballot, but Michael Heseltine was not then in a strong enough position, with 152 votes, against her 204, with sixteen abstentions, to ensure victory later in the contest. Indeed, his support dropped on the second ballot to 131, against 185 for John Major and fifty-six for Douglas Hurd, the two new entrants then. A sizeable number of MPs voted for Mr Heseltine on the first ballot to get rid of

Mrs Thatcher and then changed their votes when the choice was widened. It is a complicated exercise to ensure that the incumbent does badly enough on the first ballot to have to pull out, but that the challenger does not do so well that he or she has an undefeatable lead against new entrants.

The bias against incumbents in these rules should not be exaggerated, since Edward Heath was party leader for nearly ten years and Margaret Thatcher was for nearly sixteen years with only one fringe challenge before her defeat. The rules ensure that unpopular leaders can be removed – perhaps part of the key to the Tories' success in remaining in office for so long. All this is, however, only possible thanks to the 15 per cent threshold and the permutation of candidates that permits.

None of these manoeuvrings would be possible under Labour's simpler rules, requiring a series of ballots, eliminating those at the bottom of the poll, to find a candidate who can win an overall majority. Labour does not allow any new entrants on later ballots, so close associates of a leader who would be reluctant to stand at first because of ties of loyalty are effectively ruled out, unless the incumbent can be persuaded to stand down before a vote occurs. This has had the effect of protecting existing leaders, who have, in general, easily been able to see off challenges by candidates outside the main leadership, as when Neil Kinnock crushed the challenge from Tony Benn in 1988. Hugh Gaitskell was the last Labour leader to face a challenge to his position from prominent colleague – Harold Wilson in 1960 (whom he defeated by a margin of two to one) and Anthony Greenwood in 1961 (whom he beat by an even bigger majority). Consequently, Labour leaders have stepped down more or less of their own accord, to general surprise in the case of Harold Wilson in 1976, though party divisions and continued electoral defeats persuaded James Callaghan, Michael Foot and Neil Kinnock to stand down.

The impact of the extension of the franchise after 1981 from just MPs to the wider electoral college is difficult to estimate.

Jack Straw, a prominent member of Labour's Shadow Cabinet, has argued (1992) that the change has further entrenched the position of existing leaders. He cites the example of Michael Foot:

although there was, by early autumn 1982, the clearest recognition within the PLP that he, no less than the party, would not be done any service were he to lead it at the forthcoming election, there was no effective means by which he could be replaced. Had the old system [of election by MPs] been in place, there almost certainly would have been a contest in late 1982, and history might then have been a little different.

Each of the leaders elected over the period has received the support of a majority of MPs, but that may, in part, have been affected by the existence of the wider electoral college and by the public disclosure of how MPs had voted (in contrast to the previous secret ballots). Punnet (1992) argues:

Ironically, in the case of Michael Foot's election in 1980 the decisive factor was probably not the system that was in place, but the system which was about to be introduced. It is unlikely that Foot would have defeated Healey in a 'normal' Parliamentary Labour Party ballot. As the electoral college was about to come into operation, however, and as it was assumed that its composition would favour a left-wing candidate, some Labour MPs undoubtedly felt that it would be politic for the PLP to select the leader who would be most acceptable to those who would soon be in control of the electoral college.

Also, some Labour MPs who later defected to the SDP are widely believed to have voted for Michael Foot rather than Denis Healey in order to make a split and the establishment of the new party more likely.

In many respects, the striking feature is how little has changed with the broadening of the franchise to elect party leaders. MPs still exercise control over who stands and when a contest occurs, while ensuring that a candidate has to be an MP. Even with its electoral college, a candidate for the Labour leadership has to be supported by 20 per cent of the party's MPs. The Tories require the support of 10 per cent of MPs for a leadership contest to occur. That reflects the central thread running through this book – the primacy of Westminster and performance in the House of Commons in the British political system. Even if, as in the case of Labour and the Liberal Democrats, party members outside Parliament have a say, the initial screening process is by MPs. Their assessment on the basis of parliamentary performance over a long period will be critical in determining who are the candidates, and, to some extent, what support they attract, even from party activists in the country. Only with a broader involvement of party supporters, as in an American type of primary system, would different criteria come into play. General electoral appeal, especially on television, would be more important than performance in Westminster and Whitehall. Jack Straw (1992) has questioned the electoral college system, in part for its cumbersome and time-consuming nature, especially if Labour were in power at the time: 'The virtue of the old system [of election by MPs] was that accountability of the leadership was more direct, that elections were swift and that it was those closest to the key qualities required of a leader – namely ability in Parliament – who exercised the judgement about who should be leader.'

At present, the choice of who may compete to become leader of their party and Prime Minister is defined by the Westminster closed shop. This does not just mean that a candidate has to be an MP but, in practice, a likely winner also has to be a current member of the Cabinet or Shadow Cabinet. Neither of the conditions – to be an MP and a member of the existing national leadership – is required abroad, even in other countries with a parliamentary system. A number of Canadian national leaders have become members of the House of Commons in Ottawa only after they have been elected to head their parties by the memberships. But they have generally been provincial leaders and Prime Ministers. Similarly, in Australia Bob Hawke was a trade union leader rather than a member of the Canberra legislature for most of his career and entered Parliament only three years before he became leader of his party and Prime Minister in 1983. In Germany, candidates for Chancellor put forward by the main parties have often been prominent as leaders of their *Länder* rather than in the Federal Government in Bonn. Even in its wildest flights from reality in the early to mid-1980s, the Labour Party would never even have considered putting forward Ken Livingstone, then the popular leader of the Greater London Council, as the alternative Prime Minister to Margaret Thatcher.

But in Britain, among members of the Cabinet at least, it counted against Michael Heseltine in November 1990 that he had been on the back-benches for nearly five years. One of the main motives of the ministers who sought to persuade Margaret Thatcher to stand down after the first ballot was to prevent Mr Heseltine from winning the second ballot. About the only common cause ministers like Kenneth Clarke, Chris Patten and Malcolm Rifkind had with their beleaguered leader after the first ballot was that they wanted to stop Mr Heseltine. They sought to allow existing members of the Cabinet to enter the contest, which could not happen while she was still in the field. The under-appreciated point in her tearful statement to her Cabinet on Thursday, 22 November, was that she had concluded that party unity and the Tories' prospects of victory at the following election would be better served if she stood down in order to enable Cabinet colleagues to enter the leadership contest – as Douglas Hurd and John Major promptly did. She regarded this as a binding Cabinet decision and was annoyed when she heard that David Hunt, the Welsh Secretary, had promised his support to Michael Heseltine. She

rang Mr Hunt to remind him of her statement, but he said that
since he had been in Tokyo at the time he did not believe he
should be bound on such a political matter. However, in an
elaborate charade he agreed to ring Mr Heseltine to ask
whether he would release him from his pledge, presumably
expecting the answer no, which he duly received.

The only exceptions to this pattern have been Bonar Law
and Ramsay MacDonald, for differing reasons. Bonar Law
had resigned the leadership of the Conservative Party in 1921
on grounds of ill-health. He then returned as a back-bencher
to join in the Carlton Club revolt of October 1922 against the
Lloyd George coalition and Austen Chamberlain, his successor
as party leader. But Bonar Law was careful to be approved as
Conservative leader before taking over 10 Downing Street.
MacDonald, while leader of the Labour Party, became Prime
Minister in 1924, never having previously served as a minister
at any level. His opposition to the First World War had ruled
out his participation in the wartime coalition governments.
One of the few Prime Ministers not also the leader of his party
was Lloyd George, who, in December 1916 became the head of
a coalition government. The Liberals then split, with Asquith
remaining as party leader. But the idea of a leader above party
disappeared with the fall of the coalition. Similarly, for five
months in 1940, Neville Chamberlain remained as leader of
the Conservative Party while Winston Churchill was Prime
Minister. When deteriorating health forced Chamberlain to
step down, Churchill saw the importance of also becoming
party leader.

But that does not, of course, mean that all Cabinet ministers
are possible party leaders. As discussed in the previous chapter,
Cabinets are chosen to balance a variety of ideologicial, social,
regional and personal interests. Some are also going to be
good, solid workhorses, party men or efficient departmental
ministers, rather than potential contenders. Nearly half the
members of any Cabinet are never at any time likely to rise

higher, and probably never aspire to do so. But the other half, say around eight to ten, are generally people who were once leadership contenders, or who are either immediate threats to the existing leader or possible long-term future challengers. At any time what subsequently seem to be rather unlikely people are talked about at Westminster by MPs and journalists as possible party leaders. Most of this 'who should captain the test team' speculation is worthless, but it is a reminder of how fashions change. Attlee was several times under considerable party pressure, even in the aftermath of Labour's landslide victory in 1945, but he was protected by Ernest Bevin against the machinations of Dalton, Morrison and Cripps. During the Tory leadership crisis of 1963, there were five possible successors considered at one time or another – Butler, Hailsham, Maudling, Macleod and Heath – even before Home appeared on the scene, almost as an afterthought. Later, Harold Wilson was constantly worried about plots involving close colleagues like Roy Jenkins and James Callaghan. Either was a possible successor at various times during the late 1960s, as was the now largely forgotten Michael Stewart, the epitome of earnest Fabian decency.

Looking through the first Thatcher Cabinet in May 1979, there were nine past, current or future leadership contenders. Lord Hailsham had been involved in the 1963 leadership contest, Willie Whitelaw, Sir Geoffrey Howe and James Prior had all stood against Thatcher in February 1975, while Sir Keith Joseph's bandwagon was stopped by him in the autumn of 1974 after one of his outbreaks of candour. Whitelaw, Howe and Francis Pym were all possible successors to her during her first term, especially when she was forced to appoint Mr Pym as Foreign Secretary at the start of the Falklands conflict in 1982. Younger members of the Cabinet who were seen as possible long-term successors to Mrs Thatcher – nobody knew then how long she would last – included both Michael Heseltine and Peter Walker. And, once he had escaped the Scottish Office in January 1986, George Younger was occasionally talked of as a possible caretaker leader, like Michael Stewart had been twenty years earlier. But most of the rest of that Cabinet, such as Mark Carlisle, Humphrey Atkins, Nicholas Edwards and Norman St John-Stevas, never looked like possible leaders. John Nott, for a time regarded as a rising star, left, disillusioned, within just over three and a half years to build an alternative career in merchant banking in the City. Later, during the Thatcher years, Cecil Parkinson, Norman Tebbit and Nigel Lawson all had phases when they were mentioned, semi-seriously, as possible leaders. Kenneth Baker's star also twinkled in the late 1980s before he became tarnished, in part by his association as party chairman with the declining Margaret Thatcher. So he was no longer a serious runner by the time of the leadership contest. The only semi-contestants were Sir Geoffrey Howe and, after his resignation in January 1986, Michael Heseltine. But Sir Geoffrey had faded, worn down by her assaults, well before his resignation in November 1990. Meanwhile, Douglas Hurd and, after his quick moves to Foreign Secretary and Chancellor in 1989, John Major had emerged as possible inside runners.

These comments are inevitably tentative and reflect the common gossip of Westminster rather than firm statistical counts by the whips. They underline the amorphous way in which reputations rise and fall in the closed world of the Commons and how they change. It is all about how you stand at the time that a leadership contest occurs. In March 1976, for example, Denis Healey had just been involved in a bruising, and public, argument in the House of Commons with some prominent left-wingers which probably further weakened whatever slim chance he had of taking over from Harold Wilson. In his autobiography (1989), he acknowledges:

Wilson's resignation could not have come at a more inconvenient time for my chances of succeeding him. For some days I was determined not to run at all, rightly believing that my row with my left-wing colleagues, now widely publicized, would reduce my support to a derisory level. In the end pressure from my fellow ministers in the Treasury and from a range of back-bench MPs, combined with a distaste for appearing to run away from the contest, led me to change my mind.

James Callaghan, the successful candidate then, had avoided such divisive actions as Foreign Secretary.

An alternative perspective is to look at not why a handful succeed and become party leaders, but why others fail. D. R. Thorpe (1983) has considered this question in a fascinating study of those who never quite made it – the uncrowned Prime Ministers.

Their lives brought them very close to the premiership, but in each case they stumbled, as it were, on the threshold of 10 Downing Street and were denied ultimate power. Between high executive office and the supreme command is a great divide, the last rung as Iain Macleod called it, and the line of those who did not make the transition is long and varied.

He concludes: 'Perhaps the most important requirements for a successful assault on the last rung (over and above the political qualifications for the post, which Butler suggested were memory, energy, resourcefulness, asperity and experience) are patience, luck, opportunism, but above all the absence of enemies.'

Thorpe argues that those who are against you are more significant that those who are for you. He concentrates on three Tory uncrowned Prime Ministers – Austen Chamberlain, Curzon and Butler. All were stars from an early age. Partly because of his father, the great Joseph Chamberlain, Austen Chamberlain had been marked out as a coming man. After his election in 1892, the elderly Gladstone had reported to Queen Victoria that Austen Chamberlain was 'a person of whom high political anticipations may reasonably be entertained'. He was Chancellor of the Exchequer when he was forty, and became leader of the Conservative Party, but never Prime Minister. Similarly, Curzon was Viceroy of India when he was forty, and, after six years in Delhi, spent much of the rest of his life hoping to become Prime Minister. R. A. Butler became a junior minister when he was thirty and served in every Conservative Government and Tory-led coalition for the following thirty-two years, which meant that he spent twenty-six years of that period in office.

Negative choice, as Thorpe describes it, was especially important in the cases of Curzon and Butler. In both 1957 and 1963 a substantial number of Tory MPs made it clear that Butler was unacceptable to them. While many Cabinet ministers, especially the younger ones, preferred Butler in 1963, Harold Macmillan, the outgoing Prime Minister, was strongly opposed. At the end of the leadership contest in October 1963, Macmillan protested in his diary (possibly with posterity in mind, as Alistair Horne, 1989, notes) that it was 'quite untrue that I was determined to "down" Rab. It is true that of the three I would have preferred Hailsham, as a better election figure.' But he then revealed his true feelings: 'All this pretence about Rab's "progressive" views is rather shallow. His real trouble is his vacillation in any difficult situation. He has no strength of character or purpose and for this reason should not be PM.' Macmillan's real intentions were forcefully exposed by Iain Macleod in his rightly memorable *Spectator* article of January 1964 on the 'Magic Circle' after he had refused to serve in the Home administration. Macleod argued: 'The truth is that at all times, from the first day of his premiership to the last, Macmillan was determined that Butler, although incomparably the best qualified of the contenders, should not succeed him.' In that contest, many ministers and MPs also made known their strong opposition to the choice of Hailsham, especially after his histrionic performance at the Tory conference in Blackpool. Following the news that the sick Macmillan intended to stand down as Prime Minister, Hailsham dramatically announced at the end of a lecture that he was intending to disclaim his peerage. He wanted to take advantage of the legislation passed earlier that year as a result of Tony Benn's long campaign to enable those who inherited peerages to renounce their titles. Hailsham's behaviour and the resulting demonstrations resulted in a determination by many to stop him becoming Tory leader. The result was the emergence of the then Lord Home as a second choice.

Thorpe's thesis about negative choice can be applied more widely. Twenty-eight years after the 1963 contest, Margaret Thatcher was as determined to prevent Michael Heseltine succeeding her as Harold Macmillan had been to block R. A. Butler. After she withdrew from the contest herself, she was active in phoning round Tory MPs to rally support for John Major. Earlier, Hugh Gaitskell became Labour leader in 1955 in part because of a desire to stop Aneurin Bevan and Herbert Morrison. As the quotation from Patrick Gordon Walker at the beginning of the chapter underlines, Attlee held on as Labour leader long enough to make Morrison look too old to take over. He disliked Morrison, whom he regarded, on the basis of ample evidence, as disloyal and liable to divide the party. Attlee timed his departure in a way that helped ensure that Gaitskell would succeed him as leader. After Gaitskell's death, George Brown, the obvious right-wing candidate, faced strong resistance because of his unstable personality and behaviour. An anti-Brown feeling benefited Harold Wilson, then a somewhat ambiguous standard-bearer of the left. Denis Healey also never became Labour leader because of the strength of opposition to him among Labour MPs. In his own view (1989):

An important factor in my defeat [for the leadership in 1980] was the number of enemies I had made by the many unpopular measures I had been obliged to take as Chancellor ... When I was a student Communist one of the favourite topics for discussion was 'Who will do the dirty work under Socialism?' In later life I discovered that the answer was 'Denis Healey'. The Defence Ministry and the Treasury were regarded by Labour politicians as the graves of ambition. Nevertheless, I do not regret the political price I may have paid for my work as Defence Secretary and Chancellor; I have always been in politics in order to do something rather than to be something.

As important as negative choice has been a determination to win and succeed. Austen Chamberlain could have become Conservative Party leader in 1911 if he had really pressed, even though there would have been bitterness and divisions within the party. Again, in February 1922, when the coalition was facing trouble, Lloyd George offered to resign as Prime Minister in favour of Chamberlain. But he declined, even though it offered an opportunity to take the political initiative and reunite his party. But he believed that Lloyd George was the best available Prime Minister and wanted the coalition to continue. In different circumstances in May 1940, Lord Halifax, clearly favoured by the Tory establishment and by the King to take over from Neville Chamberlain, did not press his claims against Winston Churchill. This was, in part, because he was a peer. He also thought that Churchill might be the better Prime Minister to run the war effort.

A similar lack of single-minded ruthlessness has also proved fatal to later contenders, notably Butler. He could certainly have stopped Home in 1963 if he had acted decisively, and he had been promised support by several key Cabinet ministers on the critical evening. But he did not insist, as Macmillan may have assumed. Enoch Powell, who like Macleod refused to serve in Home's administration, comments (in Thompson, 1971), characteristically, about Butler's reluctance to strike then:

Certainly, for becoming a Prime Minister a man must be ready to shoot it out. He must be ready to see his rivals off, no matter how. He mustn't mind blood on the carpet. You see, Rab Butler had it in his hands. He could have had it for one shot and we gave him the weapon. We said, 'You see, Rab, look at this, this is a revolver; we've loaded it for you, you don't have to worry about loading it. Now you see this part here, it's the trigger, if you put your finger round that, all you have to do is to squeeze that and he's dead, see?' Rab said, 'Oh, yes, thank you for telling me, but will it hurt him, will he bleed?' We said, 'Well, yes, I'm afraid when you shoot a man he does tend to bleed.' 'Oh,' said Rab, 'I don't know whether I like that, but tell me something else, will it go off with a bang?' We said, 'Well, Rab, I'm afraid we must admit you know, a gun does make rather a bang when it goes off.' Then he said, 'Well, thank you very much, I don't think I will. Do you mind?'

Lord Hailsham was also involved in the discussions initially aimed at preventing Home from becoming Prime Minister. He recalls (1990) a meeting with Butler and Maudling:

I placed my cards on the table. I said that if we all declined to serve in it, Alec would not be able to form a government and that I no longer regarded myself as a candidate. But Rab then said that he had already given his word to Alec. I cannot remember what Maudling said. But it did not matter anyway. Ferdinand the bull had preferred to sniff the flowers rather than take what would have been his if he had wished it.

The absence of a sufficiently large blocking group of enemies and a single-minded determination to succeed are necessary conditions for election as a party leader and entry to 10 Downing Street. In the October 1963 case Butler and Hailsham suffered from the first and, in Butler's case, the second, leaving Home, to whom few really objected, as the beneficiary, even though he could not be regarded as ruthless. The balance of these factors also explained the success of Baldwin in becoming Prime Minister in 1923, Macmillan in 1957 and James

Callaghan in 1976. In other cases, leading politicians have failed to become Prime Minister because they have been unwilling to mount a challenge. As I suggested earlier, incumbents are in a strong position, especially in the Labour Party. That is why the average service of Prime Minister is longer than that of any other Cabinet minister. There have been only twenty-two leadership contests since the early 1920s, eleven for each of the main parties, and in only seven cases was the existing leader challenged. Prime Ministers and party leaders do not discourage this tendency.

Most party leaders are elected when the existing occupant steps down more or less voluntarily. Apart from the factors listed above, the key is to appear the right leader for the time – as, for instance, John Major did in November 1990. He looked the appropriate man to take the Tories on from the Thatcher era in a reasonably united way. Similarly, John Smith looked, both by experience and by position in the party, the obvious successor to Neil Kinnock in July 1992. In both cases, there was a mixture of continuity and contrast, keeping the party together while offsetting the faults of the previous leader. The appeal of John Smith was that he offered an intellectual self-confidence, precision and incisiveness which Neil Kinnock appeared to lack. But a person who looks the inevitable successor at one moment can soon fade, to be replaced by another politician more suited to the times. There has been a tendency, especially in the Labour Party, to pick the right general to fight the last battle.

In his memoirs, Roy Jenkins (1991) reflects on his opportunities to become Prime Minster. At times it seemed within his grasp. For instance, if the Labour Party had won the 1970 general election, he suggests that Harold Wilson might have resigned within two of three years, 'with a strong presumption that I would then have succeeded him'. But even after Labour's defeat in 1970, he accepts that he had the option of finessing the European issue, remaining as deputy leader and being well placed for the 1976 contest.

That I did not follow that course I do not regret. The inheritance had by then become a tawdry one, and I would have been through so many humiliating compromises that I would have lost any capacity to preside over a government with verve. There was also the possibility of attempting a pre-emptive strike, first in 1968 and then in 1972 or 1973. On the first occasion it was my primary duty to get on with the job of being a beleaguered Chancellor, and again I do not regret that I was not diverted. In 1972–3 it might have been better for the future health of the Labour Party had I challenged, but had I done so I might well have achieved just about the outcome that Michael Heseltine did in 1990. I half regret I did not do that, but not on grounds of ambition.

He notes that the last appearance of the will-o'-the-wisp was in 1981–2 when, after the initial success of the SDP, 'There was a brief flickering moment when Ladbrokes' odds made me the most likely person to be the next Prime Minister.'

Even in a mellow and retrospective mood, Roy Jenkins admits:

There is obviously a qualitative difference between being Prime Minister and occupying other great offices but not attaining the highest. It is not exactly a question of influence, for some non-prime ministerial politicians – Joseph Chamberlain, Ernest Bevin and R. A. Butler for example – put more imprint on British politics than did, say, Campbell-Bannerman, Anthony Eden or Alec Home. But there is nonetheless something in Melbourne's remark that 'It is a damned fine thing to have been, even if it only lasts for two months.' It puts one in a sort of apostolic succession of forty-nine men and one woman descending from Walpole, for which no amount of explaining how narrowly or even honourably it was missed is a compensation.

9

FAILURE

'His Majesty has thought proper to order a new Commission of the Treasury to be made out, in which I do not see your name.'

Lord North's letter to Charles James Fox, dismissing him from his administration, 1774

'All political lives, unless they are cut off in midstream at a happy juncture, end in failure, because that is the nature of politics and of human affairs.'

Enoch Powell on Joseph Chamberlain, 1977

'To this writer the story of men in political office is one of inevitable tragedy. After victory, defeat eventually will come. The lucky ones die in office. The rest suffer lingering suffocation as did both Asquith and Lloyd George.'

Bentley Gilbert, *David Lloyd George, Organizer of Victory, 1912–16*, 1992

Enoch Powell's haunting sentence – which says as much about him as it does about Joseph Chamberlain – expresses the ambiguities and melancholy of many political careers. Even if Powellite gloom about the nature of human affairs can be overdone, few political careers end as MPs would have wished. Loss of ministerial office after a reshuffle or after a government's defeat at a general election, and the loss of a seat in the Commons itself, mean that the rise up the ministerial ladder is often cut short involuntarily. However, even where the circumstances of removal from office or from the Commons are unwelcome, most politicians still look back with pride on what they have done. There is an acceptance that, along with the pain of defeat or of disappointment, they recorded some achievements and would not have pursued any other career. The degree of satisfaction with life in the Commons is higher among older MPs than middle-aged ones still facing up to the frustrations of a political life. Of course, most people in any career have to accept that their youthful ambitions will not be fulfilled, and they become reconciled to lesser achievements.

In politics, however, the end is often open and brutal. Politics is, after all, a career for the unusually ambitious. And while there are many prizes – in the junior and middle ranks of government or as a shadow spokesman – they are seldom retained for very long and there are many fewer prizes at the top. The process can appear arbitrary and talent may be rewarded only in occasional bursts. Loss of office, and indeed of your seat in the Commons, can be sudden and often unpleasant – though for those who do remain MPs there is no formal retirement age. This is unlike, say, permanent secretaries, who have to go at sixty. For many ex-ministers there is ermined exile in the House of Lords – a significant consolation for the failed, wounded and retired. Aside from the Lords, however, there is little of the cushion of other jobs, where executives in their fifties and sixties can gradually reduce their workloads and move towards retirement. In politics you are either in or out of office. In many respects that is good – a reminder that politicians are, both as members of the Commons and as ministers, at the whim of the electorate, who can, and do, dismiss them. Life should not be too secure or else there will be complacency and self-satisfaction, as affected some Tory ministers and MPs after their run of election victories from 1979 onwards.

Politics is an extreme example of an occupation – like sport or the performing arts – where life at the top can be relatively brief and the process of decline can be bruising. Just as there are few more embarrassing sights than a sportsman, a previous star player, trying to keep going at the top for just another season or two longer and failing, so the end can be humiliating for a politician on the way down and out. The reasons for the decline of a sports star or singer are usually physical – over-used and tired bodies and vocal cords. But in politics, while physical stamina is very important, and under-appreciated, the key is timing. Politicians generally have a period when their views, their faction and their party may be in tune with the times. But these factors seldom work in their favour for ever. A relative handful of politicians can survive the twists and turns to continue at the top for a long period.

Norman Tebbit and David Owen were both at the top as nationally known and influential politicians for almost the same period, from 1981 until 1987. This was when Norman Tebbit served in the Cabinet and David Owen was a dominant figure in the new Social Democratic Party, and then its leader for four years. Although he had been Foreign Secretary from 1977 until 1979, David Owen had not then been a national political figure. It was not until the formation of the SDP in 1981 and his own prominent role in the political debate over the Falklands war in 1982 that he became nationally prominent. Both men were products of the breaking, or at least the splintering, of the mould of British politics which occurred in the first half of the 1980s, caused as much by Margaret Thatcher as by the divisions within the Labour Party. They both spoke for the spirit of the times in their very differing ways – Norman Tebbit for the new, upwardly mobile support-ers of the Tory Party (to use the revealing title of his autobiogra-phy) and David Owen for those wanting, in his words, a tough and tender approach (tough on economic and foreign policy and tender on the welfare state). But after the 1987 general election, their time in the limelight came to an end. Norman Tebbit, who had been seriously injured in the 1984 Brighton bombing and whose wife had been left partially paralysed, decided to leave the Cabinet. He appeared at times disillu-sioned, in part with his leader, and was a discordant, if distinctive, voice on the back-benches for five years. David

Owen's career faded with the splitting of the original SDP after the merger with the Liberals in 1987–8 to form what became the Liberal Democrats. The disintegration of his own independent SDP, after a brief life, left him looking increasingly isolated. His voice seemed out of tune with the times, especially as the Thatcher era ended and the new Liberal Democrats revived. So he eventually accepted that his career as a Westminster politician was over.

William Waldegrave (1985) has suggested that most leading politicians have a finite period of real influence:

In politics everyone has fifteen years – putting aside the superstars – when their weight can really matter and they have enough experience to use it. But for the whole of that fifteen years you may be in opposition or the wrong section of your party may be in power. To go into politics in the way that I have done, or any of the people who want to be ministers, you have got to recognize that you are taking a gamble and you may just miss.

Mr Waldegrave may even have exaggerated the period of influence of most politicians, whether or not his or her party is in government or opposition. This is best measured by the period a politician is in a Cabinet or Shadow Cabinet. This has applied even if a party is in power for a longer period. As pointed out in Chapter 7, the rate of turnover of Cabinet ministers was as high during the Thatcher years as in earlier periods, when governments moved in and out of power more often.

Members of the Thatcher Cabinets served at that level for an average of just over eight years, including earlier service as members of the Shadow Cabinet or the Heath Cabinet. That average was, of course, boosted by the thirty years which Lord Hailsham enjoyed as a Cabinet minister, from the Macmillan era up to when he was dropped as Lord Chancellor after the 1987 general election. Sir Keith Joseph had twenty-four years as member of the Cabinet and Shadow Cabinet under four

Tory leaders. Margaret Thatcher managed twenty-three years, Willie Whitelaw twenty-two years, Peter Walker twenty years (not all continuous), Lord Carrington nineteen years and Sir Geoffrey Howe eighteen years. But more typical were the eight years of Michael Jopling (including his period as Chief Whip), the seven years of John Nott or Sir Ian Gilmour and the six years of Norman Tebbit. A few had less than the life of a Parliament at the top level. Peter Rees managed barely two and a quarter years before being dropped and John Moore just over three years. Peers are regarded as even more dispensable, often surfacing for two or three years at the top level before disappearing into obscurity again. The same pattern has been true of earlier Cabinets. Of the twenty-three-strong Cabinet formed by Harold Wilson in 1964, only nine survived until the Labour defeat in June 1970. The higher-quality Cabinet formed by Harold Wilson in March 1974 proved to be more durable; some thirteen out of twenty-two were still in office when the Callaghan Government lost in May 1979.

Few of the departures are voluntary, in the sense of a minister leaving office feeling he or she has achieved all they want to do and being content to spend more time with their families (in the phrase immortalized by Norman Fowler in January 1990) and/or to pursue other interests. Of the eleven ministers who left the Wilson/Callaghan Cabinets between 1974 and 1979 (two of whom joined after March 1974), four retired voluntarily, one died in office (Anthony Crosland), one resigned because of a disagreement over policy (Reg Prentice) and the other five were in effect sacked, mainly when James Callaghan replaced Harold Wilson in Downing Street. Under Margaret Thatcher, fourteen ministers left voluntarily, sixteen were dropped or sacked, and eight resigned as a result of disagreements with her or because of their conduct in office. Margaret Thatcher had the flexibility provided by large Commons majorities to do largely as she wanted in her reshuffles. Even with the more limited scope of a small majority, John

Major felt he had to remove Norman Lamont as chancellor since he had become very unpopular.

Although many of those who have left office are seen as casualties, many go on to have a rewarding life, obtaining as much or more pleasure outside the Commons. As reported later in this chapter, Barbara Castle bitterly resented being dropped by James Callaghan, but she developed a successful second political career after 1979 as a member of the European Parliament. George Thomson left the Commons in his early fifties to become one of Britain's first Commissioners in Brussels and then had a successful career as chairman of the Independent Broadcasting Authority and on the boards of several companies. This was at a time when his contemporaries were suffering the frustrations of Labour's divisions. Others, on both sides of the Commons, have prospered in business – Anthony Barber and John Nott in banking, Richard Marsh at British Rail and Alf Robens at the then National Coal Board.

One of the often repeated myths of contemporary political comment is that ministers never resign nowadays unless forced out of office. The evidence from the above is rather to the contrary. Three of the Cabinet ministers who resigned during the Thatcher era did so because of disagreements over the conduct of policy with the Prime Minister (Michael Heseltine, Sir Geoffrey Howe and Nigel Lawson) and three (Lord Carrington, Humphrey Atkins and Leon Brittan) because of alleged failures in their record in office. The remaining two, Cecil Parkinson and Nicholas Ridley, left because of personal gaffes. There are no, nor have there ever been, clear guidelines about when, and why, a minister should resign, as shown by the refusals of Lloyd George and Rufus Isaacs to resign over dubious financial practices in the Marconi scandal in 1912. The alleged doctrine of responsibility by ministers to Parliament for the actions of their departments has been steadily redefined away from responsibility for administrative actions by subordinates, of which they are often ignorant, to the narrower definition of decisions specifically taken by ministers. But even here responsibility is in practice nebulous. The most famous example of a minister allegedly behaving honourably in accordance with the old textbook doctrine is Sir Thomas Dugdale's resignation in 1954 over the Crichel Down affair, a case of blatant maladministration by civil servants. But subsequent evidence has shown that the real reason Sir Thomas believed that he should resign is that he had lost the confidence of his fellow Tory MPs. Most resignations are for that reason rather than on grounds of some clear principle. As Cecil Parkinson (1992) makes clear in his memoirs, the reason he resigned in October 1983 was that he felt he 'had become a liability to the Government' and 'should resign'.

Nine years later David Mellor used similar language when he resigned as National Heritage Secretary in September 1992. This followed a two-month saga of allegations in the murkier tabloids about his affair with an actress and, much more significant in the end, revelations in a libel case about his acceptance, while a Cabinet minister, of very generous hospitality from the daughter of a prominent Palestine Liberation Organization fund-raiser and from a property developer. David Mellor insisted, and the Prime Minister accepted, that he had not breached any guidelines on the conduct of ministers, but he concluded: 'It is too much to expect of my colleagues in Government and in Parliament to have to put up with a constant barrage of stories about me in certain tabloid newspapers.' Mr Mellor's resignation coincided with a difficult time for the Major Government because of its forced decision to float the pound – in effect a devaluation. He said that one reason for his decision to leave was that, at a time when he would have liked to be seen as a tower of strength, he was 'perceived by some as a point of weakness'.

Only a minority of ministers return to government after a resignation, and, if they do, they seldom attain their previous heights of influence. The breach with the former leader and

Cabinet colleagues is often too great for previously close relationships to be re-established. Events have moved on, so the minister who has resigned looks like a figure from the past. Some ministers see themselves as indispensable and believe their departure will topple the sitting Prime Minister. But in most cases the immediate row is soon forgotten, as they are themselves. The classic example is Lord Randolph Churchill, who electrified Tory politics during the 1880s and was made Chancellor of the Exchequer by Salisbury in 1886. But in a failed attempt to assert his power within the Cabinet he resigned in a dispute over the defence estimates that December. He later said that he never thought his offer to resign would be accepted, as it was by Salisbury in a calm and unruffled manner, rather as Harold Macmillan dismissed the departure of Peter Thorneycroft and his Treasury team in 1958 as 'a little local difficulty'. Lord Randolph admitted a few days later that Salisbury had probably been glad to get rid of him. When talking about a possible successor, someone suggested the name of Goschen, a financial expert and a Liberal Unionist, and he said, 'I had forgotten Goschen', while scoffing at the idea. Later, after the latter had been appointed as Chancellor, Lord Randolph saw one of the people in the discussion and admitted, 'You were quite right; I forgot Goschen' (in Rhodes James, 1959). Lord Randolph never served as a minister again. Many politicians since then have thought they could call a Prime Minister's bluff and have forgotten that there are always Goschens around to take their places.

In many cases a resignation marks the culmination of a long period of disenchantment and tension, as seen, for instance, in the departures of Aneurin Bevan in 1951, George Brown and Ray Gunter in 1968, or of Michael Heseltine in 1986, Nigel Lawson in 1989 and Sir Geoffrey Howe in 1990. The minister gradually becomes more distanced from the Prime Minister and his or her senior colleagues. It is generally only those who have been forced to resign over a particular incident, while retaining the confidence of the Prime Minister, who have returned. Sam Hoare was back in the Cabinet, as First Lord of the Admiralty, just six months after having to resign as Foreign Secretary over his pact with Pierre Laval. Similarly, Hugh Dalton was back in the Attlee Cabinet, if only as Chancellor of the Duchy of Lancaster, within six months of resigning as Chancellor of the Exchequer over a Budget leak. Dalton remained a very important figure within the Labour Party for some years.

These experiences have been typical of those former Cabinet ministers who have returned to office after resigning. Of the twenty-one Cabinet ministers since 1945 who have resigned because of a policy disagreement, their conduct in office or a personal matter, only six have later returned to office. And just one has come back to a more senior post than the one from which he resigned. The exception was Harold Wilson, who left the Attlee Cabinet in 1951, along with Aneurin Bevan and John Freeman, in the row over Hugh Gaitskell's Budget proposals and health service charges. His next ministerial post, more than thirteen years later, was as Prime Minister. The others who returned – Hugh Dalton, Peter Thorneycroft, Reg Prentice, Cecil Parkinson and Michael Heseltine – all accepted less senior jobs, in Mr Prentice's case at minister of state level in a government of a different party – Tory rather than Labour. Mr Heseltine moved sideways since he resigned as Defence Secretary and returned in November 1990 as Environment Secretary, a post he had previously occupied up to January 1983. Along with Harold Wilson and Anthony Eden from an earlier era, Mr Heseltine is one of the few ministers not to have disappeared into obscurity on the back-benches after his resignation. All three returned to office only because of changed circumstances. Anthony Eden was brought back by Neville Chamberlain when the Government was broadened in September 1939 at the start of the Second World War. Harold Wilson had to wait for a full turn of the electoral cycle before returning to office, though he was a leading member of the

Shadow Cabinet for most of Labour's years in opposition. Michael Heseltine's return, after nearly five years on the back-benches, occurred when John Major replaced Margaret Thatcher in November 1990.

There are also rare cases when ministers step aside, more or less voluntarily, and then return, but again not usually to their previous seniority. The most unusual instance in recent years has been Peter Brooke, who left the Cabinet after the April 1992 general election. This was generally regarded as the end of his ministerial career after thirteen years as a whip and minister, including two and three-quarter years as Northern Ireland Secretary. He then unsuccessfully sought to become Speaker of the Commons, but was widely seen as rather old-style, and he was defeated by Betty Boothroyd. But within less than six months he was back in John Major's Cabinet as National Heritage Secretary after the resignation of David Mellor in September 1992.

In the mid-1960s, Patrick Gordon Walker was in the unusual position of being a Foreign Secretary without a seat in the Commons for three months after he had been defeated at Smethwick in the October 1964 general election. He had to resign the following January after he was again beaten in a by-election specially created for his benefit at Leyton. He subsequently won back the seat in the March 1966 general election. He returned to the Government and the Cabinet in January 1967 as Minister without Portfolio, and then for eight months as Education Secretary, before finally leaving office in April 1968 without anyone noticing. After his brief period as Foreign Secretary, he never regained his former authority or prominence after he returned to the Commons.

Comebacks are always difficult, even when it is a matter of returning to the Commons rather than to ministerial office. Roy Jenkins left the Callaghan Government and Westminster politics in the autumn of 1976 to take a four-year spell as President of the European Commission. His return could not

have been more spectacular, since he was one of the Gang of
Four who launched the Social Democratic Party in the spring
of 1981. He fought, and narrowly lost, the Warrington by-
election that July, remained in the limelight during the SDP's
rise for the rest of that year and returned to the Commons
after the Glasgow Hillhead by-election in March 1982. But, as
he has himself admitted, he never regained the command over
the Commons which he had enjoyed in his prime in the late
1960s and 1970s. In part, it may have been because he himself
had changed; in part, it may have been because of his rivalry
with David Owen; in part, it may have been the open hostility
of his former colleagues in the Labour Party; and, in part, it
may have been the changed nature of the Commons itself. Roy
Jenkins himself says he found it difficult to adjust to not
speaking from the dispatch box. He was used to the sense of
command – and the cheering troops behind him – which he
had when on the front-bench. But whatever the reason, Roy
Jenkins made much less impact returning to the Commons
than he did, at least for a time, on British politics as whole.
On a less elevated level, many other former MPs who return
after a gap of several years, perhaps a couple of general
elections, remark on how difficult it is to adjust. The character
of the Commons changes and develops.

The most well-publicized ends to careers are of Prime Ministers. Of the eighteen this century (excluding John Major), only
five went voluntarily, largely on grounds of health and age –
Salisbury, MacDonald, Baldwin, Churchill and Wilson. And
Churchill, the oldest of the lot, went only after a lengthy
struggle by his colleagues to prise him out of office and in spite
of serious, and justified, misgivings on his part about his
successor, Eden. A further four left office either because of
terminal illness or ill-health – Campbell-Bannerman, Bonar
Law, Eden and Macmillan – though in Eden's case he would
probably have been forced out of the premiership anyway. Of
the remaining nine, four – Attlee, Home, Heath and Callaghan

– left Downing Street because their party was defeated at a general election, and Balfour resigned ahead of an almost certain defeat. That leaves four – Asquith, Lloyd George, Neville Chamberlain and Margaret Thatcher – who were removed from office as a result of internal party revolts. In all, less than a third of this century's Prime Ministers left office happily at the time of their choosing.

Defeat at a general election can be brutal enough, but even more so when it is precipitated by defeat in the House of Commons, as happened memorably in March 1979 when the Callaghan Government was beaten by a single vote on a no-confidence motion. In a brilliant piece of descriptive writing from his insider's viewpoint as a Tory MP, just over a year later Robert Rhodes James (1980) recalled the mood and scenes in an article for the *Listener*. After the vote was announced, there was bedlam:

Margaret then rose to ask the Government's intentions, and Callaghan announced an immediate general election with a defiant confidence and spirit that one could only admire. A group of Labour back-benchers began to sing 'The Red Flag' somewhat reedily; there was a sporadic and swiftly doomed attempt from our side to respond with 'Land of Hope and Glory' . . .

In the Lobby there were wild scenes. Bitter enemies, although nominal colleagues, virtually hugged one another. A Conservative peeress was startled to be much kissed. Margaret went to the Whips' Office for champagne and was greeted with a roar of exultation from her exhausted aides.

Ironically, the one occasion when a Prime Minister in late middle age left voluntarily has also been the source of the greatest mystery. When Harold Wilson stepped down aged sixty in March 1976, many politicians and commentators wondered why. The public explanation that he had always said he would do so two years after returning to Downing Street somehow did not seem sufficient to many people. There must therefore have been some deeper, more sinister reason, and many conspiracy theories have been born. But Wilson's earlier promise, and tiredness of the infighting in Downing Street and the Labour Party, seem reasonable and plausible. Ben Pimlott (1992) discusses in detail the various theories for Wilson's departure and concludes: 'The conspiracy theories that have been designed to solve what some have seen as the riddle of Wilson's early retirement do not add up. The straightforward explanation for his departure, that he left because he had lost the desire to carry on, requires no amplification.'

In most cases, the incumbent Prime Minister loses his or her previous sure political touch. That happened in the cases of both Asquith and Margaret Thatcher. There are striking similarities between the events of December 1916 and of November 1990. Both Prime Ministers had lost the confidence of close Cabinet colleagues – in Asquith's case over the conduct of the war and in Thatcher's over policy towards Europe. But at the heart of the problem were doubts about their political judgement in running the Government. What cost both Asquith and Thatcher the premiership was less the conspiracies and intrigues against them than their own failings. In their very differing ways, they both believed they had become indispensable and had forgotten that they were mortal. Both were also given poor advice. Bentley Gilbert (1992) comments:

Asquith, the bastion and fortress of Liberalism, contrived his own demise, not for tiring of, but for loving too well, the office he held. When confronted with a man who would do anything to win a desperate war he was helpless. In retrospect, one must conclude Lloyd George destroyed him easily. Perhaps Asquith's future monument might display not an arm holding an upraised sword, but a question mark.

John Grigg (1985) similarly argues:

The longer he stayed in the post the more natural and right it came to seem to him that he should occupy it. However tired he may have been in other ways, he was never tired of being Prime Minister. His attitude became increasingly proprietorial, and any suggestion that he should relinquish the office, or even a significant share of its power, was resented by him almost as a monarch might resent the threat of usurpation.

Yet a measure of flexibility on his part might have enabled him to stay in office, albeit with Lloyd George having a greater say in the running of the war.

Margaret Thatcher never contemplated defeat; in her famous phrase, she intended to go 'on and on'. But she centralized power in the hands of herself and the small staff around her, often ignoring advice. The ideal time for her to retire would have been May 1989, on her tenth anniversary of becoming Prime Minister, when she could have departed amid widespread praise and acclaim for what she had achieved in shaking up British social and economic attitudes. But by staying on she ensured that her end would be bloody and bitter. Not only did she press ahead with controversial measures, such as the poll tax, but she also fell out with close colleagues who had created what became known as Thatcherism alongside her, notably Nigel Lawson, who resigned in October 1989, and Sir Geoffrey Howe, whose resignation speech just over a year later precipitated her own downfall. It was appropriate that Sir Geoffrey, previously her most loyal and long-suffering colleague, should have plunged in the knife. As he said in his speech in the Commons on 13 November 1990:

The conflict of loyalty is between loyalty to the Prime Minister – and after more than two decades together the instinct of loyalty is still very real – and the loyalty to what I perceive to be the true interests of this nation. That conflict of loyalty has become all too great. I no longer believe it is possible to resolve that conflict from within this

Government. That is why I have resigned. In doing so I have done what I believe to be right for my party and my country. The time has come for others to consider their response to the tragic conflict of loyalty with which I have myself wrestled for perhaps too long.

The key to the events of November 1990 was a calculation of political survival on the part of her colleagues, both in the Cabinet and on the back-benches. Enough of them believed they could not win an election with her still as Prime Minister to undermine fatally her position. She could have survived, at least on the mechanical calculation of winning four more votes on the first ballot of Tory MPs. But she would have been grievously wounded and the pressures against her would have mounted again within a few months. She was never likely to change her style and reach out to her critics – long-serving Prime Ministers are seldom that flexible. The end, when it came, was humiliating for her, as the accounts of her tearful final Cabinet meeting on 21 November 1990 underline. She may have remarked then, 'It's a funny old world', but her behaviour over the years after she left office revealed less ironic detachment than bitter hurt at being deprived of what she believed was rightfully hers. It was a delightful coincidence that a long-prepared television version of Michael Dobbs's novel about a Tory leadership contest, *House of Cards*, was shown at the same time as the real battle in November 1990. Ian Richardson, playing Chief Whip Francis Urquhart, is shown looking at a photograph of Margaret Thatcher. He says: 'Nothing lasts for ever. Even the longest, the most glittering reign must come to an end some day.'

However, the switch from being Prime Minister to being out of office can be harsh. Alistair Horne (1989) records that on the very day Harold Macmillan resigned in October 1963, when he was dozing in his hospital bed still recovering from a serious operation and from a series of meetings with senior colleagues and the Queen about the succession, an engineer from the Post Office knocked on his door, arriving to remove – with what seemed like indecent haste – his scrambler telephone. '... I said: "Hell, I was Prime Minister two hours ago, you might leave it a bit." "No," he said, "that's the rule." So that was the end of my power, which has never been restored. Curious ...' It seemed a sad way to go; but then the same could be said about much of Macmillan's life.

After he resigned in 1976, Harold Wilson also found adjusting to retirement a shock, not only because he had been so fully committed to being Prime Minister but also because he was now a much less important and newsworthy figure.

The end can be as tough for other members of a government when asked to leave at a reshuffle. Many Prime Ministers have recoiled from being butchers and have often bungled large-scale reshuffles, as Harold Macmillan did on the 'night of the long knives' in July 1962, when he replaced a third of his Cabinet. Few have been as brisk as Clement Attlee, as Kenneth Harris (1982) noted in his biography:

One junior minister was summoned precipitately to Number 10, to be congratulated on the work of his department, he thought. 'What can I do for you, Prime Minister?' he said as he sat down. 'I want your job,' said Attlee. The minister was staggered. 'But – why, Prime Minister?' 'Afraid you're not up to it,' said Attlee. The interview was over.

Some thirty years later, Barbara Castle never disguised her disappointment at being dropped from the Cabinet by James Callaghan after he took over from Harold Wilson in March 1976. She recounts in her diaries (1980) how Callaghan quickly came to the point: '"I don't want to soft-soap you, Barbara. I must reduce the average age of Cabinet and I want to ask you for your portfolio." I felt detached.' After some further discussion, and pauses,

Jim burst out: 'Harold said to me that the worst thing about this job would be the parliamentary questions. It isn't that: it is this.' 'Harold thought that, too,' I replied sweetly, 'that's why he didn't do it.' Another pause and Jim said with a semblance of briskness: 'So you will let me have a letter saying that you are putting your job at my disposal in order to make way for someone younger.' 'Oh, no,' I replied even more briskly. 'So you are going back on what you have just said,' replied Jim with a show of nastiness. 'Not at all,' I replied. 'What I have said is that I have no choice. But I am not doing this voluntarily. I want to stay to finish my legislation [on pay beds in hospitals]. And that is what I shall say in my letter to you. And I shall hold a press conference to spell this out. I shall go on to the standing committee on the bill and shall defend it line by line.' 'Heaven help your successor,' he replied mournfully. 'Don't worry, Jim,' I said cheerfully. 'I shan't attack you personally. I shall just tell the truth.'

Barbara Castle notes that some months later she was chatting to Merlyn Rees, a close Cabinet ally of James Callaghan, who recalled how much Jim had hated dismissing her. 'He told me it spoilt his day,' he remarked apologetically. 'It spoilt my session,' I retorted.

The blow is no softer even when it is long expected. There had been rumours throughout the spring and summer of 1985 that Patrick Jenkin, then Environment Secretary, would be dropped in the expected Cabinet reshuffle that September, along with Peter Rees, Chief Secretary to the Treasury. The rumours were never denied by Downing Street. Mr Jenkin had anyway been under fire for his handling of the abolition of the Greater London Council and the metropolitan counties. But it was still a shock when the end came, as Jenkin said in an interview the next day on Radio Four's *World at One* programme. The Prime Minister started her meeting with him by saying she had some bad news. He then told her that he did not want any job in government and to start again in some other department, such as Energy. He told the BBC interviewer that he was disappointed to be losing office. I don't think anybody would be surprised at that, particularly when you have been on the front-bench as long as I have. To be suddenly out of it, there are real withdrawal symptoms, real momentary pain, but no, not bitterness at all, because I understand absolutely what the Prime Minister had to do. She had to bring new faces into the Cabinet. I feel they could not be nicer faces to make way for.

Even some of the voluntary departures from Cabinet reflect an acceptance that there is no prospect of further advance. After more than two and a half years in the arduous post of Northern Ireland Secretary, James Prior (1986) noted in his memoirs how he 'hoped very much that I might be able to move to one of the major departments of state. However, it was clear to me that Margaret had no intention of offering any of them to me.' He then received an approach from GEC, the leading industrial company, to become chairman and he raised the matter with Margaret Thatcher. 'I was not surprised when she jumped at the idea. It seemed an easy way out for her and she covered herself brilliantly by saying, "But, of course, Jim, there will always be a job for you in my Cabinet." She did not go on to say what job.' In the following weeks, when he was working on an important Northern Ireland initiative, there was considerable pressure on the Prime Minister to change her mind and try to keep him in the Cabinet. 'But she did not attempt to do so and it was quite obvious therefore that she preferred to have me out of harm's way. It was equally obvious that the sooner I got out the better.' Eventually, after the news had leaked out prematurely, partly thanks to Prior's usual candour, he left the Government in September 1984. While there was a courteous formal exchange of letters, he notes in his memoirs that:

Until the time came to leave, I did not realize how unhappy I had been in the Government during those last few years. Although I am totally committed to its Irish policy – and was indeed its architect – and although Margaret now backed it wholeheartedly, I was also a member of Cabinet responsible for British policies. But over these I had no control and less real influence; what is more I felt distinctly uncomfortable about some of those policies.

For ordinary back-benchers, losing your seat can, of course, be as traumatic as losing office. There is a sense of deprivation, of loss, which is difficult to accept. After the prominence and the status – if not the power or the money – there is suddenly nothing, not even a title, unlike in America, where former members of Congress are known as Senator or Congressman. Sir Anthony Beaumont-Dark lost his Birmingham seat at the age of sixty having entered the Commons in his late forties following a long career as a stockbroker. He felt (1992) sorry for those who became MPs at an early age and then lost their seats: 'They have done damn all with their lives but politics, so they haven't got much to go back to and they haven't much to offer.'

Robin Corbett was the member for Hemel Hempstead for nearly five years in the late 1970s, and was out of the Commons for four years until returning for Birmingham Erdington in 1983. His comments (1987) are typical: 'It was terribly hurtful when I lost in 1979. You feel hurt, dirty, shabby, it's all your fault, it's worse in a sense when you live locally as well. I'd had a book in me for a time, so in order to try and cope with this dreadful situation, I wrote 20,000 words.' The adjustment back to the world outside Parliament was very hard for him:

I found in 1979 that it's very, very difficult getting back into the real world, as it were, once you've done this job. I mean, you're very much your own boss to a very large extent, and people are very suspicious of you anyway if you've been an MP. I did some public relations work and, on one of the accounts I did, the managing director said to me some months into it, rather crossly, 'You never told me you'd been a Member of Parliament,' and he was very put out about it, very put out – he was even more put out when he found out which party I was.

A similar feeling was experienced by Margaret Ewing, then Bain, one of the phalanx of Scottish Nationalist MPs elected at the two 1974 general elections. She lost in May 1979. After returning to the Commons in 1987 she noted (1988):

Having allowed for the fact that seats are won and lost on national swings, it was still difficult when I lost my seat in 1979, because when you've spent five years of your life working very hard for people, there is an ultimate sense of rejection. I wouldn't say hurt, but I did find that I was having to do quite a few therapeutic things – I painted my flat from top to toe.

Bryan Gould was in the Commons at the same time as Robin Corbett in the late 1970s, representing Southampton Test, was out for the same period and also returned in 1983 for a different constituency, in his case Dagenham. But, perhaps reflecting his more detached attitude to British politics, he claims (1987) to have been less distraught about losing:

My reaction when I lost my seat was not what most people said it would be: a very embittering experience, a sense of rejection and all that kind of thing. It was partly that I had a very good result. I'd put up my total vote, and share of the vote – the only thing was that I didn't win. When one of the attractions of politics is itself uncertainty, it seemed to me that there was no point going in if you are going to complain if things don't go right. But I was very clear that I wanted to get back in because it seemed to me the fullest use of my talents. There was a time when I felt a little pessimistic about the changes – as you start going through your forties, there's no point in thinking of yourself as a parliamentarian if you aren't in Parliament. You've got to think of something else to do. I was a television reporter and that was fun. I enjoyed that, but it was much, much less satisfying than being a politician.

As noted earlier, roughly half of defeated MPs try to return to the Commons, and just under a third on average have succeeded since 1970. That may underestimate the desire to become an MP again, since it excludes the unknown number who try and fail to become parliamentary candidates again. Of the forty-five Labour MPs who were defeated in 1979, some twenty-six fought a constituency again, including a handful as SDP candidates, while just eleven returned to the Commons over the following thirteen years. This included one, Bryan Davies, who did not come back until the 1992 election. The proportion of successful retreads, as ex-MPs returning to Parliament are known, was lower among those defeated in 1979 than the historic average. This was because of Labour's uphill struggle throughout the 1980s, especially in England, where most of the 1979 losses occurred. Most were not even partially reversed until the 1992 general election. By the late 1980s local constituency parties wanted to look to a new generation of candidates rather than to veterans who had last served in the Commons a decade earlier.

In all political careers there is a sense of wistfulness, of what might have been. If things had gone differently, an MP might have had a promising ministerial career, or even reached the Cabinet. But if your party was in opposition for a long period, or your face, or your views, did not fit at the right time, then you might have lost out. John Gorst, always an independent-minded back-bencher, is remarkably frank in his reflections on his own fate and that of his contemporaries. He has admitted (1989) that he has been rebellious and that does not get you very far in politics.

I suppose I regret that I'm not more suited temperamentally to politics. I'm not ambitious. I would have quite enjoyed a period as a junior minister but not for very long. I remember sitting in the members' dining room recently with two secretaries of state who had entered the House at the same time as me. I didn't feel from their conversation that they were intellectually my superiors, and I came to the conclusion that the very big gap between us was motivation and energy. I'm not motivated in the same way that they are – and if I had been I wouldn't have had the energy that they have to pursue my goals.

Mr Gorst highlights one of the main characteristics which distinguishes successful politicians, especially those who sustain a lengthy career at the top. They have stamina and energy. Despite their late nights, frequent journeys and demanding lives, most ministers and shadow spokesmen are remarkably fit for their ages. In most cases also, those who do not have the required qualities of decisiveness and persuasiveness get found out and do not prosper. The unsuccessful can console themselves with the thought that the process is seldom rational or fair. It is more meritocratic than those left out think, but it is still a highly arbitrary form of meritocracy.

A survey carried out by the All Party Reform Group in 1983 (and quoted in Radice *et al.*, 1990) shows a relatively high level of satisfaction. Some 63 per cent of MPs were either very or fairly satisfied. Older members were the most satisfied, followed by the youngest (no doubt delighted to be in the Commons so young), followed by thirty to forty year-olds, while the middle-aged were the least satisfied. The authors suggest that the latter were those whose ambitions were unfulfilled. 'It is reasonable to suggest that those due for retirement have already come to nurture a romantic view of what they are about to lose, while the young are still caught up in the hope and excitement of the beginning of their parliamentary career.'

For many senior MPs, any regrets at the lack of promotion are balanced by the mellowing of middle age, and the other satisfactions of being in the Commons. Sir John Hunt (1990), the epitome of moderate suburban Toryism, has said that he has enjoyed his time as a back-bencher. 'My ambitions were never really much higher than that. I never aspired to high ministerial office. If I'd wanted any position at all, it would have been leader of the House – I think I have the qualities to provide a bridge between the Government and the Opposition.' Sir David Crouch (1984) has acknowledged that he would have liked power:

I have been a very ambitious person and I'm sorry I've never been given ministerial office. I would have liked it, particularly in Health, for example, or Industry and Foreign Affairs. But I'm certainly not disillusioned, frustrated or embittered by not having had this opportunity. I still treasure the opportunity of being an MP and being able to exercise a little influence.

Some younger MPs see a less happy picture as they observe their older colleagues. Edward Leigh commented in 1990, when he had become a junior minister, that, looking around the Commons, 'I see too many old men who are bitter because they have spent their lives being terribly ambitious when fundamentally we are losers in politics. Even Mrs Thatcher had to lose, and if we fail to put family or personal priorities first, we are doomed to awful disappointment.' There are few things sadder in the Commons than seeing a former minister in early middle age who has been sacked, or who has had to resign, wondering how he is going to spend the rest of his parliamentary career or whether he should leave the Commons and look elsewhere. None the less, the need for sympathy should not be exaggerated. A number of Tory ex-ministers do pretty well financially out of office. And even if a ministerial career lasts only a few years, just being an under-secretary means that he or she has made good – like being capped for your country at sport, however many caps you get. The expanded select committee system has provided at least a partial alternative – hardly a golden parachute for former ministers, but at least a well-padded mattress. And perpetual back-benchers have, on the Tory side at any rate, the consolation for their vanity of a knighthood or the chairmanship of some party committee. There is at least some deference to seniority left in the House of Commons.

In general, while many MPs regret not having ascended further up the greasy pole, they are satisfied at what they have achieved, not least merely being in the Commons. However frustrating it may be to wait around at the summons of the whips, to sit and not be called in debates and to be ignored when you are, most MPs share Trollope's much-quoted view that 'to sit in the British Parliament should be the highest object and ambition of every educated Englishman'. Peter Archer, Solicitor-General from 1974 until 1979 and a Labour MP for twenty-six years until the 1992 general election, noted (1991) just before his retirement the old story of the knights of Oxfordshire who fled the country on being told that they had been selected and contrasted that with his own views and experience. He reflected on his 'student contemporaries presiding in the Court of Appeal, enjoying the gracious style of a Cambridge college, or simply inviting me to their country mansions. Yet I have never spoken with one of them who would not have been an MP, offered the choice. I would choose politics again, assuming, of course, that I got past the selection procedures.'

Even those who almost got to the top of the pole seek to hide their disappointment. R. A. Butler claimed in a BBC interview in 1966, just over a year after he had left the Commons:

It has always amused me in politics why if you don't happen to reach the one top job, how you're supposed not to be a success; surely if you're not made Pope in the Roman Catholic Church you could be a perfectly good Cardinal. So don't let young people think there is only one top; there have got to be several tops; and let them all feel satisfied that if they go right through it and do their best, they can't all reach the one top, because there's only one man does that roughly every ten years.

That is true. But even the most well-balanced and creative senior politicians who have tried, and failed, to become Prime Minister must wonder at what they might have achieved. Apart from R. A. Butler himself, several other prominent politicians in the last generation have tried to be Pope but have had to settle, with greater or lesser degrees of contentment, for being memorable Cardinals. The list includes Roy Jenkins, Denis Healey, Willie Whitelaw, Sir Geoffrey Howe, Douglas Hurd and Michael Heseltine.

As discussed in the previous chapter, Roy Jenkins several times approached the top of the greasy pole and came to terms with not doing so. As he has reflected (1991):

One reason that I was not more tantalized by these more or less near misses is that I always sensed that I would enjoy being Prime Minister more when it was over than while it was taking place. This thought set a limit to the thrust of my ambition . . . So, although I think that I was a decisive and even an adventurous politician at various stages in my life, and had more sensible views about how to lead a government than many of those who have actually done it, I none the less lacked at least one of the essential ingredients of a capacity to seize power. I may have avoided doing too much stooping, but I also missed conquering.

But for Roy Jenkins, as for most politicians, however far they progress up the greasy pole, and whatever compromises they have to make, there is the consolation of having achieved things which they might otherwise not have. For Roy Jenkins, it was mainly achievements in office. Those who climb to the top of the greasy pole, or near the top, have a more agreeable and varied life than most of those who remain outside on some stand of principle. For most MPs, the consolation is service to constituents, challenging Whitehall or the town hall over a housing case, or over a social security payment, or over an immigration problem. However important the spur of personal ambition, few politicians can survive the vicissitudes of a parliamentary career and succeed without what Denis Healey has called a 'sense of vocation'. In the end, a political career has to be about more than just climbing the greasy pole.

10

CONCLUSIONS

'Gaining a seat in the House of Commons is the most important single event in any British political career. Up to this point, all is fantasy and, from the point of view of non-political observers, vanity. After it, anything is possible. For Parliament is a tiny talent pool, without much talent in it, from which governments of several score ministers are drawn. Anybody representing a major party who enters the Commons, with even a modest amount of vigour and judgement, is likely to achieve prominence sooner or later, if he or she so chooses. Harold Wilson did so choose.'

Ben Pimlott, *Harold Wilson*, 1992

'My reluctance to enter politics directly had been rooted essentially in the fear that I was not cut out for public life, and that I would find it intolerable to make the compromises required of a party politician. On reflection, however, I came to realize that almost any alternative which met my desire to do something useful about the state of the world would have the same disadvantages, while offering less opportunity for effective action.'

Denis Healey, *The Time of My Life*, 1989

'There is a feeling at Westminster that to leave university, come and work at Central Office, become a special adviser and go into the Commons, and after three months wander around with a permanent expression of amazement that you are not in the Cabinet is not necessarily in the best interests of the Conservative Party.'

Senior Tory MP and party office-holder, quoted in
The Times, 24 August 1992

The British Parliament, and hence government, is increasingly dominated by career politicians – by men, and a few women, who have dedicated most of their adult lives to entering the Commons, staying there and advancing to become ministers or spokesmen. The conclusion of this book is unmistakable: the balance has shifted towards the full-time politician.

The signs, listed in earlier chapters, are many and varied. They include the growth of ancillary political jobs (public affairs consultants, special advisers, full-time union officials, full-time council leaders and chairmen of committees), the willingness to commit yourself to fighting several seats before entering the Commons; the desire of most to stay at Westminster; and the high rate of recidivism by defeated MPs seeking to return. Not all Tory MPs are like those described in the quotation at the beginning of the chapter and not all Labour MPs are former party officials or council chairmen, but increasing numbers are. The range of experience of many MPs is narrower than in the past, and their dedication to politics is greater. The real difference is the degree of dependence on politics not just as a livelihood but as a mark of status and esteem. Moreover, in part because of the skills developed from an early age and in part because of the degree of commitment, these career politicians are the ones who tend to rise fastest and furthest at Westminster.

By contrast, late entrants start with the disadvantage of unfamiliarity about the means of advancing their careers. It is no coincidence that it has been the Cambridge generation of the late 1950s and 1960s, with all its precocious political interest and ambition, that has prospered, while many small businessmen and professional men who have entered the Commons in their late forties and early fifties have languished on the back-benches. There are, of course, exceptions. Nigel Lawson, Douglas Hurd and Michael Howard, for example, did not enter the Commons until well into their forties, though the first two had served on the political staff of Tory Prime Ministers and the latter had fought hopeless seats in his late twenties. More typical in recent Cabinets, however, have been

Norman Lamont, Michael Portillo, Malcolm Rifkind, William
Waldegrave and John Major himself, all of whom entered the
Commons in their thirties and in several cases became ministers
before they were forty.

The most conspicuous recent example of a successful late
entrant has been Paddy Ashdown, who first became politically
involved in his mid-thirties and was elected to Parliament
when he was forty-two. But his appeal, especially as the head
of a self-consciously anti-establishment third party such as the
Liberal Democrats, has been that of the outsider, the politician
who has not been a member of the Westminster club. He has
drawn parallels with the anti-politics themes offered by Ross
Perot during the 1992 presidential campaign in America. Although a competent Commons performer, Paddy Ashdown
does not enjoy its rituals and nuances, in the way that someone
like John Smith does. Mr Ashdown is not popular at Westminster, because he is seen as a somewhat self-righteous outsider,
distancing himself from the manoeuvrings of the political
game. Few other late entrants, defined as having no previous
political involvement until, say, their late thirties, have succeeded. The switch in careers has come too late. Few even of
those who have been local council leaders before becoming
MPs have succeeded at Westminster. The rules of the parliamentary game are different and, in general, are learned relatively young.

The American experience similarly reflects the impact of the
rise of the career politician. Alan Ehrenhalt (1991) has argued
that: 'The typical person who gets elected now is someone
who grows up in the political process. Politics is a vocation for
them.' He describes a pattern in which young men, and women,
get out of college, go to work in the Capitol on the staffs of
Senators and members of the House, go back home to run for
office, and then return to Washington as legislators themselves.
They are good candidates because they have connections with
the political establishment, including access to finance. The

modern Congressman is like a professional athlete drawn into
the competition by temperament and trained to measure success by his winning percentage, and unable at the age of forty
or forty-five to end his obsession with running, even if he or
she no longer needs to run very hard. Gary Jacobson (1992)
has concluded in the latest edition of his classic study of
congressional elections that: 'Other things being equal, the
strongest congressional candidates are those for whom politics
is a career. They have the most powerful motive and the
greatest opportunity to master the craft of electoral politics.
They are most likely to have experience in running campaigns
and in holding elective office.' He notes that ambitious career
politicians have the greatest incentive to follow 'a rational
strategy for moving up the informal, but quite real, hierarchy
of elective offices in the American political system'. Even those
challengers who successfully ousted incumbent Senators and
members of the House during the 1992 campaign on the basis
of an anti-politics/anti-Washington appeal were in themselves
mainly state and local legislators. It was a younger generation
of career politicians defeating an older generation.

In a study of what differentiates candidates from each other,
Linda Fowler and Robert McClure (1989) argue:

Ambition for a seat in the House [of Representatives] more than any
other factor – more than money, personality or skill in using television, to name just a few examples – is what finally separates a
visible, declared candidate for Congress from an unseen one. Even
among the declared candidates, it is the force of ambition that most
often turns up the critical difference between the winners and the
losers, because only intense motivation can overcome the high political, personal and financial hurdles that law and custom impose in a
politician's path to a seat in the US Congress.

Ambition is the dynamic force which ensures an apparently
endless supply of people willing to contest for public office
and to produce change in the political system. Without

ambition the political system would seize up and decay. As in so many other ways, James Madison was right in arguing in the Federalist Papers:

Those ties which bind the representative to his constituents are strengthened by motives of a more selfish nature. His pride and vanity attach him to a form of government which favours his pretensions and gives him a share in its honours and distinctions ... Duty, gratitude, interests, ambition itself are the cords by which they [representatives] will be bound to fidelity and sympathy with the great mass of the people.

In Britain, has the growing influence of dedicated career politicians really produced a very different system? In a sense it was always thus. Reading any diary or memoirs about British politics from the late eighteenth century onwards shows that the successful have, on the whole, been the driven, the fiercely ambitious and the committed. It is this view of politics driven by personal ambition which is celebrated in the novels of Disraeli and Trollope. The latter remains the most widely read, or at any rate most often mentioned, British political novelist. Characteristically, his is the politics of personality rather than of principle. Members of the Major Cabinet of 1992 would find much in common with the Baldwin Cabinets of the 1920s and 1930s, while John Smith is recognizably in the tradition of the clever lawyer/politician, like Asquith.

The change has been in the balance. There are now more committed, full-time politicians, for whom their careers at Westminster are the centre of their lives, both financially and socially. There is no longer a self-perpetuating aristocracy which regards service in Parliament and government as part of their inherited duties. The aristocrats and gentry who dominated the nineteenth-century House of Commons may have been as interested in politics as today's members. But they were not wholly dependent on their membership of the House for their incomes or standing in the community. Lord Salisbury and Gladstone had an importance separate from their activities at Westminster. Now, leading politicians are only prominent because of their membership of the Commons or the government. Many have little life outside Parliament. One factor is dedication and ambition, but as important is the increased opportunity to live off politics. The rise in the pay of MPs – and the growth of ancillary political occupations – has meant that more people can be full-time politicians, whereas in the past only those in government or financially supported by trade unions could survive financially without another income, either from business interests or from inherited wealth. But now there is greater financial flexibility. A result of this change is that there are now fewer successful businessmen or prominent trade union officials in the Commons. Instead, there are more consultants and research officers.

The shift towards more full-time politicians does not mean that ambitions are necessarily being frustrated. The system has adapted. The number of ministerial – and shadow – posts available has risen sharply this century. Supply has, as so often, increased to meet demand. Provided they have managed to stay in the Commons for more than two general elections, and provided their party is in power, MPs have virtually an even chance of at least becoming a whip or a parliamentary under-secretary. With usually only a handful of exceptions, there are normally good reasons why the perpetual back-benchers have been excluded. Similarly, the growth of the select committees during the 1980s has offered, at least in part, an alternative career structure for the back-bencher.

But what are the advantages and disadvantages of the rise of the full-time politician? The main plus is a degree of professionalism, in the sense of an awareness both about the political process and about how to achieve results. There are fewer gentleman amateurs who are content to let ministers run the country, or, if themselves a minister, to let civil servants run their departments. That is anyway necessary because of the extension of the role of government, which makes greater demands on a minister. A more extensive, even intrusive, government requires more committed politicians in charge. More MPs now are aware of how the social security system works. Being in office, or a shadow, is more of a full-time occupation, requiring a full-time commitment and a lengthy apprenticeship.

What is in doubt is whether an apprenticeship spent concentrating on getting into Parliament and staying there is the right one. As Richard Rose (1987) has pointed out:

A British politician does not set out to become a Cabinet minister, but to enter the House of Commons. Experience in the Commons does not lead naturally to the work of a minister, as primary school leads to secondary school. Becoming a minister is as much a change for an MP as going out to work is a change for a schoolboy.

The central questions are whether the system chooses – throws up might be more vivid and accurate – people with the right backgrounds, knowledge and experience to become effective ministers and shadow spokesmen. Or, more broadly, whether the process by which parliamentary candidates are selected produces MPs who are representative of their constituents, responsive to their needs and the interests of the community as a whole. There is, at the very least, some doubt as to whether either of these points can be answered satisfactorily. There is, of course, no formal method of measuring the effectiveness of politicians. Judging the record of MPs by the value of the pound, or the growth of public spending, or the weight of legislation could be a tempting and diverting exercise, but not one that is helpful to the main question. There are too many other factors involved apart from whether or not politicians have a full-time career commitment. Any answer would depend on your partisan view of the worth, or otherwise, of public spending or of Parliament passing huge tomes of acts. There are no objective measures of whether someone is a good or bad representative or minister.

None the less, active government is a characteristic, and possibly a result, of an age dominated by the rise of the full-time politician eager to be busy. This does not necessarily mean 'big government', or a rapid growth in public spending, though both have been associated with legislatures dominated by career politicians. Equally, such legislatures have sought to rein back the size of government and to reduce public spending. So the distinguishing feature is not the scale of government but rather its level of activity. That reflects the desire of career politicians to do something, to find an outlet for their ambitions. Change is the order of the day. Active government initiating a heavy legislative programme has been as much a product of the Thatcher era as of the earlier collectivist phase since 1945.

In America one of the main complaints by conservative Republicans against Congress is that the growth of the full-time career politician has created an institutional bias not only in favour of the aggrandizement of their own personal position (in terms of the size of their staffs and perks) but also in favour of 'big government' and high public spending. Yet that partly reflects Republican frustration at the continued domination of Congress by the Democrats. Alan Ehrenhalt (1991) has argued that the new breed of legislators has been 'drawn to political careers for different reasons. What stands out, though, is that for most of them the commitment to a political life has been accompanied by a positive attitude towards government itself as an instrument for doing valuable work in American society.'

In Britain the rise of the full-time politician is related to active government, whatever the level of public spending. A career politician is by definition not a traditional conservative; he or she wants to do things. That in itself is not necessarily a bad thing. The question is rather whether the activities of politicians have become divorced from the aspirations and needs of the electorate. Has the career politician become more ideological, or, alternatively, more opportunistic? A good case can be made for either view. There is both the firmly committed politician motivated by a clear ideology and the legislator determined to retain his or her seat and to advance his or her career in face of the shifts of party and public opinion. At the height of Thatcherism in 1981, Anthony King argued:

The rise of the career politician has been associated, not with a lowering of the political temperature, a move away from ideological politics to a single-minded preoccupation with vote-maximizing, but rather with the reverse. By any measure, British politics from the late 1960s onwards have been more heated, more ideological and less consensual than for a long time past.

Professor King suggested that a contributory factor has been the rise of the career politician and he lamented the fact that, 'The demise of the non-career politician has led to a certain loss of experience, moderation, detachment, balance, ballast even, in the British political system.'

A decade later, and after the end of both the Thatcher era and Labour's flirtation with Bennism, the link between the career politician and ideological politics looks less clear. From 1987 onwards Neil Kinnock's leadership of the Labour Party was characterized by an abandonment of previous ideological positions and a shift towards policies intended to maximize votes. Similarly, John Major's arrival in 10 Downing Street was marked both by the abandonment of some of the more entrenched features of Thatcherism, such as the poll tax and hostility towards the European Community, and by the approval of higher public spending in areas such as health and education in order to deal with the concerns of voters. Indeed, the *coup* against Margaret Thatcher in November 1990 can be seen as a desperate act by career politicians determined to ensure their own survival. As the ideologists in both main parties frequently complained, they were on the fringes and no longer in the mainstream. The dominant career politicians saw that they had to adopt a more consensual approach in order to retain, or to win, office. That does not mean that they did not have views, or political values, but rather that they wanted, above all, to avoid defeat. These experiences do not satisfactorily resolve the ideological versus opportunistic debate about career politicians. Perhaps the answer is the healthy democratic one that the instinctive ideological views of career politicians hold sway only when the Opposition is weak, as in the early 1980s, and that the overriding priorities of ambition, and of remaining as MPs and ministers, reassert themselves when there is closer competition between the parties, as in the early 1990s.

None the less, politicians are increasingly a caste apart in Britain. The early chapters of this book showed how many future MPs first become politically involved, and in many cases committed, in their teens or early twenties – that politics becomes their life at this early stage. While they may not be able to live off, as against for, politics until they become MPs, they are still dedicated to becoming members of the Commons. Any occupation they pursue is treated as ancillary to this ambition and, increasingly, future MPs are already full-time politicians. This has cut them off from the interests of many of their contemporaries and when they enter the Commons their background is more limited than would have been true in the past. That does not mean that MPs do not have views or are not ideological. Often that is what triggers, and sustains, their commitment to the political life. Moreover, the qualities which get them selected as parliamentary candidates – a solid resumé of political work, fluency in making a short speech and answering questions and an apparent knowledge about contemporary politics – are ideally suited to the already committed rather than to the interested but so far uncommitted. The closed shop operates at a very early stage.

Even a politician with as broad a range of interests as Roy Jenkins has complained (1991) that he was too politically concentrated between the ages of eighteen and thirty-two. 'I devoted too much attention to politics at Oxford. I was too eager to get into the House of Commons, for anywhere, almost anyhow, and when I got there I was too much of a party loyalist, thinking more about the game than about the merits of issues.' That is true of many other politicians of lesser distinction. For them, ambition appears to be all. They have not filled out as people, let alone as politicians. They lack what Denis Healey has famously described as 'hinterland' – that is, a range of interests outside politics. Surprisingly few MPs are well read, or in touch with intellectual or artistic developments.

After arriving in the Commons, the qualities which secure an MP's preferment, whether in government or in opposition, are primarily those of performance in Parliament itself. Executive ability, in managing a department or in handling a Whitehall committee, is seldom known or noticed. What matters is an ability to think and argue on your feet, to handle a difficult question or intervention well. As Dennis Kavanagh (1990) has argued:

Political skill is shown within the parliamentary arena. Approval among this parliamentary élite is more decisive than a popular following in reaching the top in British politics ... Acceptability to colleagues at the levels of party, Parliament and Cabinet have attracted and rewarded a personality and style in which qualities of reliability, self-restraint, and trustworthiness have figured prominently.

These qualities are important in so far as a minister's job concerns handling the Commons or appearing in a television or radio studio. But they do not cover the development of policy or managing a vast Whitehall department – though that aspect of a minister's responsibilities may be reduced by the hiving off of large areas of administration into separate executive agencies.

Aside from the questions of training and preparation is the more basic issue of whether the current career pattern of British politics produces the best available ministers and, equally, whether it makes the best use of MPs themselves. At present, there is a tendency to believe that an MP eager to reach the top has to be elected to the Commons in his or her thirties, or at any rate just afterwards, join the front-bench within two or three years of being elected and then rise steadily thereafter. If any of these steps is missed, a candidate or MP is then seen as doomed to fail. He or she has missed a bus which will generally not return. An early start and a rapid rise are true for many of the real high-flyers, from Winston Churchill to Margaret Thatcher, though Churchill did have ten years out of office from his mid-fifties to his mid-sixties. But there are a few intriguing exceptions. Harold Macmillan had to wait for nearly sixteen years after he was first elected, until he was aged forty-six, to become even a junior minister for the first time. His rise then was rapid. There are other less eminent examples given earlier of successful late entrants to the Commons.

The present system discriminates against those who cannot adapt their lives to the necessary career pattern of early commitment and increasing devotion of time. There are three main categories of the excluded: women, still less than a tenth of the House of Commons, even after the big rise at the April 1992 general election; ethnic minorities, just six MPs; and, more generally, those with successful careers outside politics. Ethnic minorities, whether of Asian or Afro-Caribbean origin, still find it very difficult to get selected for seats outside areas with a high ethnic-minority population. Five out of the six MPs have come from London. There is limited evidence in mainly

white seats that voters will discriminate against a black or
Asian candidate, almost certainly contributing to the defeat of
John Taylor in Cheltenham in April 1992. That in turn makes
constituency parties more reluctant to pick such candidates.
The other two groups suffer because their lives do not fit in
with the requirements of a political apprenticeship. These
range from the demands of raising children for women in their
twenties and thirties, which conflict with evening meetings, to
the male orientation of much local political activity. Byron
Criddle has quoted (in Butler and Kavanagh, 1992) the views
of one Labour Party official that the failure to increase black
or female representation significantly in safe Labour seats in
1992 was attributable to the widened franchise: 'Particularly in
safe, largely old industrial seats, the wider membership was
less likely to share fully the relatively progressive opinions of
party activists on such matters.' The obstacles to those successful in other careers have been discussed in earlier chapters and
primarily relate to time and the increasing professionalization
of all careers.

Even granted the present background of MPs, it is doubtful
whether the best use is being made of the available talent. For
instance, recruiting people on to the front-bench within a
couple of years of being elected may be too early. They may be
clever but insufficiently experienced. They are often dropped a
few years later with years of active political life ahead of them.
Some former ministers might well do better in office after
several years on the back-benches than when they first served
in office. For instance, David Howell was a classic example of
a career politician, first elected to the Commons aged thirty
after having been a journalist and director of the Conservative
Political Centre. He became a minister in the Heath Government aged thirty-four, serving in four different departments.
He was Energy Secretary and then Transport Secretary in the
first Thatcher Government, before being dropped in June
1983, aged forty-seven. He was never seen, either by his fellow

MPs or by the public, as a heavyweight Cabinet minister. But since leaving the Government he has gained reputation and influence as chairman of the Foreign Affairs Select Committee since 1987. That experience would make him a much better Cabinet minister in the second half of his fifties. But such returns to office are rare. Once out, few return. It is rather like the old eleven-plus examination: there is little allowance for later development.

Politicians themselves are increasingly worried about the implications of the rise of the career politician. The big influx of full-time politicians into the Commons at the April 1992 general election created a reaction in both the Conservative and the Labour parties. Shortly after he became Conservative Party chairman following the general election, Sir Norman Fowler made known his desire to broaden the base of candidates, to attract more women and more people in their forties and fifties who have had successful careers outside politics, in business and the professions. Andrew Mitchell, the party vice-chairman in charge of candidates for a time after the 1992 election, said: 'We have to get across the message that there is no hidden barrier at forty. Often people who are older have a great deal of experience of life and we want to persuade them to come forward and present themselves for selection.' One of the targets in what is partly a head-hunting exercise is the successful businessman in his forties who wants a change of direction – 'Someone with a lot of experience of how the economy works out there would be of great benefit to the party.' Such people would obviously have had to show a prior interest in politics and been active at a local and constituency level, but not with the degree of involvement and commitment of many younger, full-time politicians. Andrew Mitchell has said that arriving in the Commons after being a special adviser or working in Conservative Central Office had disadvantages, since constituency parties were worried that such people did not have enough experience of life.

The desire to shift the balance away from the Oxbridge career politician is, as Sir Norman has freely admitted, more than a little ironic, since he himself was a prominent member of the Cambridge generation, which, as described in Chapter 3, has epitomized the rise of the career politician. None the less, after the 1992 election there was discontent among senior Tory MPs and whips about the quality, experience and attitudes of some of the new entrants. With an average age of forty-one they were the generation of Thatcher's children. Most took over from retiring MPs in safe seats and were too young to have had much experience or memory of the Tories' years in opposition. Not only were many of the sixty-three regarded by their more senior colleagues as bumptious but they were seen as naïve and rebellious, in part because of their inexperience.

Parallel complaints were heard on the Labour side, about the predominance of full-time politicians, whether party or union officials or councillors. The absence, on the one hand, of manual workers and, on the other hand, of successful professional men and women was noticeable, and regretted, by party leaders. There were few genuine voices of the people, as opposed to their university-educated surrogates. Few Labour MPs or candidates had been successful in the private sector and had experience of business. Many more came from the public sector, working in teaching, the health service or local government. Writing in the September 1992 issue of *Fabian Review*, Hilary DeLyon and Damien Welfare argued that the Labour system of selecting candidates amounts to an 'absurd parody of the free market'. The electoral college, in which a wider range of party and union members has a say, has meant that local parties are increasingly choosing candidates they know, because they are local party activists, because they are union or Labour Party officials, or because they have a national name. In all three groups white men predominate. Of the twenty-two candidates selected in seats vacated by sitting

Labour MPs in April 1992, eighteen were white men, one was an Asian man and only three were women. Moreover, fifteen of the candidates were local, eight were current or former union officials, two were current or former Labour Party employees, three were MEPs and two were former MPs. The authors acknowledge the advantages of being local for campaigning in a marginal seat 'but it carries the danger of limited experience outside the constituency, and too narrow a view of issues and their wide impact across the country as a whole'.

Nevertheless, there is little public dissatisfaction with MPs and Parliament as such, as opposed to the performance of whichever party happens to be in power at the time. A Market & Opinion Research International survey for the Rowntree Reform Trust in 1991 showed that nearly three-fifths of the sample thought that Parliament worked well; the proportion disagreeing was higher among supporters of opposition parties and the further away from London someone lived. Some 43 per cent were satisfied with the job their local MP was doing for the constituency, and 23 per cent were dissatisfied. Moreover, turnout has remained high in British elections and support for fringe candidates has been minimal. But that does not mean the MP is contributing to the national debate, or is a good potential minister.

In the rest of Europe, there have also been complaints about politicians. Kurt Biedenkopf, prime minister of Saxony, has (1993) called for a different kind of leader. 'We need people who do not make politics their prime career from scratch. People who have not gone through a process of selection in which you can be successful only if you are so slick, so without contour and so groomed to the organisation that you can go through all the hoops all the way up. We have our own forms of *nomenklatura*. People are getting fed up, and not only here. It is the same in France, in Britain, in Italy, and in the US.'

The American public is also dissatisfied with the performance of Congress, in part because of a series of scandals about

financial perks enjoyed by its members and in part because of
the deadlock on many issues produced by a division of party
control for much of the 1970s and 1980s between the executive
and the legislature. Polls conducted during the 1992 presidential
campaign showed that 70 per cent of American voters disap-
proved of how Congress was handling its job. The dissatisfaction became focused on a dislike of the increasing dominance
both of Congress in Washington and of state legislatures by
full-time politicians. In spite of what William Schneider (1992)
has called 'a strong emotional and philosophical commitment
to citizen legislatures', most individual states have seen an
increasing professionalism among members of their legislatures. Their main focus is on getting and staying elected, and
this means avoiding risky positions. 'Representatives spend a
great deal of time making sure they do what their constituents
want. They spend less time working collectively to make good
public policy. Because representatives concentrate so completely on making sure the voters know them and like them,
the institution cannot make tough choices.' By contrast,
'amateur legislatures are more representative of the population.
They bring real world experience to legislative procedures and
a pragmatic perspective on the issue. Citizen legislators could
be said to take more risks because they are less dependent on
their legislative careers. They have something to fall back on.'
The dislike of full-time career politicians in America has also
been associated with worries over the large influence of special
interests whose backing is needed by candidates to finance
expensive television advertising campaigns. This is not an issue
in Britain in view of the tight controls on local campaign
spending, though there are questions about the lack of disclosure of large financial contributions by wealthy people to
the Tory Party centrally.

This dissatisfaction has been expressed in a populist revolt
against incumbent legislators and in a demand for term limits
restricting the length of time anyone can serve either in state

legislatures or in Congress. During the 1992 presidential campaign, the Ross Perot phenomenon was the most widely discussed aspect of the populist revolt against the existing political
establishment. But the rejection of an unprecedented number
of incumbent Congressmen was in many ways a far more
significant expression of this discontent. It was in part an
instant response to the demand for term limits and was seen as
showing why such mechanistic restrictions were unnecessary.
The call for such limits was not new in 1992 and had gained a
victory in the post-Second World War era when an amendment
to the American constitution was approved (the 22nd Amendment) which has limited presidents to serving two terms, or a
total of eight years. This was a reaction to Franklin Roosevelt,
who was elected president four times, though only served a
couple of months of his fourth term before his death.

The demand for term limits on congressional service has
reflected a mixture of Republican dislike of Democratic domination of Congress and general public dissatisfaction with its
performance, supported by almost nostalgic ideas about a
citizens' Congress. There has, in particular, been a reaction to
the near certainty of re-election for members of the House in
the second half of the 1980s. Even with voluntary retirements,
this meant that the turnover was only about 10 per cent,
compared with about 40 to 50 per cent in the nineteenth
century. But the low turnover of the second half of the 1980s
may have been exceptional and reflected the generally quiescent
political mood of that period. During the 1970s, for example,
there was a high turnover of members of Congress. By the
early 1980s three-quarters of Senators and members of the
House had served fewer than twelve years.

The advocates of change have generally proposed two six-
year terms for members of the Senate (a total limit of twelve
years) and between three and six two-year terms for members
of the House of Representatives (a total of between six and
twelve years). Such limits were approved by votes in fourteen

states, including California, in November 1992. The supporters
of the change have argued that it would bring in members
with 'a more varied experience' and those 'closer to what's
going on in their states'. Arguing against term limits, Thomas
Mann (1992), a leading American political analyst, has maintained that the problem is not individual accountability, since
voters show no signs of suffering from inattentive or unrespon-
sive representatives. What is needed, he believes, is a change in
the electoral system that once again allows the outcome of
hundreds of congressional elections to build up cumulatively
to a meaningful national decision. This means having elections
that are more party-based and less candidate-centred. He suggests that term limits are the wrong medicine. 'Natural turnover [from voluntary retirements, progressive ambition and
election defeat] is preferable to an arbitrary scheme that unnec-
essarily restricts a democratic electoral process.'

Term limits would, he argues, be likely to turn into a floor,
rather than a ceiling, as would-be candidates defer their challenge and await the forced retirement of incumbents. Moreover, the candidate-centred character of American elections
would not disappear even if careers were forcibly shortened.
Thomas Mann argues that what is needed is a Republican
Party willing to compete more energetically at a local level,
and campaign-finance reforms which remove the advantages
of incumbents and strengthen the hands of challengers. His
worry is that term limits would eliminate many of the members
most inclined to legislate in the national interest, would shift
power from elected politicians to unelected officials and private
interests, and would strengthen the administration at the expense of Congress.

Such rigid solutions as term limits have had little appeal in the
very different political system of Britain, which remains party
rather than candidate-centred. Such limits would, indeed, be
difficult to introduce unless there were fixed-term Parliaments.
Moreover, under the British arrangements where members

of the Commons constitute the bulk of the executive, any formal limit on the length of service as an MP would dramatically change the composition of governments by excluding many well-qualified and experienced members. After all, John Major was highly unusual in becoming Prime Minister after only eleven and a half years' service in the Commons. Margaret Thatcher had to wait nearly twenty years, as did Edward Heath. Any shorter limit would be arbitary in its impact and any longer one would be largely meaningless, an empty gesture.

The only comparable process in Britain has been the introduction by Labour from the early 1980s of the mandatory reselection of its MPs during the course of every Parliament. Apart from an initial flurry of deselections at the height of the Bennite phase in the 1979–83 Parliament and when the SDP split was occurring, relatively few MPs have been deselected in subsequent Parliaments, generally 3 per cent or less of sitting members who want to stand again. In most cases, special circumstances have been involved. Most members who are assiduous in maintaining relations with their local parties do not have any trouble even if they take a distinctive ideological position. Deselections are even rarer in the Conservative Party, and local constituencies are often reluctant even to get rid of members in their seventies. Despite rumours of retribution against the more prominent critics of Margaret Thatcher before her downfall, only Sir Anthony Meyer, who had dared to stand against her in December 1989, was rejected by his local party, and he was over seventy by the time of the April 1992 general election. Otherwise, the main parties have to rely on a combination of an improved parliamentary pension scheme, gentle persuasion and, in the case of the Tories, the reward of knighthoods to ease out older members sitting for safe seats.

The main British proposals have concerned the type of candidates being picked. In part, this has been through the initial screening process at Conservative Central Office and the attempt publicly to encourage the selection of more candidates aged over forty, more successful businessmen and more women. Apart from exhortation and informal guidance, there is little that Conservative Central Office can do in view of the independence of local parties. Moreover, for all the talk of encouraging successful businessmen and executives to become MPs, large employers need to change their own attitudes and behaviour, so that middle-managers are not penalized in their careers for being politically active. The Industry and Parliament Trust has been trying to remedy this problem by its contacts with both the main political parties and, equally significantly, its business members. The Trust has launched a political service initiative to reverse the decline in the number of new MPs with business experience. Fewer than a quarter of nearly fifty corporate members covered in a survey had policies that supported employees who wished to become politically involved. Consequently, the Trust has drawn up a declaration committing member companies to regard political participation as something positively to be encouraged. As a further stage, a model corporate policy has been designed, drawing on parallel initiatives in Canada and Sweden and upon the best practice of some British companies. This states that leave (paid or unpaid) should be given for political activity, such as electioneering, canvassing and attendance at party conferences, paid leave should be provided for candidates adopted by a political party to stand for election and extended unpaid leave should be provided for a minimum of one parliamentary term for those elected. There should then be continuity of pension and private health rights and guarantee of return to employment at the same level of seniority if defeated after one term. For all these good intentions, it remains to be seen how far the present rigid career patterns of British business can be broken down.

Any change also requires local parties to take a wider view of the necessary qualifications for becoming a parliamentary candidate and not just look for a long record of local service or a period as an adviser in Whitehall or in Conservative

Central Office. Supporters of changing the way Labour Party candidates are picked, like the authors in the *Fabian Review* article quoted above, see virtues in the Conservative system of screening potential nominees by interviews and assessment, so that the national party determines quality (up to a point) and the local party chooses the candidate. The authors believe that Labour should be encouraging, as a first requirement, the head-hunting of prominent party members to join the pool of possible candidates, to be followed by pre-selection training and assessment procedures.

The Labour Party has made more formal changes in its rules of candidate selection. But, as noted above, widening the franchise from a few dozen on the local management committee to the whole local membership has favoured already known local candidates and a few national names. The increasing trend towards locally based candidates can mean that they lack a perspective on national issues. Good local MPs are not necessarily good national spokesmen for the party. Widening the franchise to include all party members may, however, create opportunities for those with a public reputation and name, though not necessarily deep involvement as a party activist. This happened in the internal elections by all members for the old SDP's national committee when Anthony Sampson, Julia Neuberger and Polly Toynbee all got elected as well-known public figures in their own right rather than because of their specifically political records. Moves towards picking candidates by primary elections in which all supporters of a party, rather than just its paid-up members, choose the party's nominee may attract people who would not naturally play much part in politics. While attractive in some respects in broadening the democratic process, primaries would require some form of registration of party affiliation, as in America. Pressures for the inclusion of at least one woman on every short list, and talk of quotas for numbers of women candidates, have probably helped increase the number of women MPs, though, as in the past, many represent marginal seats.

Changes in the electoral system could also affect the types of candidate and MP chosen. Moves away from the present single-member constituencies might increase diversity. But there is no magic formula. Much depends on the precise system chosen. The single transferable vote, as operated in the Irish Republic, would encourage the trend towards locally based candidates even more than the present system. This is because the main focus is on candidates in local competition gaining a slight edge of preferences in multi-member constituencies. An additional-member system, as in Germany, is more flexible, though the balance of candidates would depend more on who determined the party lists. But it could allow more women and ethnic minorities to become MPs.

But if there are only likely to be gradual changes in the types of candidate being picked, to offset the rise of the career politician, are there ways of altering the basis on which ministers are chosen to secure a wider choice? The convention that the vast majority of ministers must be members of the Commons, and have served an apprenticeship there, limits what can be done. In one sense such conventions are sensible in that a key part of any minister's job is persuading his or her parliamentary colleagues of the merits of Government policy. Parliamentary and related skills of persuasion do matter. Richard Rose (in Vibert, 1991) has noted the lack of success of importing outsider experts in as ministers – not least because they may be seen as the representatives of the special interests and pressure groups from where they originate. 'Outsiders normally fail because they are amateurs as political ambassadors representing a department within Whitehall, in Parliament and to the public.' Professor Rose has also raised the possibility that civil servants might play a more prominent role, but this would risk further undermining the political impartiality of the Civil Service if it involved them becoming public spokesmen for a department's policies in a more partisan way than they now are. Instead, he has suggested developing a policy directorate combining the complementary skills of the minister and civil servant. This would bring together a dozen or so MPs, civil servants and, if appropriate, outside experts, with the aim of mobilizing more expert advice, and would be similar to the French Cabinet system.

From his own mixed experience of dealing with the Commons when he was a departmental minister in the second half of the 1980s, Lord Young (1990) has suggested a number of possible reforms to get round the difficulty of involving outsiders in government at the highest level. Some of his proposals are minor, such as allowing ministers in the House of Lords to have the run of the Commons while they are in office. He has also gone further in suggesting that all Lords ministers should be allowed to answer departmental questions on the floor of the Commons, as they already do before departmental select committees. More radically, he has proposed allowing the Prime Minister of the day the right to bring in one or two unelected outsiders to the Cabinet who would be allowed full membership of the Commons during their period of office. This would be with the aim of bringing outsiders in for short periods to play a part in the political process and then depart. He has acknowledged that the last suggestion would be rejected by all in the Commons. Lord Young's ideas are worth considering, though outsiders would still suffer the disadvantages of never having been members of the Commons – as he did himself. The addition of one or two eminent outsiders to the Cabinet would, under whatever basis they served in Parliament, make at most a marginal change to the type of people at the top of British politics. The career politicians would still rule. During wartime there were successful examples of bringing outsiders into major Cabinet posts, such as Sir John Anderson, and Lords Woolton and Beaverbrook. But that worked only because accountability to the Commons was less important during the war. Churchill's attempt to repeat this experiment with his overlords in his 1951 Government failed.

Another approach might be to reform the membership of the House of Lords, as proposed by Labour and the other opposition parties. A more representative second chamber – possibly filled by a mixture of election and nomination – might have the power and standing to have more senior ministers sitting there, not just spokesmen for departments in the Commons. This might facilitate the flow in and out of government, and in and out of politics, which is desirable. But the Commons will take a lot of persuading, not just to permit the growth of a potentially strong rival but also to surrender its role, at least in the twentieth century, of being the chamber from which almost all senior ministers are chosen.

The most practicable – and therefore British answer – to the rigidities described above is to introduce greater flexibility both in the selection of candidates and in their promotion within Parliament. The parties need to broaden their bases of selection and Prime Ministers need to drop some of the old ideas of hierarchy. It should become more normal for someone to serve a few years in government, then possibly go back to the back-benches, before returning to government in a more senior position with greater knowledge and experience. That used in practice to be achieved during the 1960s and 1970s when parties alternated in power. Under the conditions prevailing since 1979, greater imagination is needed to secure the maximum out of the available talent.

Similarly, it should no longer be impossible for leading politicians to spend some time in Parliament, including a period as a minister, before taking up a prominent public appointment outside government, and then in time returning to the Commons. That is much easier said than done in view of the way parliamentary candidates are chosen. But such moves in and out of the national legislature are common in the rest of the European Community, in part because of the proportional representation systems there. It is revealing that only Roy Jenkins of Britain's Commissioners in Brussels since

1972 has subsequently returned to the Commons. Most of the rest have gone to the House of Lords. But up to the Second World War service in some major Imperial role, whether as Viceroy of India or as a colonial governor, was regarded as a normal part of the career of many politicians. However, few such proconsuls ever returned to the Commons. Those, of course, were the days when it was possible for peers to hold senior posts in a government. Acceptance of the fact that someone might move in and out of a career in government, and even in and out of the Commons, might improve the quality of ministers and those in leading public positions. It will be revealing, for instance, to see whether Chris Patten returns to mainstream British politics after his term as Governor of Hong Kong finishes. A similar interchange between the Westminster and Strasbourg Parliaments might have a mutually benefical effect on the handling of EC issues. It is curious that when many business and commercial organizations are becoming more flexible in their career structures to maximize the use of their talent, the political world is not.

Any changes in the type of people who become politicians are likely to be marginal in the short-term. Politics will remain a separate calling, even a vocation, that attracts the very ambitious, as it always has. Where change is needed is not among the high-flyers, the stars who will rise to Cabinet rank, but among those whose ambitions of reaching the top are always likely to be frustrated. It is here that there needs to be greater flexibility in the selection and service of MPs, so that elected politicians are no longer a separate caste but are more representative of the electorate as a whole.

In the end, what attracts people to the ascent of the greasy pole – even if very few reach the top – is fascination with the enigmas and illusions of power, as John Grigg (1985) has noted about that contrasting duo, Asquith and Lloyd George:

Above all both men were fundamentally bold and adventurous characters, with a driving passion for power. This is not to say that they craved it entirely for its own sake; on the contrary, they needed it as much as artists need their materials or craftsmen their tools. Desmond MacCarthy once overheard a woman asking Asquith whether he liked being Prime Minister. This question only elicited a dubious rumble. 'Don't you enjoy having so much power?' 'Power, power? You may think you are going to get it, but you never do.' 'Oh, then what is it that you enjoy most in your work?' 'Well ... perhaps – hitting nails on the head.' Lloyd George might have said the same.

SOURCES AND BIBLIOGRAPHY

Adams, Jad, *Tony Benn*, Macmillan, 1992

Adonis, Andrew, *Parliament Today*, Manchester University Press, 1990

Allen, Graham, *House Magazine*, 13 January 1992

Alton, David, *House Magazine*, 4 December 1987

Amery, Julian, interviewed by Allan Massie, *Sunday Telegraph*, 21 June 1992

Amery, Leo, *Thoughts on the Constitution*, Oxford University Press, 1947

Anderson, Bruce, *John Major*, Fourth Estate, 1991

Archer, Peter, 'Thoughts before Going', *House Magazine*, 28 October 1991

Atkins, Robert, *House Magazine*, 17 June 1991

Bagehot, Walter, *The English Constitution* (with an Introduction by Richard Crossman), Collins, 1963

Baker, David, Andrew Gamble and Steve Ludlam, 'More "Classless" and Less "Thatcherite"? Conservative Ministers and New Conservative MPs after the 1992 Election', *Parliamentary Affairs*, Vol. 45, No. 4, October 1992

Barron, Kevin, *House Magazine*, 7 May 1990

Beaumont-Dark, Sir Anthony, *Guardian*, 18 May 1992

Beith, Alan, *House Magazine*, 5 July 1985

Biedenkopf, Kurt, interview in *Newsweek*, 24 May 1993.

Biffen, John, *Inside the House of Commons: Behind the Scenes at Westminster*, Grafton Books, 1989

Blair, Tony, *House Magazine*, 2 April 1990

Blake, Robert, *Disraeli*, Eyre and Spottiswoode, 1966

Blondel, Jean, and Jean-Louis Thiebault (eds.), *The Profession of Government Ministers in Western Europe*, Sage Publications, 1991

Blunkett, David, *House Magazine*, 29 April 1988

Brown, George, *In My Way*, Victor Gollancz, 1971

Burt, Alistair, *House Magazine*, 24 April 1989

Butler, David, *British General Elections since 1945*, Basil Blackwell, 1989

Butler, David, and Gareth Butler, *British Political Facts* (sixth edn), Macmillan, 1986

Butler, David, and Dennis Kavanagh, *The British General Election of 1987*, Macmillan, 1988

——*The British General Election of 1992*, Macmillan, 1992

Campbell, John, *F. E. Smith, First Earl of Birkenhead*, Jonathan Cape, 1983

Campbell, Menzies, *House Magazine*, 6 November 1989

Cannadine, David, *The Decline and Fall of the British Aristocracy*, Yale University Press 1990

Carrington, Lord, *Reflect on Things Past*, William Collins, 1988

Carvel, John, *Citizen Ken*, Chatto and Windus, 1984

Castle, Barbara, *The Castle Diaries 1974–76*, Weidenfeld and Nicolson, 1980

Cook, Robin, *House Magazine*, 19 March 1982

Corbett, Robin, *House Magazine*, 3 July 1987

Cradock, Percy, *Recollections of the Cambridge Union, 1815–1939*, Bowes and Bowes, 1953

Criddle, Byron, article on parliamentary candidates, *Financial Times*, 26 March 1992

Critchley, Julian, *Westminster Blues*, Elm Tree Books, 1985

——*Heseltine: The Unauthorized Biography*, André Deutsch, 1987

Crosland, Susan, *Tony Crosland*, Jonathan Cape, 1982

Crossman, Richard, *The Charm of Politics*, Hamish Hamilton, 1958

Crouch, David, *House Magazine*, 7 December 1984

Dalyell, Tam, *House Magazine*, 29 April 1988

Darling, Alistair, *House Magazine*, 18 February 1991

Davies, Denzil, *House Magazine*, 22 March 1985

DeLyon, Hilary, and Damien Welfare, 'Prime Candidates', *Fabian Review*, Vol. 104, No. 5, September 1992

Dewar, Donald, *House Magazine*, 8 February 1985

Dicks, Terry, *House Magazine*, 28 November 1988

Dionne, E. J., *Why Americans Hate Politics*, Simon and Schuster, 1991

Dixon, Don, *House Magazine*, 5 June 1989

Dod's Guide to the General Election 1992, Dod's Parliamentary Companion, 1992

Donoughue, Bernard, and G. W. Jones, *Herbert Morrison: Portrait of a Politician*, Weidenfeld and Nicolson, 1973

Dutton, David, *Simon: A Political Biography of Sir John Simon*, Aurum Press, 1992

Eggar, Tim, *House Magazine*, 22 April 1991

Ehrenhalt, Alan, *The United States of Ambition: Politicians, Power and the Pursuit of Office*, Random House, 1991

Ewing, Margaret, *House Magazine*, 25 March 1988

Fairlie, Henry, *The Life of Politics*, Methuen, 1968

Fallon, Michael, *House Magazine*, 18 November 1991

Fatchett, Derek, *House Magazine*, 15 June 1992

Fishburn, Dudley, *House Magazine*, 19 June 1990

Fisher, Nigel, *Iain Macleod*, André Deutsch, 1973

Fowler, Linda L., and Robert D. McClure, *Political Ambition: Who Decides to Run for Congress*, Yale University Press, 1989

Fowler, Norman, *Ministers Decide. A Personal Memoir of the Thatcher Years*, Chapmans, 1991

Fulford, Roger (ed.), *Greville Memoirs*, Batsford, 1963

Gilbert, Bentley Brinkerhoff, *David Lloyd George: A Political Life. Organizer of Victory, 1912–16*, Batsford, 1992

Golding, Llin, *House Magazine*, 23 July 1990

Goodlad, Alastair, *House Magazine*, 14 November 1988

Gorst, John, *House Magazine*, 13 March 1989

Gould, Bryan, *House Magazine*, 20 October 1987

Grigg, John, *Lloyd George: From Peace to War, 1912–16*, Methuen, 1985

Hailsham, Lord, *A Sparrow's Flight: Memoirs*, Collins, 1990

Hain, Peter, *House Magazine*, 1 June 1992

Harris, Kenneth, *Attlee*, Weidenfeld and Nicolson, 1982

Harris, Robert, *The Making of Neil Kinnock*, Faber and Faber, 1984

Haseler, Stephen, *The Gaitskellites*, Macmillan, 1969

Healey, Denis, *The Time of My Life*, Michael Joseph, 1989

——'Thoughts before Going', *House Magazine*, 16 March 1992

Heathcoat-Amory, David, *House Magazine*, 14 May 1990

Herman, Valentine, and James E. Alt (eds.), *Cabinet Studies: A Reader*, Macmillan, 1975

Higgins, Sir Terence, *House Magazine*, 15 March 1985

Hillman, Judy, and Peter Clarke, *Geoffrey Howe: A Quiet Revolutionary*, Weidenfeld and Nicolson, 1988

Horne, Alistair, *Macmillan: Volume 1; 1894–1956*, Macmillan, 1988

——*Macmillan: Volume 2, 1957–86*, Macmillan, 1989

Howard, Anthony, *RAB: The Life of R. A. Butler*, Jonathan Cape, 1987

——*Crossman: The Pursuit of Power*, Jonathan Cape, 1990

Howell, Denis, *House Magazine*, 12 June 1989

Hughes, Robert, *House Magazine*, 31 October 1988

Hunt, David, *House Magazine*, 11 July 1988

Hunt, Sir John, *House Magazine*, 15 January 1990

Hurd, Douglas, interview with Terry Coleman in the *Guardian*, 30 November 1985

Ingram, Adam, *House Magazine*, 22 January 1990

Iremonger, Lucille, *The Fiery Chariot: A Study of British Prime Ministers and the Search for Love*, Secker and Warburg, 1970

Jacobson, Gary C., *The Politics of Congressional Elections* (third edn), HarperCollins, 1992

Jenkin, John (ed.) *John Major: Prime Minister*, Press Association for Bloomsbury, 1990

Jenkins, Roy, *Asquith*, Collins, 1964

——*Essays and Speeches*, Collins, 1967

——*Gallery of Twentieth-century Portraits*, David and Charles, 1988

——*A Life at the Centre*, Macmillan, 1991

——'Whatever Happened to the Dignity of Public Office?', *Daily Telegraph*, 1 June 1993

Johnson, Paul (ed.), *The Oxford Book of Political Anecdotes*, Oxford University Press, 1986

Jones, Barry, *House Magazine*, 8 March 1985

Jones, Professor G. W., 'The House of Commons: A Threat to Good Government?', *London Review of Public Administration*, 16, 1984

Kaufman, Gerald, *How to be a Minister*, Sidgwick and Jackson, 1980

Kavanagh, Dennis, *Politics and Personalities*, Macmillan, 1990

Kellerman, Barbara (ed.), *Political Leadership*, University of Pittsburgh Press, 1986

Kennedy, Charles, *House Magazine*, 6 June 1988

Key, Robert, *House Magazine*, 2 December 1991

King, Anthony, *British Members of Parliament: A Self-Portrait*, Macmillan, 1974

——'The Rise of the Career Politician in Britain and Its Consequences', *British Journal of Political Science*, Vol. 2, No. 3 July 1981

King, Anthony (ed.), *The British Prime Minister*, Macmillan 1969

King, Anthony, and Anne Sloman, *Westminster and Beyond*, Macmillan, 1973

Lasswell, Harold, *Psychopathology and Politics*, Viking, 1960 (first edn, 1930)

Lawson, Nigel, *The View from Number 11: Memoirs of a Tory Radical*, Bantam Press, 1992

Leigh, Edward, *House Magazine*, 16 December 1990

Leighton, Ron, *House Magazine*, 23 October 1987

Lilley, Peter, *House Magazine*, 13 May 1991

Macmillan, Harold, *The Past Masters: Politics and Politicians 1906–39*, Macmillan, 1975

Mann, Thomas E., 'The Wrong Medicine: Term Limits that Won't Cure What Ails Congressional Elections', *The Brookings Review*, Vol. 10, No. 2, spring 1992

Market & Opinion Research International survey of public recognition of Conservative politicians, *The Economist* 3 September 1988

Marsh, Richard, *Off the Rails*, Weidenfeld and Nicolson, 1978

McLeish, Henry, *House Magazine*, 20 May 1991

McLoughlin, Patrick, *House Magazine*, 28 October 1991

Mitchell, Austin, *Westminster Man: A Tribal Anthropology of the Commons People*, Thames/Methuen, 1982

Moran, Michael, *Politics and Society in Britain: An Introduction*, Macmillan, 1989

Morris, Rupert, *Tories: From Village Hall to Westminster – A Political Sketch*, Mainstream Publishing, 1991

Morrison, Herbert, *Government and Parliament*, Oxford University Press, 1954

Needham, Richard, *Honourable Member: An Inside Look at the House of Commons*, Patrick Stephens, 1983

Newton, Anthony, *House Magazine*, 18 March 1988

Nicholson, Emma, *House Magazine*, 29 January 1990

Nicolson, Harold, *Curzon: The Final Phase*, Constable, 1934

Norton, Philip, *Dissension in the House of Commons 1945–74*, Macmillan, 1975
——*Conservative Dissidents*, Temple Smith, 1978
——*Dissension in the House of Commons 1974–79*, Oxford University Press, 1980.
Owen, David, *Time to Declare*, Michael Joseph, 1991
Oxford University Conservative Association: A History, 1924–1991, OUCA, 1991
Parkinson, Cecil, *Right at the Centre: An Autobiography*, Weidenfeld and Nicolson, 1992
Parry, Geraint, George Moyser and Neil Day, *Political Participation and Democracy in Britain*, Cambridge University Press, 1992
Paterson, Peter, *The Selectorate: The Case for Primary Elections in Britain*, Macgibbon and Kee, 1967
Patten, Chris, *House Magazine*, 15 November 1982
Pearce, Edward, *The Shooting Gallery*, Hamish Hamilton, 1989
——*The Quiet Rise of John Major*, Weidenfeld and Nicolson, 1991
Pimlott, Ben, *Harold Wilson*, HarperCollins, 1992
Pimlott, Ben (ed.), *The Political Diary of Hugh Dalton, 1918–40, 1945–60*, Jonathan Cape, 1986
Powell, Enoch, *Joseph Chamberlain*, Thames and Hudson, 1977
Prescott, John, profile in the *Independent*, 23 May 1992
Price, Sir David, 'Thoughts before Going', *House Magazine*, 25 November 1991
Prior, James, *A Balance of Power*, Hamish Hamilton, 1986
Punnett, R. M., *Selecting the Party Leader: Britain in Comparative Perspective*, Harvester Wheatsheaf, 1992
Radice, Lisanne, Elizabeth Vallance and Virginia Willis, *Member of Parliament: The Job of a Backbencher* (second edn), Macmillan, 1990
Ramsden, John, *The Making of Conservative Party Policy: The Conservative Research Department since 1929*, Longman, 1980
Ranney, Austin, *Pathways to Parliament: Candidate Selection in Britain*, University of Wisconsin Press, 1965
Rawnsley, Andrew, 'The Cambridge Mafia', *Guardian*, 10 October 1988
Redwood, John, *House Magazine*, 19 December 1988
'Register of Members' Interests on 1st December 1992', HMSO Cm 325

Review Body on Top Salaries, Report Number 32, 'Review of the House of Commons Office Costs Allowance', July 1992, HMSO, Cm 1943

Rhodes James, Sir Robert, *Lord Randolph Churchill*, Weidenfeld and Nicolson, 1959

——'The Fall of a Government: A Tory MP's View of Mr Callaghan's Final Days', *Listener*, 8 May 1980

——'Thoughts before Going', *House Magazine*, 7 October 1991

Rhodes James, Sir Robert (ed.), *Chips: The Diaries of Sir Henry Channon*, Weidenfeld and Nicolson, 1967

Richards, Peter, *The Backbenchers*, Faber and Faber, 1972

Riddell, Peter, *The Thatcher Government*, Basil Blackwell, 1983 (second edn, 1985)

——'Consenting Adults: The Subterranean World of the Whips at Westminster', *Financial Times*, 19 July 1986

——profile of John Smith, *Listener*, 2 October 1986

——'The Making of a Modern Minister', *Financial Times*, 22/23 October 1988

——*The Thatcher Decade*, Basil Blackwell, 1989 (updated and expanded under the title of *The Thatcher Era and Its Legacy*, 1991)

Rodgers, William, *The Politics of Change*, Secker and Warburg, 1982

Rose, Richard, *Ministers and Ministries: A Functional Analysis*, Clarendon Press, 1987

——*Politics in England: Chance and Perspective* (fifth edn), Macmillan, 1989

Ruddock, Joan, *House Magazine*, 8 May 1989

Rush, Michael, *The Selection of Parliamentary Candidates*, Thomas Nelson and Sons, 1969

Ryle, Michael, and Peter Richards (eds.), *The Commons Under Scrutiny*, Routledge, 1988

Schneider, William, 'Off with Their Heads: Public Resentment of Professionalism in Politics', *The American Enterprise*, Vol. 3, No. 4 July/August 1992

Searing, Donald, 'The Role of the Good Constituency Member and the Practice of Representation in Great Britain', *Journal of Politics*, 47, 1985

Seyd, Patrick, and Patrick Whiteley, *Labour's Grass Roots: The Politics of Party Membership*, Clarendon Press, 1992

Shepherd, Robert, *The Power Brokers: The Tory Party and Its Leaders*, Hutchinson, 1991

Snape, Peter, *House Magazine*, 5 February 1988

Spencer, Sir Derek, *House Magazine*, 8 June 1992

Stanworth, Philip, and Anthony Giddens (eds.), *Elites and Power in British Society*, Cambridge University Press, 1974

Steel, David, *Against Goliath*, Weidenfeld and Nicolson, 1989

Straw, Jack, *House Magazine*, 4 July 1988

——'Leave It to Us: The Election of the Labour Party Leader', *Fabian Review*, Vol. 104, No. 5, September 1992

Survey of the views of 100 Conservative MPs on the party leadership, *Independent*, 11 April 1988

Taylor, Sir Teddy, *House Magazine*, 15 April 1988

Tebbit, Norman, *Upwardly Mobile*, Weidenfeld and Nicolson, 1988

Theakston, Kevin, *Junior Ministers in British Government*, Basil Blackwell, 1987

Thompson, Alan, *The Day before Yesterday*, Panther/Sidgwick and Jackson, in association with Thames Television, 1971

Thorpe, D. R., *The Uncrowned Prime Ministers*, Darkhorse Publishing, 1983

The Times Guide to the House of Commons (Guides from 1945 up to 1992), Times Books

'Tories Plan Campaign to Attract Older Candidates', *The Times* 24 August 1992

Tyler, Paul, 'Reflections on Return to the Commons', *House Magazine*, 20 July, 1992

Vibert, Frank (ed.), *Britain's Constitutional Future*, Institute of Economic Affairs, 1991

Waldegrave, William, *House Magazine*, 19 April 1985

Walker, Peter, *Staying Power*, Bloomsbury, 1991

Walley, Joan, *House Magazine*, 5 November 1990

Walter, David, *The Oxford Union: Playground of Power*, Macdonald, 1984

Watkins, Alan, *A Conservative Coup: The Fall of Margaret Thatcher*, Duckworth, 1991

Weber, Max, 'Politics as a Vocation', in H. H. Girth and C. Wright Mills (eds.), *From Max Weber: Essays in Sociology*, Routledge and Kegan Paul, 1948

Wheeler-Bennett, Sir John, *John Anderson, Viscount Waverley*, Macmillan, 1962

Whitelaw, William, *The Whitelaw Memoirs*, Aurum Press, 1989

Wilson, Harold, *The Governance of Britain*, Weidenfeld and Nicolson and Michael Joseph, 1976

——*Memoirs: The Making of a Prime Minister 1916–64*, Weidenfeld and Nicolson and Michael Joseph, 1986

Winterton, Nicholas, *House Magazine*, 9 July 1990

Wyn Ellis, Nesta, *John Major: A Personal Biography*, Futura, 1991

Yeo, Tim, *House Magazine*, 5 February 1990

Young, Alison, *The Reselection of MPs*, Heinemann Educational Books, 1983

Young, Hugo, *One of Us*, Macmillan, 1989 (revised edn, 1991)

Young, Lord, *The Enterprise Years: A Businessman in the Cabinet*, Headline, 1990

Younger, George, *House Magazine*, 7 June 1985

INDEX